My Mistress the Queen

The opening sheet of Letter 2 showing Frieda's sketch of the Round Tower,
Windsor Castle

My Mistress the Queen

THE LETTERS OF FRIEDA ARNOLD
DRESSER TO QUEEN VICTORIA 1854-9

Edited by Benita Stoney and Heinrich C. Weltzien

Translated by Sheila de Bellaigue

Weidenfeld & Nicolson, London

First published in Great Britain in 1994 by

Weidenfeld & Nicolson
The Orion Publishing Group,
5 Upper Saint Martin's Lane,
London WC2H 9EA

A catalogue record for this book is available
from the British Library

ISBN 0 297 81435 4

Typeset by Deltatype Ltd, Ellesmere Port, Cheshire
Printed by Butler & Tanner Ltd, Frome and London

Contents

Contents

Contents

Illustrations

Between pages 144 and 145

Illustrations are numbered in the order in which they appear.

All Frieda's sketches are reproduced courtesy of Heinrich C. Weltzien

Acknowledgements

The editors are most grateful to Her Majesty the Queen for her gracious permission to publish material from the Royal Archives, without which a full understanding of Frieda's letters would not have been possible. The staff of the Royal Archives, the Royal Library, and the Royal Collection have made the researcher's task a pleasure; our thanks are due in particular to Jane Roberts, Bridget Wright, Frances Dimond, and Pam Clark for their generous assistance. The kind offices of Frau Gertraude Bachmann in Coburg brought to light Queen Victoria's comments on her new dresser from Karlsruhe. We drew on the time and expertise of Kay Staniland. R. D. Ridding, Researcher *HMS Warrior* (1860) provided a feast of information on the victualling of the Royal Navy. E. A. Sibbick proved once more that his knowledge of Osborne House is inexhaustible. With the help of Rosemary Maddy we identified the mail packet leaving Southampton. North of the border, we are especially indebted to Martin and Catriona Leslie, and to David Anderson, for their kind assistance with our task of identifying the places Frieda sketched and described around Balmoral and in Edinburgh. We were also given a warm welcome at Haddo.

Introduction

A few days before Christmas in 1854 Queen Victoria added an afterthought to her journal: 'my new dresser, Frieda Arnold, from Carlsruhe, has come since a few days ago, on three months trial, and has begun her duties.'*[1]

The Queen had had a trying autumn. 'We are, and indeed the whole country is,' she said, 'entirely *engrossed* with one idea, one anxious thought – the *Crimea*.'* The war's bloody victories, legendary bungles, and the heroic suffering of her 'dear noble Troops' fired the Queen's imagination, indignation and compassion, and involved her completely. The tensions of excitement and uncertainty, however, had not made for an easy period in her marriage where public and private life overlapped, and Prince Albert, beloved, and overworked, was beginning to show the strains of combining in one person the roles of husband, private secretary and adviser to the Queen. As ever, he got no thanks from the country and his wife was bitterly distressed that he was once again the object of ferocious attacks from the Press. At home, eight children engendered their own natural demands and worries, from the eldest, Victoria Princess Royal, who would soon be needing a husband, to the youngest, the haemophiliac Prince Leopold, born the previous year, a sickly, difficult infant. The September visit to the half-completed new castle at Balmoral refreshed as it always did the royal spirits, but on the way back to Windsor domestic misfortune struck. The Queen's second dresser, Ida Bonanomi, who for some time had not been feeling well, became too ill to complete the journey, had to be left behind, and on 15 October, died.*

The Queen, writing to her Uncle Leopold, King of the Belgians,

---

[1] All source references can be found from page 207 in the Reference Notes.

I

was sure that he would sympathise with her in having lost 'a most valued and excellent servant, my first German dresser, who had been nearly seven years with me and I may truly say was *perfection* in every sense of the word'; the news of her death 'has quite overset me'.* The Queen's aunt, the Duchess of Gloucester, quite understood; and this elderly princess trembled for her own dresser who had been with her for fifty-two years: 'if anything was to happen to Miss Gold', she told her niece, 'I should not know what to do without her, but as you are younger you may look forwards to finding a dresser that by degrees [may become] perhaps as useful though an old friend can never be replaced.'* The Duchess need not have worried; Miss Gold was with her to the last and the dresser's final office was to lay her mistress out for burial.*

The monarch's confidential servants, who occupied positions of considerable trust and responsibility, were usually found by asking quietly of other members of the Royal Family. A complicated network of relationships existed not only between members of the extended Royal Family, but between the dynasties of men and women who served them. For instance, of the women who were Frieda's immediate colleagues, the Queen's Principal Dresser, Marianne Skerrett, was the niece of a Mr Mathias, who had been sub-treasurer to Queen Charlotte; and one of the wardrobe maids, Mary Ann Andrews, born in England, was the daughter of Charles Andrews, who was in the service of King Leopold in Brussels, and known to Queen Victoria.* Mary came to the Queen on the King's recommendation.* With so many royal connections in Europe, and particularly Germany, where each small state in the confederation had its own prince and court, the network of such contacts was a wide one.

The facts about Frieda Arnold's background are few, but do reflect just this kind of link with court life. Her home town of Karlsruhe was the modest, and relatively new, capital of the southern state of Baden, ruled since 1806 by the Grand Dukes of Baden. Frieda Arnold's father, Burkhard Andreas Arnold of the Baden Artillery, born in 1797, had distinguished himself on active service, and enjoyed the high regard of the Grand Duke. In 1826 he married Marie Sophie Rossbach, daughter of the Master Butcher to the Court in Mannheim.

Friederike Jakobine Arnold, or Frieda as she was always known, was born in 1830. 'If I look back to my childhood, I see only joy'; so she assures us in the diary she wrote at the age of twenty-three. Her parents were 'loving and conscientious', and she grew up happily in the company of her five 'friendly' brothers and sisters: Georg, and Anna Barbara (or Babette), who were older than Frieda, and Ludwig, Julie and Wilhelm, who were younger.

Frieda's early years were, she remembered, pleasant and uneventful. The children spent several summers with their grandparents in the country. All was well until the spring of 1841 when Frieda was eleven, and her father fell ill. After four weeks in bed, he was moved to his parents in Liedolsheim. During the crisis, the family separated. Frau Arnold kept her eldest daughter, Babette, and the two-year-old Wilhelm with her. Georg and Ludwig went to their grandmother in Mannheim. Frieda and Julie went to friends in Langensteinbach. After about fourteen days, Frieda remembered, she was allowed to travel with her aunt to see her father, and found him very ill. Just over a week later, she and her sister were called in from their play to find everyone in tears; her father had died. The next day they went to the oak trees which her father had loved, and bound an oak wreath for his coffin. A friend, Herr Mayer, attended the funeral and told the children about it. All the officers of the Baden Artillery had been present. Within a few days Frieda and Julie returned to town and were reunited with their mother and the other children. Frieda considered this to be 'the only remarkable period in my childhood'.

Captain Arnold left his widow to rear and provide for six children, the oldest of whom was fourteen and the youngest only two. Her success, and their abilities, can be judged by their subsequent careers. Georg went on to become a professor at the Gymnasium in Mannheim. Babette taught first in Holland, then in Mannheim, before becoming director of her own institute, the Victoria School, the first school for the higher education of girls in Karlsruhe. Ludwig, an engineer, became co-founder and director of Maschinenfabrik Esslingen. Julie, who did what was so often expected of the youngest daughter, never married, and stayed with her mother. Wilhelm went to live in London, where he ran his own insurance company.

In 1841, however, all this was far in the future, which must have seemed very bleak to Frau Arnold. A *cri de coeur* she uttered in a letter written a few years later has survived: 'Oh, dear God! with all this work I cannot collect my thoughts at all . . . pity me, I am like a hunted deer who cannot find any rest from the hunters; from the outside I seem to be quiet and pleased, but who knows the tortures tearing my inner self apart? May God assist me further as before to fulfil the duties which are my lot.'*

The widow hid her troubles well; all that Frieda records of the years following her father's death are her preparation for confirmation and her first Holy Communion in the spring of 1844. She does not seem to have had much formal education – she writes of 'a period of learning', by which she seems to mean her attendance for a year at a French sewing school. The breadth of her reading, evident from the literary allusions which pepper her letters, is thus the more remarkable.

Frieda was well-read in the popular authors of her day. She was also an incurable romantic and she tended to see the world coloured by the descriptions of the masters. She inscribed one of her drawing-books with lines from Schiller. In England she was to preface a short account of a fortnight in the Isle of Wight with appropriate verses from the lyric poet Geibel. A short sea-crossing would inspire thoughts of the poet-botanist Chamisso's journey round the world; London was to be Dickens brought to life; a military review conjured up Pickwick, and a sunset at Aldershot evoked a scene from Schiller. When she saw Scotland it was through the historical-romantic lenses of the Waverley novels, of which her mother was such an ardent devotee. A drive in the Highlands summoned the shade of the young Byron and in the Crystal Palace Thomas Moore invested with oriental splendour those Fine Arts Courts which Frieda had not coloured with the lyrical melancholy of Chateaubriand. Frieda may have read the English authors in the original: her sister Babette owned a copy of *Barnaby Rudge* in English, and Frieda quotes Byron and Longfellow in English, but that was after two years in England. Dickens, Byron's poetry, Scott's Waverley series, and almost all Thomas Moore's prose as well as poetry were translated into German, often by distinguished hands.

Besides reading, Frieda was a regular attendant at the active Hoftheater in Karlsruhe and the plays she saw there became a useful shorthand for describing to her family the sights she was to see in England. It seems also that she attended lectures of a high standard at the Polytechnic Institute of Karlsruhe, most unusual for a girl at that time. Her attendance, however, is evidence more of her family's close links with the Institute than of any particular scientific aptitude in Frieda.

Money was obviously tight, and Frieda could not but be aware of Frau Arnold's difficulties, remembering how her mother was 'always ready to let us learn something useful, even if it had to be bought with great sacrifices on her part'. After the sewing school, when Frieda found herself more at home and helping a great deal in the kitchen and in the house, she asked 'with beating heart, half hope, half fear', to be allowed to take drawing lessons. Since Frieda was learning needlepoint at the time, for which the drawing might be useful, her mother consented. Drawing gave Frieda intense joy; these lessons were most important to her, and she felt that they had greatly influenced 'my future and my inner self'.

Frieda entertained very strong family feelings. Her diary concludes with an enthusiastic account of a large family wedding, lasting three days with about twenty cousins attending. 'I love family feasts so much, they are such pure and long lasting joys. Oh! no-one should quarrel with their relatives, even if misunderstandings may occur, one should always try by any means to eliminate them. Because relatives are our natural friends, given by God, and so many people so easily lose this source of joy and this support in days of need.'

The following pages in her diary were cut out. We do not know where, or for whom, Frieda may have worked before she came to England. It is unlikely that Queen Victoria would have taken on anyone inexperienced. On the other hand, there is no evidence from Frieda's diary to suggest previous work. Her sketchbooks, in which her landscapes are carefully named and dated, show that she was not away from Karlsruhe for any extended period before 1854.

It seems that Frieda came to England through an old friend of hers, Sophie Weiss, also from Karlsruhe, who had become dresser to Queen Victoria in 1852. After Ida Bonanomi's death, the Queen moved quickly to find a replacement, and on 18 November 1854, just over a month after the dresser's death, the Queen had already settled on Frieda, who was to come on three months' trial.* The new dresser's credentials were impeccable. As she was an old friend of Sophie's, they could be expected to get on together; the Queen had heard high praise of her; and her background was most respectable, her father having been a captain, and her uncle Schmidt being Hofrat or councillor. On 22 November the Privy Purse issued a bank draft to pay the expenses of 'the new dresser from abroad'.*

On 15 December 1854, Frieda's term of service with the Queen began.* The Queen described a decent, quiet and sensible girl, but enormously tall.* Within a few days she had decided that Frieda pleased her very much, being quiet and friendly and learning her duties 'unbelievably quickly' so that the Queen felt quite 'at home' with her. The Queen also remarked on what a cultured girl her new dresser was.*

What kind of world did Frieda find herself in when she arrived at Windsor? The Court of Queen Victoria revolved in a series of circles around the central figure of the Queen and the members of the Royal Family who were grouped about her according to ranks of jealously guarded precedence. Beyond and below them, as it were, circled the lords, ladies and gentlemen of the Court: members of 'Society'. The foremost of the Queen's ladies, the Mistress of the Robes, who was always a duchess, was a political appointment reflecting the Whig or Tory allegiance of her husband, so she would change with every new government. At this period the Duchess of Sutherland held the appointment. She would be present when the Queen attended state occasions but was not in daily attendance on her as were the Ladies and Women of the Bedchamber (when on duty these were known as the Ladies in Waiting) and the Maids of Honour. Their function was to keep the Queen company when she needed it, go driving or sketching or walking with her, dine with her, sit with her, and undertake a certain amount of correspondence. Letters between the Queen and the Duchess discuss these appointments, but do not discuss those of the dressers, who were very much the Queen's personal appointment and took their orders directly from her.

The dressers belonged to the hierarchy of men and women who

lived in a parallel and quite separate world, which mirrored the rank and degree of 'Society'. As the personal attendants of the Queen, the dressers were among the highest of all. These matters of rank and position were considered very important. The deportment and treatment of the servant must reflect the respect due to the mistress, to the point that the Queen issued the most detailed instructions as to the seating arrangements for her upper servants' dining table, so that someone who had only recently been promoted should not 'go over the heads of those confidential servants who are constantly in personal attendance on the sovereign'.*

One of the most confidential was Marianne Skerrett, who in 1854 had been with the Queen for seventeen years, having entered her service soon after her accession in 1837. She was called the Queen's dresser, but, according to the Queen herself, she did not act as such. Instead, she seems to have been more of a personal secretary, dealing with matters which were either beneath the dignity of a Lady in Waiting, or part of the very private world of the Queen's personal and family affairs. As the Queen put it, 'She communicated with the artists, wrote letters to tradespeople, etc.'.* She dealt in English, German and French with the lithographers and photographic colourists who duplicated the many likenesses of the Queen's numerous family. If the Queen wanted to commission a new painting from Sir Edwin Landseer, it was Skerrett who wrote to him – theirs was a long and warm correspondence. When William Simpson, whose exhibition Frieda describes in Letter 10 (*see* p.154), came to Buckingham Palace with sketches of the Crimea commissioned by the Queen, it was Skerrett whom he saw first, and then Her Majesty. It was Skerrett who answered begging letters from such as the daughter of the Queen's old singing master, Luigi Lablache. Honiton lace for the Princess Royal's wedding dress, and midwives and nurses for her first confinement were well within Skerrett's capabilities. She paid small bills incurred by the dressers and wardrobe maids, such as 'Miss Arnold's bill' for 14s. on 23 October 1857* or £1 on 31 November 1857 'for Miss Weiss and Mary going to town and back'.* She dealt with the accounts of the silk mercers, milliners, suppliers of lace and embroidery, makers of shawls, linen and corsets, the woollen drapers, the hosiers and glovers, the shoemakers, tailors, plumassiers, perfumers, hatters, straw-hat makers, furriers, suppliers of tartans and of Irish poplins, habit makers, soap manufacturers, jewellers, dressing-case makers and whip makers who all contributed to Her Majesty's wardrobe.*

Skerrett was closely involved in the business of engaging the dressers and wardrobe maids, when as often as not her letters would be to the parents of the women who were taken on, rather than to the women themselves. The letter Skerrett wrote offering the post of wardrobe maid to Mary Ann Andrews is addressed to her father, and so is the letter of November 1854 confirming her in the position: 'Mary has now been here five months which is about the time Her Majesty had fixed for a trial, and as Her Majesty is satisfied with her conduct, and manner of keeping her service, she may consider herself as finally engaged. I have mentioned this to Mary who hopes she will be able to continue to give Her Majesty satisfaction in her service.'*

Skerrett was, in the Queen's opinion, 'a person of immense literary knowledge and sound understanding, of the greatest discretion and straightforwardness'.* To others she was 'a sharp clever old maid as ever lived, and very plain spoken',* and 'most eager in her likings and dislikings'.* After she retired, in 1862, she was not replaced.

Frieda's closest colleague was Sophie Weiss, who had been promoted on the death of Ida Bonanomi to second dresser.* There were also two wardrobe maids, Mary Ann Andrews and Lydia Greatorex. All were unmarried. For the purposes of accounts, they belonged to the Department of the Mistress of the Robes. Skerrett's salary was £200 per annum; Sophie's £120, Frieda's £100, and the wardrobe maids' £80. All were paid quarterly.*

Their workplace was in the private apartments of the Queen: her sitting-room, her bedroom, and above all, her dressing-room. What was this room like? At Windsor and Buckingham Palace, the Queen – or rather, Prince Albert – modified existing arrangements, but at Osborne and Balmoral the Queen enjoyed the comforts and convenience of a custom-built layout. At Osborne, her dressing-room was situated between her bedroom and her sitting-room. In the window overlooking the sea stood her dressing-table, crowded with the multitude of little blue and white pots and dishes, and the kissing cupids among the scrolls and candles round the oval glass, of the porcelain dressing-table set which had been given to her by Prince Albert for Christmas in 1853. Along the opposite wall mirrored doors concealed a shower and a deep copper bathtub encased in mahogany, fed by hot water from the furnace in the basement. A water-closet, accessible from bedroom or dressing-room, was discreetly hidden as part of a gigantic built-in wardrobe. The dressing-table and chest of drawers were of plain and solid design, the armchair covered with a cheerful chintz and the floor with a florid carpet. On the mantelpiece, in front of the looking-glass, stood a blue enamel clock and matching candlesticks. On the walls hung studies of young women by Winterhalter, gentle southern landscapes depicting Italy and Spain, enamel miniatures of the Queen's extended family, and paintings of Tyrolean huntsmen and favourite horses.*

The 'Wardrobe' was a large room situated, at Osborne, next door to the Queen's bedroom. Unlike most of the rooms allocated to servants it had a view over the terrace where the Royal Family took their ease; and Frieda would have sat in there, sewing and mending, to the sound of the Venus fountain playing below. According to an inventory taken at the end of the nineteenth century – and Osborne saw very little change after Prince Albert's death in 1861 – the Wardrobe was furnished with three vast mahogany wardrobes, the largest of which was 13 feet 6 inches long by 5 feet 6 inches deep, with six doors, five outer drawers at the bottom, and the wings fitted with drawers and for hanging dresses, lined with holland and curtains. A bedstead was incorporated into one of the other wardrobes. A chimney glass with a mahogany frame hung over the fireplace. Also in this room there was an enclosed double washstand of mahogany, a Pembroke table, a mahogany dress stand, two stuffed easy chairs and a small mahogany boot cupboard.* A later inventory suggests there were also two mahogany ironing trestles.*

The dressers and the wardrobe maids between them carried out the functions of a lady's maid. Perhaps it would be useful, before going any further, to have a brief look at what was typically expected of a lady's maid at that period. According to that household authority, Mrs Beeton, the lady's maid must be able to 'originate many parts of the lady's dress herself'. She should be 'a tolerably expert milliner and dressmaker, a good hairdresser, and possess some chemical knowledge of the cosmetics with which the toilet table is supplied'. She must know how to clean any material, from the gauziest muslin, and finest barege, to the skirts of the muddiest riding habit; she must be able to crisp up the crushed and tumbled feathers on a bonnet, must know the secrets of cleaning feathers (if damp, hold near the fire and recurl; if dirty, clean with a paste of pipeclay; if grebe, wash with white soap); she must know how to wash lace, how to clean ribbons (recommending a mixture of honey, gin and soft soap), and how to remove grease and stains from dresses. Everything, except stockings, should be mended before washing. On sending linen to the wash the lady's maid should list everything that went out, keeping a copy, and checking everything off when it came back. The coppers, tubs and mangles of the Victorian laundry were hard on smalls: 'on its return it is still more necessary to examine each piece separately, so that all missing buttons be supplied, and only the articles properly washed and in perfect repair passed into the wardrobe.' Ironing would also be part of her duties: 'a lady's maid will also have a great deal of "ironing out" to do; such as light evening dresses, etc., which are not dirty enough to be washed, but merely require smoothing out to remove the creases', although to keep muslin dresses in order 'they almost require smoothing out every time they are worn, particularly if made with much trimming'. The lady's maid should arrange the dressing-room, toilet-table and linen, according to her mistress's wishes and habits. 'Having prepared the room . . . and made everything ready for dressing her mistress, placed her linen before the fire to air, and laid out the various articles of dress she is to wear, which will probably have been arranged the previous evening, the lady's maid is prepared for the morning's duties.' Hairdressing, according to Mrs Beeton, was the most important part of the lady's maid's office. She gives instructions on how to dress various styles, finishing off by giving the hair 'a glossy appearance by the use of pomades, or oil, applied with the palm of the hand, smoothing it down with a small brush dipped in bandoline'. She gives a few recipes for her cosmetic secrets: one 'excellent' pomade was compounded of 1½ lb lard, 1½ pints olive oil, ½ pint of caster oil, scented with spermaceti or bergamot, and finished off with elderflower water and brandy. 'A waiting maid who wishes to make herself useful', Mrs Beeton continues, 'will study the fashion books with attention, so as to be able to aid her mistress's judgement in dressing, according to the prevailing fashion, with such modifications as her style of countenance requires.'*

A memorandum in the Royal Archives sets out the duties of the Queen's dressers. It was probably written in 1866, some years after Frieda had left, but given that the Queen disliked change, and that even as late as 1897 rules for servants differed very little from the arrangements laid down early in the reign, it can safely be said to give an idea of what Frieda's duties were.

Scrupulous tidiness was a prerequisite. Everything Her Majesty took off must be looked over and anything that needed repair mended at once, either by the dresser or by a wardrobe maid. Bonnets, gloves, caps, cloaks and so on must all be inspected before Her Majesty put them on. The dressers were to see that everything in Her Majesty's dressing-room was 'right and in its place' before the Queen got up in the morning, dressed or went to bed 'so that there be no confusion or anything missing'. They must take note when anything became torn or dirty and obtain replacements. They were to 'think over *well*' everything that might be wanted before Her Majesty went anywhere, or when she went to London to hold a Court, and make sure that everything was in its right place. The dressers were in charge of the Queen's wardrobe, and were responsible for the dresses, shawls, jewels or whatever Her Majesty used from it. If they were in doubt about anything they were to ask Her Majesty about it at once. They were to see to it that all Her Majesty's clothes were 'kept properly and in their places and in proper drawers appointed for them'. Finally, they were to look after the wardrobe maids, to see that they did their duty and that their health was properly attended to.*

Many of the dressers' duties seem to have overlapped with the wardrobe maids', to whom it was made quite clear in a similar directive, initialled by the Queen, that they were 'under the . . . dressers, and must obey them'.* Their duties were 'to prepare things for the dressers, to do some ironing, and look after some parts of the dress in particular'.*

The Queen's day was a very busy one, and the amount that she did could not have been achieved without a great deal of efficient organisation. The domestic ceremonies of her dressing-room were laid out for the wardrobe maids in the minutest detail, from opening the shutters in her bedroom at 7.30 a.m., to locking all the doors last thing at night.* Her maids were instructed as to how the tables and chairs in the dressing-room were to be arranged, how the sponges and basins of water for face and hands should be set, and towels should be laid out, when they were to enter with seltzer water and camomile tea (for the eyes), when to leave the room and upon returning, in what order to hand Her Majesty the various articles of her dress and jewellery.

As soon as she was ready, the Queen swept off to breakfast with Prince Albert, and the maids and dressers tidied everything away. One was then 'on duty' all day; that is, she sat in the elegant room described by Frieda (*see* p.41), the Queen's Wardrobe, ready to answer Her Majesty's bell. At Osborne, the Queen's desk in her sitting-room was equipped with three bell-pushes, one of which was marked 'Wardrobe', which could be used to ring a bell there. The maid 'off duty' saw to the ironing, cleaning, and if necessary mending, of Her Majesty's dresses, and between three and four o'clock she took the place in the Wardrobe of the one who was at dinner.* On alternate days they could go out 'for a certain time for walking' and occasionally were able to obtain leave 'on asking' to go out at other times.* Frieda's letters bear out that free time was rare and precious.

In the afternoon, when the Queen came in from driving or walking, she changed into silk shoes and stockings. The maids then prepared the dressing-room for eight o'clock, ready for the Queen to dress for dinner, putting out warm water scented with elderflower for the hands and face, camomile tea to bathe the eyes, and the 'little round sponge' scented with eau-de-Cologne.*

When the Queen went in to dinner they prepared once more for her undressing, setting out amongst the toilet articles, candles, papers and books and the Queen's lamp.*

The Queen has left us a picture of herself in her dressing-room, last thing at night, with Prince Albert leaning against the fireplace 'talking over the company – and what had passed – such a pleasure; sometimes my maids would come in and begin to undress me – and he would go on talking, would make his observations on my jewels and ornaments

and give my people good advice as to how to keep them or would
occasionally reprimand if anything had not been carefully attended to
– my dress not well fastened or badly made . . . he would then go to
his dressing-room . . . I undressed quickly – but alas! [writing after
Albert's death, she now regrets every minute she could have spent
with him, but did not] I dawdled and read often while my hair was
doing afterwards and from ¼ p 11 – it got to ½ p 11 – often 20 m to
12 . . .'*

One unenviable duty that the dressers do not seem to have shared
with the wardrobe maids was the practice the Queen recommended
to her newly married daughter: 'Have one of your people sleeping on
the sofa in the next room; I never do otherwise . . . wherever I go – my
maid always sleeps next door – even if Papa is with me.'*

When the Queen referred to her maids' 'to a *certain* extent, peculiar
duties',* she may have been thinking of the mannish intrusion into
this feminine world of the affairs and secrets of state contained in the
innumerable leather despatch boxes that followed the Queen
wherever she went. Every morning the 'off-duty' maid, after putting
away the Queen's Journal, took away the despatch boxes and put the
newly arrived boxes and letters in the dressing-room. (Just what it
meant for Her Majesty to have the latest news, and to keep in touch
with her government, can be seen in Letter 8, in which Frieda
describes her gruelling journey from Buckingham Palace to Balmoral
in the company of the Queen's Messenger, who brought the boxes.)
The 'signing boxes', marked 'Colonial', 'War' and 'Home Office' were
left in the Queen's sitting-room. The maids were expected to be 'fully
acquainted with all the things in Her Majesty's sitting room' such as
books and drawings.* It was not easy. When the Queen and Prince
were compiling their nine 'View Albums', and six 'Journey Albums',
souvenir volumes of all the places they had seen and visited together,
gathering and arranging '*all* the prints, woodcuts, and photographs
we could get' to be pasted in, the Queen wrote that 'often my maids
mislaid some of the things and they were not put in'.*

The dressers were mainly occupied, however, with Her Majesty's
clothes.

During the period that Frieda was in England, from December
1854 to July 1859, Queen Victoria was firmly centre-stage of the

social world. She was active, energetic and busy. She stayed in London for the 'Season', from February to July, when she held levees, those afternoon assemblies at which only men were received; she stood for hours at drawing-rooms while débutantes, brides and other social aspirants were presented by the hundred. She received foreign royalty, and went abroad herself; she danced at balls, attended concerts, reviewed her troops, opened parliament, laid foundation stones, held investitures, opened exhibitions, went regularly to the theatre, rode, walked, bore her last child, and worked tirelessly at her unending correspondence on state and family matters. From Frieda's point of view, the pace was exhausting and unremitting: 'From early in the morning until late at night there are endless preparations to make and adornments for parties to help with, and my poor brain has to know weeks ahead on what day this or that ball, or this or that concert takes place.'*

The Queen was at her grandest and most formal at the levees, drawing-rooms and other formalised occasions when she dressed to personify her function as the linchpin and pinnacle of a rigidly classified society that gathered in assemblies where the entrée was governed by strict rules of breeding, morals and dress. These were the only occasions on which the Court Circular, the official account of the movements of the court, would describe what the Queen was wearing.

At a typical levee, for which Frieda could well have dressed her, the Queen wore a train of white and gold moire antique silk (clouded or watered silk), trimmed with gold blonde lace and red velvet bows. The gown, always referred to as 'petticoat,' was of white satin, also trimmed with gold blonde and red velvet bows. She wore a coronet of opals and diamonds.* At the next levee, and 'Her Majesty's costume on this occasion was much admired',* she wore a train 'of pink satin, covered with English lace and trimmed with bows of pink and white satin. The petticoat was of white satin, covered with English lace and trimmed with bows of white satin . . . on her head a diamond circlet.'* She wore this costume again two months later,* but in general did not repeat herself. During the Season of 1856, the one that Frieda likened to a battle, the Queen as usual held a levee about once a month and appeared in glittering array: in blue and white silk brocade, in white poplin embroidered with gold and coloured flowers, in red poplin patterned with gold, in maize and white. She would always wear a diadem.

Drawing-rooms were occasions of equal display. There were usually about four of them every Season. In 1856 the Queen appeared at her birthday drawing-room in 'a train of light blue silk, embroidered all over with a palm pattern in gold, silver and red; trimmed with silver blonde and bunches of orchidacean flowers. The petticoat white satin, with a bouffant of white tulle and bunches of orchidacean flowers to correspond to the train.'* On her head was a diadem of diamonds and opals. At the next drawing-room she was in white and red, the train 'of crimson silk, brocaded with a running pattern of crimson and silver bouquets, trimmed with crimson satin, silver blonde, and bows of crimson satin ribband. The petticoat was white satin, trimmed with white blonde and silver ribband.'* Her diadem was of diamonds and pearls.

The Queen's ball gowns at this period were usually pink or blue, of tulle over silk, flounced, and trimmed with lace, where diamonds nestled among such flowers as roses, lilacs or jasmine, though sometimes the trimmings were more exotic, as at the State Ball on 17 June 1856, when she opened the quadrille in a dress 'of Indian muslin embroidered with gold sprigs, and a broad gold border in bouquets, trimmed with bunches of red cactus, and green leaves ornamented with diamonds'. Her head-dress was a simple affair, of red cactus, green leaves and diamonds.* In June she was seen at a ball at the Royal Academy of Music in 'a superb dress of white glacé silk, with painted flounces of the most elegant design. Her corsage blazed with a mass of diamonds, and the heavy tiara on her brow sparkled with the richest jewels of the crown.'* In July she attended the Duchess of Gloucester's Ball in 'a magnificent dress of cerise coloured tulle . . . and a profusion of diamond ornaments'.*

When the Queen's subjects set eyes on her for themselves, however, watching her launch a ship or lay a foundation stone, they invariably commented on how plainly she was dressed – that is, if they mentioned her clothes at all; newspaper correspondents were often too far away to see, or simply not interested, but if they were pressed for column inches might throw a sop to the 'fair sex' with such informative observations as, Her Majesty was wearing 'a sort of puce dress, and carried a green silk parasol'.*

Occasionally, newspaper reports gave more detail. For the journey which Frieda describes in Letter 12, of some fifty miles through the Scottish Highlands in an unheated carriage in October, the Queen was glimpsed in 'a plain white bonnet, trimmed with blue, a grey cloth cloak, and a silk dress, without flounces, of hunting Stewart tartan'.* Frankly disappointed, the correspondent was glad to report that the next morning the Queen was 'dressed somewhat more gaily'. Apart from the Stuart tartan, this was much what any lady would have worn, as were the clothes in which she carried out her other engagements. 'In fact,' said the same observer, 'she looks just like a high-bred lady of nearly forty.'

To distribute war medals to Crimean veterans in May 1856, Queen Victoria put on 'a lilac and white dress, a green velvet mantle, and white bonnet'.* To lay the foundation stone of the military hospital at Netley in May 1856, she wore a white bonnet trimmed with red roses, a dark blue jacket and a white dress – according to a watercolour* by W. Simpson, who prided himself on his accuracy. She laid the foundation stone of Wellington College in a summer dress of white muslin, a white 'visite', or short sleeveless cloak and a white bonnet.* Reviewing troops at Aldershot in July 1856, she was thought to be looking 'remarkably well' in 'a bonnet of blue and white, trimmed with flowers of a geranium colour; a blue visite, and a barege dress of blue and white'.* The only thing that struck the same correspondent as 'particularly noticeable' in the royal costume was 'the bonnet, which, though elegant in shape and most becoming in appearance, differed considerably from those apologies for a head-dress that are nowadays worn by the fair sex'. It may be that the Queen was trying to protect herself from the ravages of the weather; reviewing troops played havoc with the complexion. After one Field Day, she told her daughter that she had 'a scorched really sore red face, but I hope powder will prevent my being too great a figure at the levee'.*

In the letters written by those directly around the Queen, such as her ladies in waiting, there is very little mention of her clothes. This may have been because the Queen merely reflected fashion, and did not lead it. As skirts grew bigger, so, a little behindhand, did the

Queen's, one of her ladies observing in March 1856, 'the Queen's petticoats much increased in circumference, which improves her excessively'.* Fashion brought its own penalties and solutions; in June 1858, the Queen confessed that 'in that dreadful heat – the stiff petticoats were unbearable, and then they lost their stiffness so completely that it was impossible to appear with all the muslins hanging down', so she began to wear a 'cage', to support the expanding circumference.*

For someone who recorded almost obsessively every aspect of her life, there is surprisingly little about her clothes in Queen Victoria's own letters and journals. Frieda's mistress took care with her appearance, wishing, for Albert's sake rather than her own, that she were ten years younger, but she did not like to be troubled with dress: 'I have plenty of low gowns – light and elegant – but I hope no great overdone elegance will be necessary.'*

Before the state visit to Paris, however, in August 1855, the Queen was definitely on her mettle, and confessed herself 'much troubled with questions of toilettes'* and we can be sure that her dressers were too. Her style in Paris seems to have met with a mixed reception; though fortunately for the Queen's *amour propre*, only the flattering reports appear to have got back to her: 'I was thought so dignified "gracieuse" and was so well-dressed (which considering all the trouble I took I am glad to hear).'* General Canrobert, on the other hand, watching the entry into Paris, saw 'a shocking toilette': 'In spite of the great heat she had on a massive bonnet of white silk . . . with streamers behind and a tuft of marabout feathers on top . . . Her dress was white and flounced, but she had a mantle and parasol of a crude green which did not seem to me to go with the rest of her costume.' The crowning objection was the 'voluminous object' on her arm, an enormous reticule 'like those of our grandmothers . . . made of white satin or silk on which was embroidered a poodle in gold.'* Usually, however, as at the Grand Opera a few days later, when the Queen was in white, with emeralds and diamonds, she was thought to be tastefully but simply dressed. The *Illustrated London News* informed its readers that 'Parisian ladies have been very busy with the Royal bonnets, the general opinion being that they were not perfect specimens of millinery'. The same report, however, concluded that 'a toilet as simple as that generally adopted by the Queen could hardly please a people who are now conspicuous for over-ornament in dress'.*

It was really only on special occasions, particularly those in her private calendar of significant dates which had some personal or family significance, that Queen Victoria would mention in her journal what she was wearing. On family birthdays she was often in what she called 'a smart new gown'* and on Christmas morning also.* At Christmas 'Dear Mama always gave me besides the actual present – something to wear – and would say "This is quite new, you must wear it; I hope you admire my new dress?" '* At dinner on her wedding anniversary, 10 February 1856, the Queen wore the new pink dress which had been just such a present, and in her hair the wreath of orange flowers in frosted gold and white enamel which Albert had designed and given her on the same day ten years previously. On the same day in 1858, she again wore jewellery which was his gift, with 'a silver moire antique dress, trimmed with lace, my big sapphire brooch (Albert's wedding present), a wreath of tulips in my hair, my dear wedding lace veil, as a shawl'.* For the Princess Royal's confirmation on 20 March 1856, 'we ladies, all, wore smart morning dresses'.* On Albert's birthday, 26 August, the dressers put out 'a quite new lilac mousseline de soie'* – a favourite summer material of a very fine soft silk, meshed like muslin. She was of course dressed with special magnificence for her daughter's wedding on 25 January 1858, in mauve moire antique and silver trimmed with Honiton lace, and 'my Regal diadem and the crown diamonds'.*

The Crimean War over, and Peace having been signed in March 1856, the Queen welcomed home her troops, whenever possible, on horseback. On 18 April she attended the first of many reviews at the new army camp at Aldershot. She left Buckingham Palace, 'already dressed in my uniform habit, but this time with a scarf, as all the officers now wear, instead of aiguillettes, and red and white feathers on my hat'.* For once, her appearance excited unqualified admiration. The *Morning Post* the following day informed its readers that, 'The Queen looked charmingly, attired in a dark green riding habit, with a round hat, from which fell a red and white feather of exceeding grace. Over her shoulder Her Majesty wore a belt of gold and tissue work, which added greatly to the effect of a most elegant costume.'

Then Her Majesty went one better. On 16 June she reviewed her troops 'for the first time wearing a scarlet tunic'.* On a 'superbly caparisoned charger' she cut a very dashing figure, 'both striking and beautiful'.* The Queen herself confessed that she was 'not a little proud'* of her scarlet tunic. It was beautifully tailored and lined with white silk. Every seam was stitched by hand, and the detailing was superb.* It aroused great interest, and was described in detail: 'of the finest scarlet cloth; the ornaments of the collar beautifully embroidered in gold and silver, the device the same as a Field Marshal's. Across the left shoulder the blue ribbon of the Garter; a brilliant star upon the left breast, and a crimson and gold net sash, terminated with gold bullion tassels. The hat was of light black felt, with a round crown, and of graceful design, having a general officer's plume of red and white feathers, and a cord of crimson and gold thrice round the crown, ending with two handsome gold and crimson bullion tassels.'* *The Times* was not alone in being very taken with 'the effect of a piquant and graceful costume'.*

All summer long the returning heroes were welcomed by their dashing Queen mounted on her charger, but when she attended a Review on 7 November 1856, the Queen was in her carriage, in a silk dress 'of mazarine blue, with a jacket of fine merino of a maroon colour, trimmed with three narrow rows of velvet of the same colour. Her Majesty carried a miniver muff of very minute proportions.'* Her Majesty was four months pregnant.

 This was her ninth and last child, Princess Beatrice, born 14 April 1857. The Queen's long experience had made her an expert on how to adjust her wardrobe to the expanding months of waiting. When the Princess Royal was expecting her first child, the Queen sent her well-tested, practical and thrifty advice. She discussed expertly the relative merits of boned and elastic stays, and advised her daughter to have two new pairs made in six weeks or two months. 'On no account' was the expectant mother to lace tightly round the waist or have her dresses too tight, 'it is very bad'. The Queen went on to recommend: 'Be sure and put by all your usual-sized stays to wear them hereafter – and keep these different large ones and let Sophie [her daughter's dresser] write the date upon each as you change them in succession; it is of great use – hereafter.'*

Because of the Queen's pregnancy during the early months of 1857, Frieda and her colleagues were spared the business of dressing Her Majesty for drawing-rooms and levees, but the Queen was still as busy as ever. She received diplomats and dignitaries, carried out her usual business, went to the theatre, and kept up her meticulous standards, which included dress. As she explained to her daughter, 'This is more than ever necessary now, when one is apt to feel uncomfortable and disinclined to do anything and therefore must be determinedly struggled against. You know dear, that I always to the last hour dressed properly of an Evening: and it is essential to bear this in mind.'* The only concession she seems to have allowed herself was to have her hair 'just twisted' early in the morning, and then 'made' later in the day.*

For her confinements, the Queen always wore the same night shift.* Afterwards she would stay in bed for some days, and then move into her dressing-room on a sofa. The Empress Eugénie sent her 'a lovely lilac silk peignoir, trimmed with guipure lace'.* No ordinary garment this; for the lace was good enough to appear in public, and when the Prince of Wales was confirmed, the bodice of the Queen's blue silk was trimmed with guipure lace 'off the Empress's dressing gown'.* After Princess Beatrice was born on 14 April the Queen adhered to her usual programme, dressed fully for the first time on 28 April, and dressed for dinner for the first time on 30 April.* Dressing for dinner meant a low-cut gown, with the blue sash of the Order of the Garter across it, jewels and often natural flowers in her hair.

At her children's christenings, the Queen wore her wedding lace and a white dress, in a way that celebrated the connection between the sacrament of marriage and the offering of this new life to the service of God.

The end of a life was marked with as much ceremony. On the complicated subject of mourning, the Queen was most concise: 'Court mournings are short and worn here for all crowned heads and sovereigns etc who are no relations – but private Mourning we wear as long as we like.'* On 2 March 1855, Tsar Nicholas I of Russia had set her quite a poser. While England and France were still at war with Russia, he died. The Queen ordered 'an IMMEDIATE search to be made for Precedents as to the Court going or not going into mourning for a sovereign with whom at the time of his decease England was at war'.* The Lord Chamberlain supplied a list of all Court mournings ordered for foreign sovereigns from the year 1700 to 1815. The Court did not go into mourning on that occasion, so Frieda and her colleagues had no need to get out the black dresses and gloomy crape, although in the same year the Court went into three weeks of mourning for the Dowager Queen of Sardinia, prolonged another week for the Duke of Genoa.* In November 1856 the Queen's half-brother, the Prince of Leiningen, died. 'The Queen put on a black gown immediately,' wrote her Maid of Honour, Eleanor Stanley, 'we have no orders yet about it, but of course it will be silk and crape; and a six months mourning.'* She describes the Queen in 'silk with crape folds to the very top, and black crape collars and sleeves, not to mention a black crape scarf over her shoulders.'* Court mourning did not necessarily put a stop to Court functions. While still in mourning for her aunt the Duchess of Gloucester, the Queen attended a State Ball in a black silk dress, trimmed with black lace and black ribbon and white water-lilies with green leaves; the whole ornamented with diamonds. On her head was an opal and diamond circlet with white water-lilies and green leaves.* Distributing the first Victoria Crosses to Crimean veterans in the now 'usual' scarlet riding coat, she wore round her left arm 'the customary token of military mourning – a band of black crape'.*

As though all this were not enough, it is clear that the Queen's dressers helped out for other members of the family. It was nothing unusual for the Queen's half-sister in Germany to send over a hat so that Sophie Weiss could refurbish it for the season.* The trousseau and wedding of the Princess Royal would have meant an enormous amount of extra work for the dressers. The Queen took a great deal of trouble over her daughter's clothes and could not rest until she had heard from her how they had been received in Berlin: 'I am anxious to know how *all my* toilettes succeeded.'*

Queen Victoria became the world's most famous widow and bequeathed to posterity an image indelibly steeped in black, but when Frieda helped to look after the Queen's wardrobe, we must imagine the young German dresser among cupboards and drawers filled with colour: the lightest of summer dresses in the softest white or lilac silk; the grandest brocaded court trains of red or gold or silver; ball dresses of pink or blue tulle; lace in silver or gold, Honiton lace, French lace; ornaments of roses, jasmine, orchids, diamonds, emeralds and rubies; ribbons of pink satin, red velvet, tartan, crimson satin. We may imagine Frieda and Sophie hurrying between wardrobe and dressing-room and laying out for the Queen a 'train of maize and white glacé ground, lamé with silver and brocaded with bouquets of green leaves and red and gold berries, trimmed with silver blonde',* adjusting the hang of the straw-coloured flounces of the white tulle 'petticoat'; Monsieur Nestor, the coiffeur, having already set in Her Majesty's hair the diadem of diamonds and opals which she was wearing on this occasion. They held out matchless jewels for the Queen to put on, such as the famous Koh-i-noor, or Mountain of Light, set in a regal tiara from which it could be detached to form a brooch; they were entrusted with rubies, emeralds, diamonds, opals and pearls. We can picture them brushing out the skirts of a dove-grey riding habit; folding up shawls of the finest cashmere; refreshing a light chip bonnet with white ribbons and pink roses; making ready wide-brimmed hats for long sunny days at Osborne; packing tartan evening dresses for Balmoral; putting away handkerchiefs like the one the Queen left behind at Haddo, a fountain of white lace embroidered with a sinuous V; shaking out the rich folds of crimson satin of the mantle of the Order of the Bath, or the dark-blue velvet of the Order of the Garter. We may imagine Frieda's clever fingers, trained in the French sewing school, arranging in readiness for the Queen the scarlet velvet, spotted ermine and tassels of gold on the robes of state.

There is no doubt that working for Queen Victoria was very demanding. The hours were long, the pressure unremitting, and the Queen's position and personality such that only the best would do. There are several instances during the Queen's long life of her maids' health breaking down; though how much this was due to the exigencies of the job, and how much to the maids' own state of health, is impossible to tell. Frieda herself is a case in point. We know that she was receiving medical treatment for an unspecified condition in the summer before she left royal service.*

The Queen liked it when her dressers and maids were 'intelligent and quiet and yet quick and active'.* Mary Andrews when being offered her post was told 'a good memory and activity are the things which Her Majesty considers to be indispensable'. After good memory, the Queen added in her own hand, 'good temper'.*

During Frieda's time, the Queen tried out a new dresser for her daughter. Bennett was described approvingly by the Queen as 'respectable and sedate-looking – and is said to dress hair – and make dresses extremely well – is accustomed to travel, and has always been liked in houses where she was living before'.* Further comments, after the Queen had tried out Bennett herself, show that Queen Victoria expected harmony and teamwork in the women around her. It is also obvious that she consulted them and valued their opinions. The Queen thoroughly recommended the new dresser to her daughter as: 'exceptionally quiet and of a very peacable unassuming disposition, handy and quick in dressing – dresses hair well and evidently is a thoroughly experienced lady's maid. My dressers like her and say she is most anxious to do well and live at peace. I have (tiresome as it is) had her every day into my room.'* She urged her daughter to be 'very patient and indulgent at first. Papa has all the ennuis of breaking in his new valet.'* The thought process is all too clear.

Queen Victoria's comfort and wishes came first, but by her own lights, and compared to many of her contemporaries, the Queen was an understanding employer. When her daughter married and went to Berlin, to be welcomed with endless celebrations, the Queen spared a thought for others who would be feeling the strain, asking, 'How do your poor maids bear this hurry scurry?'*

Although most of the Queen's surviving remarks about servants date from after Frieda's term of service, they help to reveal her attitude to those who were in close, daily contact with her. The Queen looked on her personal servants 'as belonging to her family'.* She felt that with any servants 'The chief thing, is treating them kindly'.* This she was obliged to stress more than once: 'Civility and consideration for the servants is another thing which the Queen is *very* particular about.'* Those who forgot, did so at their peril. Prince Arthur, her favourite son, bringing home military manners, earned himself a thundering rebuke; he must not 'treat servants etc like many do, as soldiers, which does great harm and which especially in the *Queen's home* is totally out of place and she will not tolerate it'.*

Once in a position of privilege, royal servants were expected not to abuse it. When Mary Andrews became dresser to Princess Helena in 1866, when the Princess married, it was made clear to her that it was her duty to 'make no difficulties' on any occasion, 'and treat all the other servants with perfect civility'.* At the end of a memorandum, initialled by the Queen, laying out the duties of the wardrobe maids, this was again emphasised: 'Her Majesty expects that they will be perfectly civil [to] all the other servants in the House – friendly and obliging to those who are in immediate attendance on Herself.'*

The relationship between the Queen and Frieda was a professional one in a domestic setting, but the Queen took an interest in Frieda's life, as she did in all those about her. Frieda's sightseeing bears the stamp of the Queen's interests, from the water-colour exhibition by Crimean Simpson, who worked for the Queen, to the Crystal Palace, one of the sights of London in which the Queen took the deepest interest because of its connection with her husband. An ardent theatre-goer herself, the Queen made sure that Frieda saw typical English theatre. Authority for Frieda's visit to Gosport must have come from very high up indeed, given that the Admiralty were cautious to the point of paranoia about visitors. Permission for Frieda to stay at Osborne in September 1855 would almost certainly have to have been requested from the Queen. There cannot have been much time during dressing, with the Queen receiving letters, or, in the evening, writing out the order in which her guests were going into dinner,* for much conversation, but there is evidence that they did discuss events: the Queen laughed heartily when told that long-legged Frieda had been taken for a 'petite anglaise' in Paris. Queen and dresser had one strong interest in common, and the Queen, who could turn out a dashing sketch herself, indulged Frieda's passion when, on Christmas Eve 1857, amid the usual 'joyous bustle', Her Majesty distributed her presents, and Frieda received 'a circular box of colours', a 'roll up case of pencils', and a 'block book'.* This was most unusual. Normally, the dressers and maids could expect something like a silk dress, a piece of jewellery, or a pair of sable cuffs, and indeed, the majority of Frieda's Christmas presents from the Queen were of this conventional order. In 1855 she was given a brooch of three gold rings and a turquoise-blue enamel ribbon with a carbuncle and small pearls;* in 1856 she received a gold étui for needlework;* in 1858, a pair of gold hairpins;* all similar to the presents given to her colleagues. Frieda sent home a careful drawing of each.

It is one of the characteristics of Frieda's job that she and her like were generally invisible to the people they served. The better the servant, the less she was noticed. The Queen, in her Journal, was somewhat unusual in according her servants the dignity of referring to them by name. Princess Beatrice, however, who edited her mother's journal after the Queen's death, and rewrote it, burning the original as she went along, rendered their shadowy figures invisible again.

How effectively Princess Beatrice erased their persons can be judged by comparing her copy with earlier copies of parts of the Queen's journal, such as that for 9 August 1845, in which we can see that the movements of her personal servants mattered to the Queen: 'I undressed as quickly as possibly and then Singer, Peneyvre, Rebecca and Dehler set off for Woolwich. Skerrett and Margaret return to Osborne.'* Princess Beatrice's version reads: 'undressed as quickly as possible, the maids having to leave for Woolwich.'*

The Princess's alterations have also had the effect of obliterating records of the dressers' functions. About 1881 the Queen's account of the state visit to Paris was printed for private circulation. In it the Queen records how 'the Empress gave me a beautiful bouquet holder of diamonds, pearls, and rubies, with the stems of enamel. She said nothing beyond hoping I would take the bouquet; and I felt shy about accepting it, and inquired through my dresser of her dresser, who then said she hoped I would retain it. It is quite lovely.'* The Queen's journal, as copied by Princess Beatrice, omits this delicate little negotiation via the dressers and simply reads: 'I felt shy about accepting it. It is quite lovely.'*

In the light of such censorship, and the absence of any comparable accounts of palace life from other royal servants, Frieda's record of her time in England is all the more interesting and valuable. Frieda's viewpoint is curious and unique; here is an intelligent, articulate voice from the vanished, otherwise silent world of the hierarchy which underpinned the workings of Queen Victoria's court.

Note on the text

The letters printed here were begun within a few weeks of Frieda's arrival at Windsor, and cover the first two years of her term of service. They are written on both sides of thin, flimsy paper, like airmail paper, occasionally bearing the stamp of Buckingham Palace, Osborne, or Balmoral. They are directed not to individuals, but to a small circle of people: 'To my friends, as a part of me from my heart, as they have been poured out. The tale is without plan, without order, only for you, remember me!' So reads a note on Letter 2. Each of the twelve letters describes a different aspect of Frieda's life in England, and she repeats herself only at the specific request of her readers. The letters are to a certain extent self-conscious and carefully planned, prefixed with epigraphs and the ready quotations, often inaccurate, as though she were quoting from memory, which are a part of Frieda's make-up. Once she gets going, however, Frieda expresses herself very spontaneously. The handwriting is rapid and not very careful, she crosses her lines and often writes down the side of the paper; but there are few changes of mind or crossings out. The style is slightly untidy and breathless. No censorship is involved other than Frieda's own discretion.

The letters have remained in the possession of Frieda's family until the present day. The ink from Frieda's hurrying pen is eating into the paper, and they are becoming unreadable, a process which must have begun in her own lifetime, as there is a late nineteenth-century copy of them, much easier to read, but which has been bowdlerised in line with more prudish mores than Frieda's. The translation was done after careful photocopying of the originals had helped to separate the writing on the front and back of each page. These photocopies were used for the translation. Frieda's spellings of English names and places, often phonetically rendered, have been silently corrected.

Letter 1

OSBORNE HOUSE AND
WINDSOR CASTLE
1855

Frieda began to write almost as soon as she had settled in. This letter covers January 1855, spent at Osborne and Windsor Castle. Usually, the Queen went to Osborne for a few days before Christmas; this winter, however, what the Queen called 'the state of affairs' had made her postpone her visit until January.

Frieda's description of Osborne is interesting. The house was entirely the creation of Prince Albert, built between 1845 and 1850 as an ecape from the trammels and ceremonies of life at Windsor and Buckingham Palace. From the Italianate style in which it was built, to the furniture and ornaments which filled it, and the trees and plants on the surrounding estate, all was a reflection of his taste. It was not universally admired, and the German Frieda is one of the few voices to speak in praise of the German Prince's creation.

Frieda was a timid sailor, and subtitled this letter 'Second improved version of a sea journey'; her first, the crossing to England, cannot have been a comfortable experience.

On Friday 5th [*January*] we were to go to Osborne, in the glorious Isle of Wight, for three days. The packing on the 4th shall be passed over in silence, because there is nothing agreeable and much that is disagreeable about it. A wardrobe maid and one dresser had to travel with the baggage, the other with the Queen. I was sent with the baggage, because this arrived two hours later, and I as a stranger could not be among the first to arrive. One of the wardrobe maids, Mary,[1] a girl from Brussels, went with me. She is a very good, well-brought-up and well-educated young girl, who has been here for only six months, and who speaks good German and English and excellent French, which she has been teaching me a little; we often talk together and I learn a great deal in this way.

And so we two, accompanied by two men-servants, who fetched us from our rooms at seven o'clock, were taken along endless corridors to a big gateway which I had never seen before, where stood a magnificent travelling coach, packed high with luggage and harnessed with four horses. We climbed in (whether the four horses were there because of our weight or that of the luggage I leave you to decide). Another carriage, loaded entirely with baggage and accompanied by a manservant, followed us.

The moon was still shining quite clear and bright. We had a special locomotive, because there was no train at that early hour. We stayed sitting quite at ease in our very comfortable carriage, which was then lashed onto another, on the rails. Very soon we were moving along with the greatest rapidity, and we were confronted with a spectacle which was rich compensation for our lost sleep, as we had been busy until past midnight the previous day. The moon disappeared, and for a few moments all was quite grey and dark; then all at once a bright streak appeared in the sky, and the vast horizon was illuminated with such enchanting beauty that one was quite swept away by it. The spectacle changed every minute, which is so characteristic of this country in general: the weather often changes completely within a quarter of an hour. Sometimes we could see nothing, and seemed to be enveloped in a cloud of smoke coming from the engine and completely swallowing up our carriage, for we were travelling incredibly fast; then came a gust of wind and the landscape lay revealed before our eyes again, quite changed, and glowing with an increasingly lovely light. So it continued for about half an hour until daylight – a day like the most beautiful springtime; the sun was clear and bright, and we had not seen such a fine day for a long time.

And so our journey continued until half past ten. There was always something new to look at. We passed towns and country houses

---

1 Mary Ann Andrews, appointed wardrobe maid 1 July 1854; remained with the Queen until 5 July 1866, when she became dresser to Queen Victoria's third daughter, Princess Helena.*

which were of great interest to us because of their – to us – quite strange and curious architecture. Mary was delighted to be able to see the country through which we were passing for once, as hitherto she had always been asleep on this journey. I would not let her sleep; she would have missed too much. Once the train stopped, and we consumed some breakfast which the man-servant had pointed out to us in the side pockets of the carriage at the beginning of the journey: it consisted of ham, capon, bread and butter and port-wine. It had been provided so that we should eat before the sea-crossing.

At half past ten we arrived in Southampton. We climbed out and were taken on board the *Ruby* by one of the men-servants. The other stayed with the carriage. The *Ruby* is a steamship, which had been hired just for us. We were quite alone on the deck, where we had to wait for an hour and a half until the two carriages had been loaded onto a lighter, which was attached to the ship. It was a delightful interlude for us, as the weather was so favourable. The harbour in which our ship lay was very large and extremely busy, full of ships lying at anchor, some of them enormous, mostly merchant ships, many of them bound for America. I observed all this closely, and then took out my sketchbook, and drew a point of land stretching out into the sea, two big ships, and an expanse of sea; it made quite a nice little picture. I wrote, not without pride 'On board the *Ruby*' beneath it: I could not help thinking of Chamisso's Rurick.[1] I felt so well and cheerful that I decided on no account to leave the deck, for I was really frightened to death of the cabin. At last we set sail; the sea was like a clear mirror, the sun shone brightly, not the slightest breeze stirred. As the shore grew farther and farther away, and the sea spread itself out ever wider before us, a strange and wonderful mood came over me: I could not tear my eyes away from the view, while the ship moved so little that one had the impression that everything else was moving away, while we stood still. The Captain was so amused at my delight with the sea that he summoned up a little French – his was half rusted away with disuse, while mine was new and Parisian beside it – and showed me the quietest spot on the deck, where he advised me to

[1] Adelbert von Chamisso (1781–1838), German romantic poet and botanist, was appointed 'natural scientist' on a Russian expedition round the world from 1815 to 1818 on board the Brig *Rurik* and recorded his impressions in *Reise um die Welt*, acclaimed as one of the finest travel books of the century.

walk up and down throughout the crossing, as I would feel the movement of the ship less if I myself kept moving. It was so beautiful. Other ships sailed past us; I felt quite well. Until about three-quarters of an hour later, when the sky quite suddenly became black, the helmsman put on his waterproof, and the movement of the ship began to grow very violent. The Captain urged us to go below: it would soon be raining and the wind was too strong to hold an umbrella. We went below, but hardly had I reached the cabin when I felt the wretched sickness coming on. I put my shawl over my head, wrapped myself in my coat, and went up on deck alone, where it was much better; I held onto a rope so as not to be knocked over by wind or dizziness. The view was spectacular: the waves rose very high, and it began to rain a little. To me it seemed like a storm, although in fact for the sailors it was nothing more than what Herr Maier used to call a *sprinkling*. The rain lasted only ten minutes, but the sky stayed grey and misty. Until then I had managed to suppress mild bouts of seasickness thanks to the impressive spectacle before me; I tried to subjugate the flesh to the spirit; although I could hardly stand and was shivering violently, I forced myself to think that it was more beautiful than uncomfortable, and I began to sing softly 'The ship glides through the waves'; it surely could not go on for much longer. Then all at once the sun came out, piercing the mist, and the coast of the lovely Isle of Wight lay revealed before our eyes. In front of us was a charming little town [Cowes] built right on the edge of the sea. In a few minutes we were at the quayside. We went ashore, and had to wait a little until the carriages had been hauled up. Four fine horses were standing ready, and were harnessed to our carriage; we climbed in, and in a quarter of an hour we were at the gates of a palace whose splendour and magnificence shall be described on another page, or rather, merely hinted at, for who could describe it? I shall only add here that I was very pleased to have seen a ship's captain at last, for one so often reads about them. He certainly did not look romantic: he had a very red face and was not at all cultivated. As we stood on the shore with the old servant I felt as if I were in a play; he was wearing a coat just like Meyerhofer in the 'Sohn auf Reisen'.[1] A crowd of children

---

[1] A comedy in two acts by Leopold Feldmann (1802–82), performed at the Hoftheater in Karlsruhe once, in 1852.

gathered around us, and adults too, staring at us, because we belonged to the Queen's household. They had no inkling how little I was to be envied.

Osborne House

The house is built on a small hill and is entirely in the Italian style: it consists of a large house in the centre with terraces and arcades, joined on either side to two pavilions with towers. Compared to Windsor the whole building is like a house of cards; but it has such a charming, fresh and cheerful aspect. One feels transported to the South. The air is mild and soft, not healthy for long periods, except for very few people. Around the house are the most delightful grounds, with fountains, the most magnificent statues, and a splendid array of vases, like the biggest ones they have in the Art Gallery at Karlsruhe, behind railings; here they stand out in the open, between laurel and myrtle bushes, and they stay outside the whole year round. The road leading into the park is marked by two wonderful stags[1] carved in stone. The splashing of fountains is everywhere, and there are lovely grottoes cut out of stone, with marble[2] figures. On one side one sees the endless expanse of the sea, which from here, ten minutes' walk away, looks so smooth that the ships seem to be standing on glass or ice. Not far away there are farmhouses, foresters' cottages etc. Here everything looks as small as a doll's house compared with grandiose Windsor. But everything is designed to enchant the senses. Nature and Art flourish with a Southern splendour and profusion. Whereas in Windsor one is overawed by the might and size of the Castle and wishes to learn about it, here one wishes only to revel in the enjoyment of Art and Nature. Inside, everything is so lovely, so bright and cheerful, everything smiles at one. The works of art accumulated here are innumerable. The main corridors have magnificent mosaic floors, great glass doors through which the sea is visible, and statues and large candelabra alternating with each other.

[1] Not in fact stone, but zinc-bronze copies, by Messrs Geiss of Berlin, of the statues by Christian Rauch (1777–1857) which stood at the entrance to the park of Glienicke at Potsdam. Purchased by Queen Victoria at the Great Exhibition 1851.
[2] Most of the statues on the terrace were bronze. One or two were plaster.

The candelabra are about twice as tall as me, of glass all the way up, or many are of pale-blue porcelain, set with porcelain pictures in the form of medallions, and some are of a quite extraordinary size: these came from the Exhibition.[1] All the busts and statues are of white marble. In the middle, in a niche like a shrine is a marble figure of the Queen[2] with crown and sceptre. The ceilings are painted. The pictures which adorn the walls of the many rooms are choice works of art. The portraits are mostly by Winterhalter. In the Queen's sitting-room hangs the magnificent painting by Winterhalter which was in the Exhibition, 'Girls at the water'[3] – the Bergmüllers have a daguerreotype of it. It costs 12,000 fl. There are wonderful scenes from the Scottish Highlands by the celebrated animal painter Sir Edwin Landseer. One of them,[4] as big as one wall of our room, shows two Scotsmen hunting stags. There are paintings by Koekkoek,[5] by Achenbach:[6] everything that is excellent is here. In one small room the walls are hung with original drawings which are wonderful; two by Lindemann-Frommel[7] reminded me of home – they are the original drawings of the published lithographs by him. Some of the fireplaces here are lined with mirrors, right into the hearth, which

[1] A pair of crystal cut-glass candelabra, manufactured by Osler and Co., arranged for fifteen lights, the shafts formed of prisms three feet long, and the whole standing eight feet high, were given to the Queen by Albert on her birthday in 1848, and were lent to the Great Exhibition.

[2] By John Gibson RA (1790–1866), in classical Greek drapery, wearing a coronet and holding a wreath in the right hand and a scroll in the left. A replica of the statue at Buckingham Palace, and given to Prince Albert by the Queen on his birthday in 1849.

[3] *Florinda* by Franz Xaver Winterhalter (1806–73) was given to Prince Albert by the Queen for his birthday in 1852. She paid £1000 for it in two instalments of £500.* Winterhalter would have had a strong local connection for Frieda, since his highly successful career as portrait painter to the royalty of Europe began when he became portrait painter to the Grand Duke of Baden in 1834.

[4] *The Deer Drive* by Sir Edwin Landseer (1802–62) hung in the Council Room. This vast canvas which measured 96 x 139 inches had been bought by Prince Albert in 1847. Landseer is the only painter who has no connection with Karlsruhe that Frieda singles out from the multitude whose work hung at Osborne.

[5] Barend Cornelius Koekkoek (1803–73), poet, lithographer, landscape painter; one of a large clan of Dutch painters. In 1845 King Leopold of the Belgians gave Prince Albert the landscapes *Morning* and *Evening*, which were hung at Osborne. Frieda may have known his *Bergwald*, which was in the Art Gallery at Karlsruhe.

[6] Two Italian landscapes, also called *Morning* and *Evening* had been given to the Queen by Albert for Christmas 1854. They were by Oswald Achenbach (1827–1905), pupil of his better-known elder brother Andreas Achenbach. Work by an Achenbach (without a Christian name) was listed as hanging in the Grand Ducal Art Gallery of Karlsuhe in 1852.*

[7] Karl August Lindemann-Frommel (1819–91). Genre and landscape painter, watercolourist and lithographer. Pupil of his adoptive father, Carl Ludwig Lindemann-Frommel, who had been Director of the Gallery in Karlsruhe since 1824.

makes a splendid effect; some are of pale-blue porcelain painted with blue flowers. In some rooms the walls are painted with light-blue glossy oil-paint, and the carpets are red. In fact there is a magnificent array of carpets here.

Nearly all the men-servants sleep in another house that cannot be seen from here, a few minutes' walk away, so that it is quite quiet in the house: they are taken there in a waggon each night at eleven o'clock. We have our rooms on the third floor, above the Queen. Here my size is an advantage, for as space is in general limited here, we have very small rooms. The beds are not very big either, and thus a bigger one had to be arranged for me, so that I can lie full length.

A strange thing here is that all trees are the same height, and quite round, as if they had been cut off; I thought this had been done on purpose, but it is the sea wind, which is at its strongest at just this level, and which prevents the trees from growing any taller: they look as if they had been sawn off. The result is more strange than attractive. The Prince's valet, Herr Löhlein,[1] a very good man, a forester's son from Coburg, who has already been here for seven years and is married to an Englishwoman, was kind enough to take me around for two hours, while the Queen was at church, and to show me everything. We went down to the sea-shore, and I looked for shells, which made him roar with laughter, and he said that in six months I would not be looking for them any more. He also took me to a small hill quite nearby, where a charming little Swiss cottage[2] has been built for the children. On the ground floor is a sweet little kitchen. The floor and walls are of porcelain, and it is equipped with lovely shining kitchen utensils. The children sometimes breakfast there. A gardener and his wife live there. The upper floor, which has a pretty carved balcony running right round it, consists of a small dressing-room with a couch and toilet articles; a little dining-room, which is wonderful, with chairs, tables, walls of most beautifully carved wood, and a carved pianino too, supported by carved figures. Then there is

---

[1] Rudolph Löhlein came from Coburg in 1847 as Prince Albert's *Jäger*, literally, huntsman, but used at Queen Victoria's Court to mean personal outdoor servant. In 1860 he became the Prince's valet. After the Prince's death he became an 'Extra Personal Attendant'. He retired in 1884 and died in 1896.

[2] The first stone was laid by the royal children, in the presence of their parents, on 5 May 1853.

another small room with eight glass cupboards, one for each of the children;[1] in these they keep choice examples of shells, stones, beetles, butterflies, moss and flower collections. How I should have liked to take just one stone with me for Georg.[2] The Swiss cottage is also surrounded by eight little gardens, one for each child; when they are here they work in their gardens, and there is a little house with the sweetest little garden tools.

Once when I had a free moment I drew the view from an empty guest room, just above the Queen's room, which has the most beautiful outlook over the sea. Good Sophie is always helping me to snatch a brief hour for this purpose, and rejoices with me whenever I manage to draw something. Of course it always has to be done quickly, and is therefore never completed. And yet perhaps because of this I have achieved a style which is more artistic, and which I have always found rather difficult. I enjoyed my stay immensely, and I shall be glad if we go there again, although the Queen's staff, without exception, dislike staying there, and all prophesy that I shall not always like it so much. But I shall never believe that. For one has more free hours here, and consequently I do more drawing, and that is enough for me. The air here does not suit Sophie very well; and the others, mostly married men, being so far from London where their families live, are quite cut off here, and hence they do not like it. For me, to be a few hours further away from home makes no difference, and I am cut off anyway; so if the climate suits me, I have no objection to the Queen going to Osborne.

Journey from Osborne to Windsor

This time I travelled with the Queen,[3] so you must hear how it went. Having managed to survive the flurry of packing, we were told at two o'clock on Tuesday the 9th that the carriages were ready. We got into a smart, light carriage, and drove down to the shore about five

---

[1] The Royal Family was still incomplete. Queen Victoria's ninth and last child, Princess Beatrice, was not born until 1857.

[2] Georg Arnold (1827–96), the oldest of Frieda's five brothers and sisters.

[3] For Her Majesty this journey was routine; her account of it in her Journal for 9 January 1855 reads 'started at 2 "à grand regret", reaching Windsor at ½ p. 5'.*

minutes' away, where a boat with the Queen's flag took us out to sea to join the steamer, an enjoyable little trip; another boat was waiting for the Queen, for she always comes last, so that the ship can leave immediately after she arrives.

This small steamer,[1] built specially for the Queen, is very neat and dainty, most comfortable and attractive; the sailors are all dressed in fresh clean uniforms, with coloured ribbons on their caps, and beaming with pride because they have the privilege of carrying the Queen in their ship. An admiral, a captain, and a lieutenant, in full dress uniform, received their sovereign, with heads bared. This time too the weather was very favourable and everyone stayed on deck. The ship got under way so amazingly fast and moved so quickly that it seemed scarcely possible. This time we went quite a different way, to the biggest English seaport, Portsmouth. The crossing was extremely interesting. After an hour and a quarter we were already close to the shore. In this harbour there were numerous large warships,[2] with their entire crews ranged on their decks: they bristled with sailors everywhere, up to the highest topmast, on ropes and rope ladders. Hardly had our ship been sighted when they began to fire salvoes, and as soon as we came near three loud 'Hurrahs!' rang out from all sides. Countless little boats, each with a naval officer and a few soldiers, came far out to sea to welcome us, waving their caps and shouting hurrah.

The train[3] was quite close to the shore, so we had only to walk along a carpeted passage to find ourselves in a comfortable carriage. Here a detachment of soldiers[4] was drawn up, playing 'God save the Queen'. Again we moved off with astonishing speed, stopping nowhere, so that we were already in Windsor by five o'clock. I had felt so well during the crossing; it was so calm, and I have never enjoyed watching the waves so much. But the cruel gods of the sea demanded

[1] The *Fairy*, commanded by Captain the Hon. Joseph Denman. The Court Circular for 9 January 1855 makes no mention of the admiral; possibly Frieda mistook the uniform.

[2] The Court Circular for 9 January 1855 records that Her Majesty steamed up to Gosport 'under the usual salutes and ceremonies'. When the Queen went to Osborne just a few days' earlier, the crews of the '*Victory, Illustrious, Himalaya* etc.' cheered the Queen loudly and the usual salutes were fired by the *Esk* and the *Duke of Wellington* at Spithead.*

[3] In the Royal Clarence Victualling Yard at Gosport. The station, private, and for the use of Her Majesty, belonged to the London and South Western Company.

[4] Grenadier and Light Company of the Royal Wiltshire Militia.

their sacrifice nevertheless. 'Thy stillness only hides the traitor's mask.' Next morning I awoke with a fearful headache which tormented me the whole day. After that I had a sleepless night, unable to summon up the strength to banish thoughts which haunted me like ghosts. Then a day in bed, followed by a night full of the loveliest dreams of home: sometimes I thought I was at home; sometimes you were beside me, dear Mother, and sometimes it was another of my dear ones. The next day I spent in an armchair, and that night both ghosts and sweet dreams were overwhelmed by a deep sleep. I awoke next morning feeling stronger again, but with a heavy cold, which was the prosaic end of the whole episode. All this time good Sophie was very kind to me. The Queen sent a friendly little man in a black frock coat and kid gloves to see me twice a day: it was Mr Brown[1] the Household doctor. He took my pulse, gave me large doses of medicine and brought me pills in such a pretty little box that one was almost glad to have to take them. He said I had a very good constitution and all would be over in two days. It was just that Germans were bad sailors, he said; but they get used to it. It always irritates the bile, and a little seasickness is healthy if it is not too violent, he said. Sophie, who also had a headache, was violently sick on the first evening, and that cured her, but for a little exhaustion. Madame Nickel,[2] of whom I wrote to you, also came to see me every day; she is so kind and good to me that I feel under a great obligation to her. She also came to England when she was young, after losing her parents, and has not forgotten how strange one feels, so she takes care of the Germans with genuine kindness.

I almost forgot to mention the crowds of people, particularly children, who stood packed together along the barriers on either side of the railway, for mile after mile, shouting and waving their hats. And what sort of children? I shall only say: our little darling,[3] even in his most ordinary clothes, is a dandy compared to these children.

I never could grasp the idea of magnetism, but now it is clear to me, since my sea-crossing. Not that I think of it as being like the

---

[1] Dr Henry Brown, Apothecary to the Household at Windsor Castle from 1837 to 1866.
[2] née Lisette Singer; her husband, Johan Carl Eduard Nickel was Conductor of Music of Her Majesty's State Band.
[3] Presumably Frieda is referring to her youngest brother, Wilhelm Arnold (1838–1910).

irresistible power of the sea. No, it is rather that I now have proof that there are forces which work so powerfully on man, both physically and mentally, that his own will is powerless to stop him giving in to them. Yes, we creatures of the dry land should stay at home away from the water. If I win the lottery one day, I shall found an institution for German girls who have to leave their country against their will. But for fear of actually winning it and having to keep my word I shall not buy a ticket. For when would I see you again if that happened? What would happen to my old, tried friends? Just wait: when I come back some day, I shall be much bigger, and people will look at me with amazement and horror; but on the other hand I shall be so weighed down with happiness that perhaps I shall be just the same size as before, except with a few deep lines on my face, when you see me. You all sent me such warm New Year's wishes, for which I thank you a thousand times: I am sure they will not be without beneficial effects.

Now let me tell you how I began the New Year. On the last day of the year I was on duty, and at just a quarter to twelve I was free to go to my room.[1] I sat down quietly at my table, read a sermon by Herr Hausrath[2] for the last day of the year, and had just finished when the lovely sound of many bells announced the New Year, and I opened my hymn book at the hymn 'The greater the Cross, the nearer Heaven'. After I had read it through I thought of all those at home, wished them all happiness, and then slept very well.

On New Year's Day the Queen gave a grand concert,[3] to which extremely distinguished lords and ladies were invited; we had the honour of dressing her for it, and were given tickets for a little musicians' gallery, like the one in the Museum Hall, where the most

[1] Queen Victoria and Prince Albert had spent a quiet evening; they had dined alone and read a meditation on the close of the year.

[2] Friedrich August Hausrath (1805–47), a theologian who lived in Karlsruhe, a close-knit community: he was tutor to Carl Weltzien, whose son Alexander later married Frieda's daughter Victoria.

[3] The Queen also enjoyed the evening, writing in her Journal for 1 January 1855: 'After dinner we had some very fine music in St George's Hall, really the finest of any of these performances we have had. There was an orchestra of 140 and a chorus of 75 ... All the neighbours, etc., were invited.'

senior servants of the Queen and the Prince were seated. It began at ten o'clock and ended at half past twelve. How pleasantly surprised I was when I beheld a group of ladies dressed in white and gentlemen dressed in black on a raised platform, and saw from the programme that we were to hear first of all Beethoven's *In Praise of Music*, then the Walpurgisnacht. Madame Clara Novello,[1] soprano, Madame Weiss,[2] contralto, Mr Sims Reeves[3] and Mr Weiss,[4] performed the solo parts wonderfully. The chorus was from the Italian Opera[5] in London. The whole performance was highly successful, particularly Novello, who is an enchanting singer. I listened with rapt attention, and was especially moved by the Walpurgisnacht, which was still so fresh in my memory: I could hear the German text throughout, although all were singing in English. At the end of the concert Novello sang 'God save the Queen', with a wonderful accompaniment, as the Queen was leaving the hall. It sent cold shivers down my spine: all the greatness of the nation lay in that thrilling sound. Unforgettable. I only wish my St Cecilians[6] could have heard the concert with me; if only Aunt Babette[7] had been able to see it all – what a wealth of diamonds! The hall in which the concert took place is magnificent: it is tremendously long, and the ceiling and walls are painted with brightly coloured coats of arms of great families, and decorated with weapons. Another time I shall describe the Throne Room, for today I think you have had enough. Farewell, and a thousand thanks for your dear letters. My replies to each will follow little by little. Write to me again. I read all my letters every day and sometimes when I am alone, I read them

---

[1] Clara Novello (1818–1908). Achieved fame as oratorio singer. Appeared regularly before royalty at state concerts.

[2] née Georgina Ansell Barrett (1826–80).

[3] John Sims Reeves (1818–1900). Enjoyed a long and successful career as an operatic tenor. Particularly admired in Handel oratories.

[4] Willoughby Hunter Weiss (1820–67). Vocalist and composer. Especially admired as an exponent of oratorio music. Perhaps best known, in his own day, as the composer of the hugely popular 'The Village Blacksmith', set to Longfellow's words.

[5] The name given to the theatres where opera was sung in Italian. These singers came from the Royal Italian Opera, Covent Garden Theatre, opened in 1846 with Michael Costa as musical director. Some of the singers also came from the Sacred Harmonic Society, an amateur choir which sang at Exeter Hall.

[6] A choral society in Karslruhe.

[7] Anna Barbara Rossbach, b. 1812, youngest sister of Frieda's mother.

out loud so that I not only read them, but hear them too.

I remain, as always,
Your loving Frieda
Be true to me too!

Windsor Castle

One can see the full extent of the Castle, and even then not all of it, from only one side. From there it gives the impression of a small citadel, because of its thick walls and numerous towers. It is of a dark-grey colour almost throughout, except for a few small areas which are of red brick. The whole Castle is built of handsome stones of exactly the same size. It has so many towers, both large and small, that one simply cannot describe them all. On both sides are beautiful terraces; on the side on which the Queen's and the Prince's rooms are situated there is a large pool with a fountain on the terrace.[1] This is open to the public only on Sunday; otherwise it is reserved for the Royal Family. The other terrace[2] is rather narrower and overlooks the little town of Windsor, and Eton which is nearby, well known for a college where the sons of the English aristocracy study. There is a magnificent old church[3] there too, which looks very beautiful in the distance. The view from this terrace makes a strong impression on foreigners because from here one sees quantities of those English country houses which one hears and reads so much about: none of them have roofs, that is, they have such small flat ones that one can hardly see them for the enormous chimneys which are on every house. Indeed one sees so many chimneys everywhere here that it is no wonder that everything looks smoke-blackened.

Inside the Castle is a great paved courtyard, completely enclosed by the mighty walls of the Castle, with a wonderful fountain and a magnificent equestrian statue[4] on one side. In the building itself there are so many staircases and corridors that one can really get lost. There are carpets throughout the Castle, from the lowest corridor upwards,

---

[1] The East Terrace.

[2] North Terrace.

[3] Eton College Chapel.

[4] The statue in the Quadrangle depicts Charles II as a Roman emperor. Given by Tobias Rustat, a devoted admirer of the king, in 1680.

and great lamps hang everywhere, which are lit every evening and burn all night. The whole Castle is lighted from four o'clock in the afternoon until eight o'clock in the morning. A nice little lamp is brought into each room at twilight, and burns all night; and if one is staying in one's room, wax candles are lit. Every evening I have three thick new candles in silver candlesticks. I find the many carpets very painful for my feet; to have a cold floor to walk on for once would be a boon.

One of the finest parts of the Castle is a great corridor,[1] very wide and immensely long, which begins at the biggest staircase, the one usually used only by the Queen, and stretches from there to the dining-room and the magnificent rooms in which the Queen's guests take tea. On one side of the corridor there are enormous arched windows; on the other, opposite each window, there are huge doors, richly decorated with gold. They all lead, if not always directly, into the royal apartments and the guest rooms for the lords and peers. The most wonderful paintings are hung here, mostly scenes from the lives of the Royal Family, for instance the baptism of the Prince of Wales, the Queen in her coronation robes, her marriage, her reception of Louis Philippe.[2] There are many old hunting pictures, and portraits of members of the family and of famous English statesmen. Then there are busts in white marble of all the royal relations, on all kinds of pedestals, sometimes gilded all over; and the most beautiful vases, one of them a gift from the Emperor of Russia,[3] which is about four times as tall as me. There are many lovely bronzes of horses and of numerous historical characters. Flower-tables with fresh flowers stand near the fireplaces, where there is always a fire blazing: the whole Castle is always heated, including all the corridors. Here and there are sofas and day-beds; the doors are entirely covered with mirrors, and there are lamps standing on the most beautiful ornamental columns, which illuminate everything most wonderfully. The ladies and gentlemen walk along here to meals, and afterwards

[1] The Corridor, 550 feet long, built in order to link the rooms of the king's private apartments, was constructed 1824–8 by Sir Jeffry Wyatville, as part of the major transformation of Windsor Castle under George IV.

[2] The King of the French visited Windsor in 1844.

[3] Tsar Nicholas I presented Queen Victoria with a large malachite vase in 1839, to which Frieda is probably referring, although it appears in contemporary paintings not in the Corridor but in the Grand Reception Room.

they sometimes take exercise here. A sleeping child in white marble pleases me almost more than anything else in the corridor: it is quite charming. In the evening, when the company is at dinner, we walk about there a little.

Very close to the corridor, near the Queen's sitting-room, is a small room with a large window and a beautiful view. It has a large fireplace with a lovely mirror and vases and silver candelabra, a sofa, a few tables and chairs. This is the so-called Wardrobe, although there are no clothes in it, and this is where we sit (the one who is on duty stays there all day, the other not so long) and work, for there is always plenty to do, and wait for the Queen to ring for us. Upstairs, or rather up several flights of stairs, is my bedroom. It is quite remarkable, in fact almost uncanny, how quiet this enormous building is, and sometimes one could imagine that the Castle was quite empty. For everyone goes about their business in the most calm and orderly fashion, and because of the carpets one hears nothing at all. People speak very quietly. And yet there are so many people in the place that 300–400 lb of meat[1] are eaten every day, and certainly almost 100 measures of tea are drunk, not to mention everything else that is consumed.

The use of fireplaces everywhere for heating makes a very strange but not unattractive impression. The fireplaces in the large rooms are often very handsome; for instance, in one room where everything is almost entirely covered with gold, all the walls, there is a fireplace of white marble, with superb gold decoration. On either side stands a devil, a large figure made of iron, trying to throw a child into the fire. The black figure against the white marble makes a most striking effect.[2] Then there are other rooms entirely panelled in wood, and everywhere there are heavy damask curtains.

I still have not seen all the halls and rooms; far from it, I have seen scarcely a sixth of them, and yet I cannot possibly describe all this to you: I only want you to have a little idea of what it is like. It is quite impossible to describe the Gold Pantry.[3] It is amazing and splendid

---

[1] This is an understatement. In 1855 the daily amount of beef, lamb and pork supplied to London, Windsor and Osborne when the Queen was in residence averaged 629 lb. The average beef carcase was reckoned at 640 lb.*

[2] Frieda is probably referring to the Crimson Drawing-room, which has a chimney piece by Vulliamy, of marble and gilt bronze, with satyrs holding infants on either side.

[3] Where the gold plate was kept.

what treasures there are, heaped up there; several hundred heavy gold dishes, countless plates, the christening font[1] for the children, of wonderful workmanship, carried by golden figures, as tall as a six-year-old child. Countless candelabra of the greatest possible variety, and a great, great quantity of things which one can only stare at in amazement. A table laid with all this is really a sight worth seeing. If our table seemed princely enough as it was on the first day, now it seems quite ordinary to me. For we have very fine painted porcelain, silver knives and forks and salt and mustard pots etc.[2] Julie[3] should see the kitchen here one day; I get quite lost in it. A German, Herr Doll,[4] showed me round – everything is so neat and clean – it is about as big as the Museum Hall. There are twelve ranges, with a huge iron table in the centre which is heated from below, and on which the dishes are set. On both sides are huge fires over which roasts are suspended on spits, with great iron chains driven round constantly by a machine. On one of these fires alone five Zentner[5] of charcoal are burned every single day. At Christmas a whole ox weighing 400 lb was roasted here; it was brought to the table: that was indeed a roast beef. I saw a Welsh capon in the kitchen which weighed 24 lb – everything here is on this scale. But the greatest calm and order reigns, as if nothing was happening. There is also a confectionery kitchen and a pastry kitchen, which is very interesting to see.

---

[1] The Lily Font, made in silver gilt by E. J. and W. Barnard, was first used for the christening of the Princess Royal in 1841. It stands seventeen inches high on a lily-shaped stem decorated with three cherubs playing lyres, the bowl adorned with flowers and ivy.

[2] The dressers took their meals in the Steward's Room. Others entitled to dine there were listed in 1844 as the clerks of the kitchen, the housekeeper of the private apartments, ladies' maids, pages, Queen's messengers and valets of visitors to Her Majesty.* Other servants ate in much plainer circumstances in the Servants' Hall, sitting on long benches and drinking out of horn beakers.

[3] Julie Arnold (1832–84), Frieda's younger sister, who never married, but stayed with her mother.

[4] Christian Doll, Page of the Presence. Served 1834–82, until 1852 as a baker in the Lord Steward's Department, which might explain why he showed Frieda the kitchens.

[5] 1 Zentner is 50 kilogrammes.

Letter 2

A REMARKABLE COUNTRY,
THIS ENGLAND
1855

In this letter Frieda recounts the scenes and events of January and February 1855. The weather had turned very hard. There were sledging parties, and skating on ice eight inches thick. In the Crimea, the Queen's soldiers suffered unnecessary hardships and at home Queen and country read, in horror and admiration, of the Charge of the Light Brigade. The inept handling of the war precipitated a political crisis at the end of January and the Queen shuttled backwards and forwards in all weathers from Windsor to London on what she called 'our eternal Government hunting errand'.* When the Queen was away, it gave Frieda the chance to see more of the Castle.

My dear friends,

One day I shall show you the finished version of this little drawing in my sketchbook:¹ it makes quite a nice little picture; but until then you must be satisfied with this one, which is all that time and circumstances allowed, and I send it only because I want to describe the inside of the tower to you.

As it happened, the Queen went to London three times for half a day to hold audiences, and I was left behind, as she needed only one person to attend her each time: twice it was a wardrobe maid, and once Sophie.² So I used the time which I thus had to myself to explore the whole Castle, which is otherwise impossible, and I saw many beautiful things in the time that I had. You shall hear all about it now, for the greatest charm for me of seeing everything here is always that I

---

1 Frieda's letter begins with a sketch of the Round Tower (see frontispiece).
2 Sophie Weiss, the Queen's second dresser and Frieda's old friend, born c.1828 in Karlsruhe.

can write and tell my dear ones at home about it, since I cannot show it to you, alas. Strange as it may seem, whatever I see, I always think of home, and every different thing reminds me of a different one of you. I often wish I could show some particular object to dear Mother, or to someone else in the family or one of my dear, unforgettable friends.

While the Queen was away the first time, I explored this tower. It is the tower in which Lord Surrey and Charles II were prisoners.[1] I saw their rooms and their beds, which are still there. There are now twenty-two guest rooms[2] in the tower, beautiful rooms furnished in an old-fashioned style. The upper and lower row of small windows were small rooms[3] for prisoners who were kept in less rigorous confinement, and they are now servants' bedrooms; the two rows of large windows are the guest rooms.[4] A circular corridor decorated with carved woodwork runs round the inside, and here stands, among other things, Queen Elizabeth's jewel cabinet. All the rooms open into it. These rooms, both large and small, are remarkable for the magnificent views they command. The tower stands higher than all the rest of the Castle, and has altogether the best position. Were such places always carefully chosen for the poor prisoners, to increase their longing for freedom? In Tübingen[5] the dungeons in the Castle also have a magnificent position like this. The rooms are furnished with large, old-fashioned furniture and old pictures which have been supplanted by the innumerable new ones in the galleries, most of

[1] Henry Howard, Earl of Surrey (c.1517–1547), poet and soldier, charged with the serious offence of quarrelling in the precincts of Henry VIII's court, was confined at Windsor, though not necessarily in the Round Tower, for about three months in 1537. Charles II was never prisoner here, but his captive father, Charles I, was brought to the Castle just before Christmas 1648. There is no evidence that he slept in the Round Tower; he was allowed a choice, and probably used his usual bed-chamber in the private apartments. He left on 19 January 1649 for London to be tried and executed. During the Civil War, Royalist prisoners were held in the Norman Tower, at the foot of the Round Tower.

[2] Under Wyatville the Tower, which had been the residence of the Governor, was laid out in suites of apartments for visitors and their attendants. Frieda is perhaps optimistic as to the number of guests who could have been put up there. During the visit of the King of Sardinia in November 1855, seventeen rooms in the Round Tower seem to have been available, but only fourteen were used, to accommodate nine gentlemen (one of them William Gladstone), each with a room to himself, and their nine valets and footmen who shared sometimes three to a room, with one valet in 'The box lobby'.*

[3] Not so; the top two rows of windows were false, put in as part of the remodelling of the Castle in the 1820s, when Wyatville added thirty feet to the height of the Tower.

[4] What would Frieda's reaction have been could she have known that these rooms would one day house the Royal Archives, copies of her own letters amongst them?

[5] Frieda had visited the old university town, a day's journey from Karlsruhe, in 1852 and 1853.

them representing scenes from the life of the Royal family. Most are no great works of art, and therefore were of interest only at a particular period; but some are quite fine. Yet these old-fashioned scenes themselves fit in very harmoniously here, and one really feels transported into the past.

The rooms are more and more beautifully furnished according to the rank of the guests occupying them: the Duchess of Gloucester's[1] rooms are wonderful. Huge Gobelin tapestries adorn the walls: they are wonderfully well preserved, finer than Frau von Hay's tapestries. The heavy silk curtains look magnificent against the great arched windows. I lingered there until I suddenly saw the Queen's carriage entering the courtyard, whereupon I rushed down to her rooms and scarcely got there in time to take off her cloak.

The gate on the right[2] is the one through which I made my first entry into Windsor, and through which I still go in and out. Away in the direction of the triangle in pencil is the part in which the Queen and we ourselves live, the outer façade of which is shown in the little picture I did for Mother. On the right, by the ●, there is a long line of large arched windows, which are those of the rooms used for special festivities. I shall describe them later. Opposite the gate I go through and where the cross is drawn is the entrance which I drew for Elise;[3] on the fourth side the square is closed with windows of enormous size, giving onto the corridor which I have already described, and with various towers and doors. This inner square, a little smaller than the market place, forms the courtyard, and as it were the heart of the Castle. By far the larger part is outside it, but this part is no longer occupied or visited by the Royal Family; there is, for instance, the beautiful Chapel of St George, and many towers, walls and terraces, where all kinds of officials live. In the inner area is a small private chapel which the Queen and her Household usually attend. Behind the gate marked with a small dot everyone who has business in the Castle goes in and out; only visitors and people belonging to the Queen's Household go in by the gate on the left. The Queen's

---

[1] Mary, Duchess of Gloucester (1776–1857) was Queen Victoria's aunt; the fourth daughter and last surviving child of George III.

[2] Norman Gate.

[3] A friend of Frieda's in Karlsruhe.

entrance is on the other side, and is shown in Mother's little picture. The former underground dungeons are now used for the heating of the corridors, which is done by means of warm air. I went down there too: there are huge iron stoves like ours, full of glowing coals, like in Schiller's Bürgschaft:[1] the hot air is carried through pipes and small openings in the floors around the whole Castle, but it is not at all pleasant – and it is said to be unhealthy. Sometimes one is hit by a gust of hot air; I do not like this form of heating; it prevents me from breathing freely.

I made use of the Queen's second absence to visit the private park, and to see her dogs there. Sophie and I went out together, guided by Herr Löhlein, although the weather was cold and dank, and we walked from twelve until two around the beautiful park. One cannot go in when the Queen is there, as she likes to be quite alone. It is very large, and undoubtedly has the finest position in the whole area. There is a lake for skating: the Queen, the Prince and and the children all skate. A Scotsman[2] and his family live in a charming little house in the park[3] where the dogs are kept: they are quite remarkable, and were the real goal of our walk. MacDonald, the Scotsman, is quite the picture of a son of the wilds: he is a tall, bearded Jäger.[4] There are seven red-cheeked, blue-eyed children, and a rather pretty wife, who however chatters too much. There is an entire house built for the dogs, in a square around an open yard with a water trough constantly filled with fresh water. Each breed of dog has its own large and spacious house, with straw bedding. They are allowed to go for walks with the Queen in turn. There is a wonderful big dog given by the Emperor of Russia, like the ones the Eskimos harness to their sledges;

[1] Frieda is here mixing up two ballads by Friedrich Schiller (1759–1805). 'Die Bürgschaft', or hostage, contains no glowing coals at all. Frieda appears to have in mind 'The Walk to the Iron Foundry', in which a jealous husband, inflamed by his black-hearted huntsman Robert, plots to have his wife's servant and suspected lover, Fridolin, cast into the furnace. Fridolin is delayed by a pious detour to church; Robert is mistaken for him and thrown to the flames instead.

[2] John MacDonald, Keeper of the Royal Kennels at Windsor since 1848.* This imposing Highlander, 6 feet 3 inches tall, was a favourite model for the artists the Queen commissioned to record her life at Balmoral. Landseer in particular admired his good looks and gentle character. MacDonald died in 1860.

[3] Dog kennels with a keeper's house were built in the Home Park in 1840–1 to the designs of Henry Ashton.

[4] Literally, huntsman, but used by Queen Victoria and Prince Albert to mean outdoor personal servant.

there is another breed of dog from Constantinople, wonderful greyhounds of the rarest sort; there are families of pugs which are really quite unique, with practically human faces – all so tame, they jumped up at us so much that we had to change afterwards, thanks to the attentions of their delicate paws. Others had fine long coats; there were innumerable dogs of the most diverse and rare breed. Then again there were enormous dogs like wolves; it was a delight to see them: they all greeted us joyfully and bounded around us, which made us scream with fright at first. But then we enjoyed it very much. Before we left we had to taste real Scottish wisket [*sic*] and Scottish bread – the latter tasted like sawdust and chopped-up straw, but I ate a large piece of it because it was so curious, and out of politeness, while the wisket nearly burned a hole in my throat, although I swallowed only a drop of it, as our host was drinking our health. Nothing could persuade me to empty my glass. The polite Sophie drank a little and became almost dizzy.

During the Queen's third absence[1] the weather was so bad, with a snowstorm, that one could not go out, and so I sketched the view from the Queen's sitting-room as a winter landscape. But you must not expect anything special, for although the view was lovely, I had only one and a half hours to finish the whole thing, for there is no question of completing it later, with all the work I have to do here.

Soon after this came a day which was glorious for me: the sheer splendour of it made me quite forget the trouble and hard work it involved. It was the day on which the Queen created three Lords Knights of the Order of the Garter.[2] For this purpose a part of the Castle to which the Prince [Albert] always keeps the key was opened. Many people have to wait for years before they have the opportunity of seeing this. The Queen and all the people there wore the ancient

[1] Probably 31 January 1855; the Queen's account in her Journal of her day excursion to Buckingham Palace reads: 'Saw Lord Derby at ½ p. 11. I informed him of the resignation of the government and of my desire that he should try and form a new one . . . we had the serious impression that Lord Derby would *not* be successful . . . We returned to Windsor at 4. Snowing and blowing fearfully.'
[2] The Most Noble Order of the Garter, the highest order of knighthood in Great Britain, was instituted by Edward III in 1348. On 7 February 1855 the Queen wrote in her Journal, 'Directly after luncheon dressed for the Investiture of the Garter, which took place at 3, with the usual ceremonies. It commenced with the Dean of Windsor's investiture as Registrar, then, successively the following were invested: Lord Carlisle, Lord Ellesmere, and my kind and excellent Lord Aberdeen, whom I thought nervous.'

costume[1] of this Order: we had a great deal of difficulty arranging it all as it should be. Two little pages, young lordlings, carried the train. Of the ceremony itself we – or rather everyone who did not belong to the Order – saw nothing; but I did not fail to take advantage of the opportunity to take a close look at everything in the rooms, before and after the ceremony. This took place in the Throne Room,[2] in which stood a great table with such huge chairs around it that three people could comfortably have sat in each of them. They were covered with blue velvet, and on each was embroidered the motto which is also on the Order itself: *'Hohn it sois qui it pense'*.[3] At each place there was a gold inkwell, a sheet of paper and a pen. At the head of the table stood the throne, under a magnificent gold embroidered canopy. The throne is of ivory,[4] so wonderfully carved that one could look at it for hours and still find new and beautiful details. It reminded me of the pulpit in Strasbourg Cathedral. In this room are life-size portraits of George III and George IV, the Queen and the Prince, and many more royalties, all in the robes of the Order. The whole room and its furnishings had a most awe-inspiring effect on me, and I had to stand still in the doorway for a few minutes before I dared to go in: history in all its mighty splendour stands before one there. It is a remarkable country, this England: so great, so powerful, holding on to tradition with pedantic exactness, and yet moving onwards, indeed leading in many other respects, as for instance in industry etc. It is indeed great and remarkable, but only when

[1] *See* illustration, Queen Victoria in the robes of the Garter, by F. X. Winterhalter.
[2] The Garter Throne Room had been part of the royal apartments since the twelfth century, but its appearance as Frieda describes it dated from the reign of George IV (1820–30).
[3] Frieda must be quoting from memory; the correct motto runs *'Honi soit qui mal y pense'*, or 'Shame to him who evil thinks'; said to have been uttered by Edward III when, picking up a garter accidentally dropped by – legend has it – the Countess of Salisbury, he rebuked the knowing glances of spectators by uttering these words, and bound the blue garter round his own knee. It could be said that perhaps Frieda, having dressed the Queen for the ceremony, ought to have been able to quote the motto more accurately; it was repeated in gold thirty-six times on the Queen's enamelled collar, it blazed among the rays of diamonds in the star upon her breast, and it was written in diamonds on the blue velvet of the garter which she wore around her upper left arm.
[4] The chair of state and matching footstool, of ivory set with diamonds, rubies and emeralds, presented to Queen Victoria by the Raja of Travancore in 1851, which had been on view at the Great Exhibition. Certainly a throne to impress: every visible surface was richly carved with a profusion of animals, including the lion and the unicorn, the whole surmounted by two rampant elephants. The seat of veined alabaster was hidden under cushions of silk velvet embroidered in gold and silver.

Frieda Arnold in about 1860, after her marriage to Ernst Müller. She is wearing the brooch which was a present from the Queen at Christmas 1855.

Queen Victoria as she looked in the year that Frieda came to England.

Sophie Weiss, the Queen's second dresser, Frieda's colleague and friend.

Karlstrasse in Karlsruhe, from the Münzstätte, drawn by Frieda in 1853.

Maritime scene by Frieda, evocative of the Solent, with the Fairy, *the tender to the royal yacht.*

Osborne House from the garden, showing the flag tower where Frieda sometimes took refuge, and below it the window of the Tower Room where she slept. The royal apartments were on the first floor: from right to left, Prince Albert's room, the Queen's sitting room, her dressing room (the two corner windows), bedroom, and wardrobe room. The top floor was occupied by the nurseries.

The Pavilion at Osborne House, showing the Queen's entrance; sketched by Frieda.

Study for a painting of Queen Victoria's arrival at St Cloud, 1855; her bonnets did not win universal approval in Paris.

The Queen, dressed for a summer's day in a wide-brimmed hat, on the terrace at Osborne with Prince Arthur. She is attended by the Hon. Flora MacDonald and the Marchioness of Ely.

On the terrace at Osborne: the Queen's birthday in 1859. From left to right, Prince Leopold, Princess Louise, the Queen, Prince Arthur, Princess Alice, the Princess Royal (now Princess Frederick William of Prussia), Princess Beatrice, Prince Albert, Princess Helena.

Queen Victoria and Prince Albert in 1854. She relied on his judgement and taste in everything from foreign affairs to the set of her bonnets.

Rudolph Löhlein, Prince Albert's Jäger, or outdoor servant.

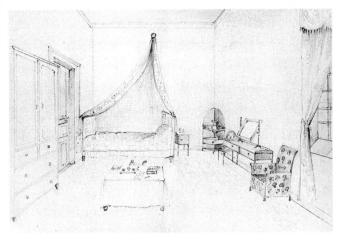

Frieda's drawing of her bedroom, probably at Windsor, since she has used a sheet of Windsor Castle writing paper.

The Jäger McDonald

The Round Tower, Windsor Castle; drawn by Frieda.

Windsor Castle from the South, by Frieda, dated December 1856. It is likely that her room was on the top floor, 8th window from the right.

Queen Victoria's dressing room at Windsor Castle as it was during Frieda's time with the Queen.

The corridor, Windsor Castle.

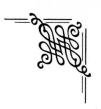

The Emperor and Empress arriving at Windsor Castle, 16 April 1855.

The Emperor Napoleon III

The bedroom prepared for the Empress Eugènie at Windsor Castle. 'You cannot imagine such magnificence', wrote Frieda.

The investiture of Napoleon III with the Order of the Garter. The Empress is seated in the foreground. 'We were all nervous, including myself', admitted the Queen in her Journal.

Queen Victoria in the Robes of the Garter. Frieda had only been with the Queen for a matter of weeks before she was required to dress Her Majesty for an investiture and wrote, 'we had a great deal of difficulty arranging it all as it should be'.

The Garter Throne Room, Windsor Castle, in the early 1870s

considered as a whole, and not in its separate parts. That is why I, for one, will never be able to think of it as really agreeable. We Germans, fragmented as we are, are nothing – alas nothing – as a whole. But as individuals, one rarely finds as much trustworthiness, as much loyalty – which makes life so pleasant – as one finds at home. Many, especially men, may prefer to belong to one great nation, and that I can understand; but what we have they would nevertheless be sorry to lose. Without this harsh division of classes, without the coldness of man towards his fellow man, without this idolatrous respect for princes and traditions, there can doubtless be no national greatness; but we good-natured Germans want to live our own comfortable, homely lives, and the general interest only ever comes second to ourselves. It is better thus, in the end; for what does everyone long for, finally? Surely it is to go back to the familiar, infinitely dear, insignificant details of home life!

Before entering the Throne Room one passes through the Waterloo Chamber,[1] which is a huge room panelled with oak and hung with pictures of all the great men who distinguished themselves in the Battle of Waterloo and at that period. But the one man without whom they would have had little opportunity to become great is not there: Napoleon is missing. Here the table was laid for a grand dinner in the evening. The table glittered with gold – I shall say no more.

The most remarkable and magnificent thing, however, is the North Corridor,[2] considerably smaller than the one I have already described, but incomparably more splendid. Through this the distinguished company passes on very great occasions. There are no paintings here, no statues, but precious stones of immense value. On both sides are deep glass cases or handsomely decorated niches full of the most costly Indian arms and treasures. These were captured in 1799 from the Indian Prince Tippo Saheb, at the storming of Seringapatam.[3] The weapons are mostly inlaid with the costliest

---

[1] Created by George IV to commemorate the sovereigns, soldiers and statesmen who had played a prominent part in the overthrow of Napoleon. Completed in 1830. Queen Victoria often used this room for formal dinners.

[2] Runs between the Brunswick Tower and the Grand Reception Room. Built by Wyatville.

[3] Tipu Sultan (c.1749–99), known as the Tiger of Mysore, who had been corresponding with the French, was defeated and killed at Seringapatam in 1799 by British troops under Major-General George Harris. The battle suppressed the last vestiges of French influence in India.

gems, diamonds etc. The throne of this prince is there, entirely of gold inlaid with precious stones. His crown, his sceptre, his footstool, all of gold and glittering with diamonds. – Then the famous bird, the possession of which in former times in India conferred sovereignty upon the owner, and many wars were waged on account of it. I shall enclose a drawing of it. Then there is Napoleon's Marshal's baton, his rifle and a cloak which was captured from his carriage at Waterloo; the sword of the Pole Lubieske;[1] the bullet from Nelson's wound which killed him; Wellington's sword; the tent of the Indian Prince, and a great quantity of the most beautiful and costly weapons – there are whole cases full of daggers and small carbines which all have golden handles inlaid with precious stones. Everything is so tastefully and fittingly arranged that one is filled with amazement and admiration both for the individual objects, and for the arrangement of the whole. The Prince [Albert] has arranged it all like this: previously the objects were either scattered or displayed in such a way that one did not have this dazzling sight of them all at once. The tent is pitched as it was, and one walks through it: it is of heavy Indian red silk worked with gold thread, quite well preserved. The walls are adorned with suits of armour and weapons, and there are curious chairs and a most extraordinary table inside. Then there is a lion's head, larger than life, of gold, with huge eyes made of diamonds.[2] It also belongs to the embellishments of the throne.

After this magnificence followed days full of exertion and fatigue: we had to pack and unpack continuously for fourteen full days.[3] And now here I am in the famed city of London, sitting in beautiful Buckingham Palace; my window looks out onto the great courtyard and I see only walls, but it scarcely matters, as I have already looked out of every possible window in the vain hope of seeing houses; but

---

[1] Probably the sword which had belonged to several Polish kings including Jan Sobieski (grandfather of Clementina Sobieska, who married Prince Charles Edward Stuart – 'Bonnie Prince Charlie') and Stanislas Poniatowski, who gave it in 1787 to Sir Ralph Payne, who presented it to George IV.

[2] In fact a tiger's head. The eyes and fangs are of rock crystal.

[3] Since returning from Osborne, the Queen had been in residence at Windsor. She spent the night of 2 February at Buckingham Palace, returned to Windsor on 3 February, and left again on 15 February, staying at Buckingham Palace until 15 March.

all one can see is greyness, except for the occasional chimney, and that is all. The dirty air here defies all description. Once when Herr Moll said to me, in his high-pitched self-important tones, 'In London, one has to change one's linen several times a day', I laughed, and thought to myself, Prussians always have to exaggerate; but it was no exaggeration! We live in a very healthy, open part of the city, for on three sides of the Palace are huge parks; there are houses only on one side, and no factories near by. In spite of this, however, every time I come into my room my table is quite black, my armchair is speckled with little black particles, and my lovely shining silver candlesticks are quite tarnished in two days. One can never leave any article of clothing lying about, and even in the cupboards everything gets dirty. The air is a heavy grey mass; on my first day I was almost frightened when I glimpsed through this mass a great round fiery ball, quite dark red in colour: that is what the sun looks like here! The entire horizon is dark grey but for this smouldering sphere, whose glow pierces the smoke and fog. Its rays are rarely strong enough to break completely through; indeed this sun has no rays, and I realise now that it is only the rays which dazzle the eyes, for one can quite easily look into the sun itself. I understand so well now how poets can say 'The sun rose blood-red over the battlefield', which I had always thought was only a poetic expression. Yesterday a few lonely rays of sunlight broke through, casting a dull glow over everything, and all over the Palace I heard nothing but constant praise of the lovely day!

One of the Prince's valets, an older man, who has been with the Prince since he was eleven years old, a French-speaking Swiss, whom Sophie knows well, Herr Cart,[1] a very pleasant friendly man, showed me where to go out and walked with me around this huge city for three hours. My head swam with all the people, carriages and enormous black buildings. The Houses of Parliament have such a

[1] Isaac François Daniel Cart. After his death in 1858 the Queen wrote of him 'Cart was with Albert from his seventh year. He was invaluable; well-educated, thoroughly trustworthy, devoted to the Prince, the best of nurses, superior in every sense of the word, a proud independent Swiss, who was quite *un homme de confiance*, peculiar, but extremely careful, and who might be trusted in anything. He wrote well and copied much for us. He was the only link my loved one had about him which connected him with his childhood, the only one with whom he could talk over old times. I cannot think of my dear husband without Cart! He seemed part of himself! We were so thankful and proud of this faithful old servant, he was such a comfort to us.'*

colossal doorway that the people going in and out look like flies. The magnificence of the shops and the churches, the beautiful Thames with its ships and bridges, everything is so grand, so massive and yet so gloomy and melancholy that one has to see it to be able to understand. But in spite of all the wonderful things one sees here, and however worthwhile it is to come here in order to gain a true impression of a great nation, I should not like to live here; a simple, peaceful little place is after all better in the end. Perhaps I am too small to feel at home in a place of such size, but I cannot help thinking that there is more happiness to be found in a little nest in Germany than here. The poverty that one sees here in the streets is frightful. The winter is so extraordinarily cold that the poor nearly freeze to death, and many have already died of starvation. The rich, meanwhile, roast on one side and freeze on the other: these fireplaces that they have are no good at all for really cold weather. I have never been so cold in my whole life as I was for two days at the Palace. We arrived in bitter weather at this huge building that had stood empty for a long time;[1] in spite of all the heating, the tomb-like atmosphere only disappeared after several days' occupation. Now the weather has suddenly become warm: the ground is covered with black mud, and the air is dark and thick. I sit here at midday with a light, for daylight has not yet arrived today. If one opens a window, one sees only smoke, which the fog prevents from rising, and one hears only a constant dull roar from afar, the noise of the carriages driving around in the city. It is cruelty for human beings to have to live in this great prison all the time; it weighs on one like a heavy burden. I always console myself with the thought that it is really very interesting – a miserable consolation when one cannot draw a single breath without swallowing smoke. 'A kingdom for a single ray of sunshine.'[2] – Yes, you must learn to appreciate the joy of being able to breathe. Here one could become a sun-worshipper. The wretched children who run about in the streets here – it always makes me quite melancholy when I see them. I have been forbidden to take money with me because of the pickpockets,

[1] Between July 1854 and 15 February 1855 the Queen had only spent four nights there. At this period in the Queen's life, she was usually at Buckingham Palace for most of the time from February to July.

[2] A transmutation, frequently done in German, of Shakespeare's 'my kingdom for a horse', *Richard III*, Act V, scene iv.

and ladies in particular must never give a beggar anything. I saw a frightful-looking man with one arm and two little half-naked children walking around the streets, singing for alms; hundreds of people went by, and I did not see a single person giving him money. He sang on regardless; I had no money on me and I think I would have been too frightened to give him anything, he looked so dreadful. I was quite horrified by him, but above all by the people who could walk coldly by such misery, as if nothing were wrong. There are children who play organs – some people keep gangs of these homeless creatures – and who are sent out in the morning, and if they do not earn a certain sum to bring back they are beaten. They play and sing, often until late at night, for which they receive from their masters shelter and food, but what kind? Many of these unfortunates prefer to stay in the streets all the time, without any form of shelter, occasionally getting something to eat from kind hands. Many of them must die of hunger in the winter. It is *Uncle Tom's Cabin*[1] come to life. And beside it, the wealth and magnificence! Oh! London is a fearful place; one must turn to ice if one is to be happy. But extraordinary, noble, wonderful it remains nonetheless. Farewell, enough for now, think of me and be content with the cosy old town.

To end with, a few more words about London. The sun, the kindly life-giving sun, has been shining brightly even here, for a few days, and has found its way into people's hearts, through fog and walls, so that the poor creatures, strangers unused to the noise, who were almost ready to give themselves up to despair, have been given new life and cheer. Yes, London is a different city when the sun shines. No doubt it is the same everywhere, you will say; but nowhere as much as here, for nowhere else is the sun so heavily veiled. Oh! one learns to love it twice as much, one clutches anxiously at it, for only too soon it has slipped away. One walks about the huge city with pleasure and enjoyment, no longer terrified by its size, as long as one can see the dear sun like God's loving eye shining down upon it. Only if one has felt the burden of the English climate can one feel the strength, the ever enlivening power of the sun. I feel as if I had come out of a

[1] By Harriet Beecher Stowe (1811–96), published in 1852, sold in hundreds of thousands, and contributed so much to popular feeling against slavery that it has been cited as one of the causes of the American Civil War.

mineshaft into the light of day. Last night too, for the first time, I saw the stars, which I had looked for in vain each evening: 'You poor people, you have not even the stars', I could not help sighing. But now they too are here, although not quite so bright as at home, indeed rather pale and dull. I see so much that is wonderful that I often have to spend the evening carefully ordering it in my mind, so as to draw from it all lasting value, and not a bewildering chaos. Farewell.

Letter 3

―――――

LONDON, WINDSOR, AND
THE VISIT OF NAPOLEON III
1855

This letter was written during March and April 1855, when the Court was mainly at Buckingham Palace.

London

*A*nd now something on the beloved subject of the theatre – which will make you all prick up your ears. Yes, it is worth telling, although I can only use words for what should really be seen.

Well, the theatre began at seven o'clock, and ended at midnight, which is very moderate here, for the English can devour at one sitting, without getting tired, as much mental nourishment as the huge quantities of roast beef and plum pudding which their well-organised stomachs can take. A further pleasure was the drive there and back through the brightly lit streets, which took about half an hour.

First there was a performance of a play, *The Rivals*,[1] which interested me only because it was well acted, and the actors were playing such typical English characters. But although this play is said by connoisseurs to be excellent, it did not appeal to me. It was all so shrill, so vehement; there was no tenderness in it; taste is so immeasurably different here from ours. The actors were all very tall, fine figures, with an expressiveness which I cannot hope to describe; this is very much prized here. It was indeed quite remarkable; even if I had not been able to understand a word of English, I would have understood the whole play simply from the faces. I did understand it

―――――

[1] The first comedy by Richard Brinsley Sheridan (1751–1816). It had been revived in the autumn of 1854.

all: that is, I could imagine what I could not understand. With a good pair of opera glasses, my eyes were fixed on the actors' faces all the time. It makes an extraordinary impression upon one; there is perhaps nothing so capable of giving the appearance of reality as this; one ceases to be aware of the theatre itself.

Then came the chief reason for my having been sent there: a pantomime. This is something which is performed here in England each year from Christmas until Lent, and which provides the only Carnival celebration there is, for one sees nothing in the streets or anywhere else here, not even in kitchens and at the pastrycooks.[1] It consists of two full hours of tableaux and tomfoolery, which succeed each other at such unbelievable speed and with such amazing variety, both serious and comic, that the effect is quite indescribable. It is very typical, and is found nowhere else in such perfection as here. Kean,[2] the celebrated actor, to whom this theatre belongs, arranges one of these pantomimes each year, and it is performed every evening from Christmas until Shrove Tuesday. At the moment he is ill, but I shall see him acting later. Tales of magic, fairy stories, were performed in the most beautiful, enchanting manner, such as only the liveliest imagination could devise. The ballerinas who played the fairies were so charming and pretty, with such sweet expressiveness, that I could not take my eyes off them. It was like a parade of beauties, enhanced of course by the lighting, which gave an ever-changing play of colours; they were not like those ugly, common-looking chorus girls at home: no, so noble, so proud they all looked, that one was tempted to believe that they really were fairies.[3] Among other fairy-stories there was *Bluebeard*: when the inquisitive wife opens the room and sees the twenty-one beheaded wives inside, they were all standing

[1] The word Frieda uses, *Schmalzhäfen*, is not directly translatable. *Schmalz* is dripping rendered from pork or goose and *häfen* is a Baden dialect word for cooking pots. The dripping was used in southern Germany to fry traditional pastries for 'Fastnacht', the southern German version of Carnival, a celebration which took place in the week before Lent began, when the streets would be full of masked revellers; parades, balls and parties were held; towns and villages turned upside down. Performances of this pantomime 'Harlequin Bluebeard', did not in fact end with the beginning of Lent; Shrove Tuesday fell on 20 February 1855 and the Queen took her children to see a performance on 2 March.

[2] Charles John Kean (1811–68), actor-manager, who from 1850–9 ran the Princess's Theatre in Oxford St, W1.

[3] The attendants of Preciosa the Good Fairy, and 'her servants of all-work, but principally engaged in cooking Bluebeard's goose'. So characterised on the playbill that was printed, as was frequently done for productions the Queen saw, on white silk.*

there, and at one stroke, as the door opened, all the heads fell off. There were many such tricks[1] and scenes from life and from politics which were quite hilarious. Among other things there was a street riot in which the policemen were given a drubbing which frightened me so much that I can quite understand that workman in Paris who took his stick and leapt onto the stage to join in the fight. All in all I still cannot understand how they escaped injury, for they hurled each other about, heads thudding on the stage – and this they do every evening! And if the Glass Palace[2] was being shown, Harlequin and Columbine would be carrying on with their foolishness all the while. It is impossible to describe it all; it has to be seen.

Osborne

I shall only mention the last, magnificent tableau now: this was a huge ship,[3] with sailors and soldiers fighting at sea and at length gaining the victory. The whole crew consisted of almost a hundred five- to six-year-old children, mostly of the same height: it was such a delightful sight that the pitiful impression that such poor children ought in principle to make on one was quite overcome by sheer enchantment. Only at home, and on calm reflection, did I begin to feel sorry for the poor little things. They acted so charmingly and portrayed feelings of fear and pugnacity with such ardour that I was quite swept away. Several were wounded or killed, and dragged away by their comrades, expressing pain with such realism and force, although such young creatures cannot yet have any idea of what it is, and finally hoisting their flag high on the mast with such shouts of

[1] As for instance the scene, promised by the playbill, in which Bluebeard's wedding breakfast 'was ultimately **dished** by a new Patent Steam Apparatus, under the immediate superintendence of the inventor, Bluebeard himself, who, mistaking his own invention, not only blows up his cooks, but himself and the wedding breakfast also'.*

[2] After scenes in demonic strongholds, enchanted gardens, Turkish villages, Bluebeard's castle, and the illuminated Temple of Concord and Transformation, the second half of the pantomime held up a comic mirror to current events. In scene 10 Harlequin and Columbine danced 'a character *pas de deux*' in front of 'a distant view of the Crystal Palace at Sydenham', which had opened the previous June (*see* Letter 4)*

[3] Scene 13 took place 'On the quarter deck of the *Royal Albert* of 131 guns fully manned by an able-bodied crew averaging from five to six years of age'. The *Royal Albert* was launched by Queen Victoria on 13 May 1854, amid great excitement. It was the largest ship in the world, 3760 tons, 276 feet and manned by a crew of 1100. It was laid down in 1842 and was originally intended to be a sailing ship of the line, but was altered to steam three-quarters of the way through construction.

jubilation! Real talent, or a high degree of artistry, is needed for a performance like that.

I went also to see the National Gallery, full of wonderful old paintings by great masters whom I shall not name with my poor pen: I have already been unforgivably bold in describing the indescribable. But you can imagine everything which I, alas, cannot put into words.

London

A second journey to Osborne[1] has passed off happily and to my great satisfaction; and if I continue thus describing my travels to you, you will have too many descriptions of the same journey. Yet however often I have to cross the sea it is always new and delightful, and so it will not vex you to accompany me once more.

I left here[2] at half past six in the morning, and we arrived at Osborne at two o'clock. It was a cold, but fairly clear morning, and we travelled by train to Southampton; not a pretty region, but I observed it closely because it is so different from home. Although there was still snow on the fields here and there, in this country nature does not take on that dead, cold aspect that it has at home in winter. Even if the meadows lack the fresh green colour of spring or summer, there is still life in them, if only faintly, and I am reminded of an invalid who drags himself painfully through the winter, and is then revived by the rays of the spring sun. This makes a gloomy impression on me; I prefer a death-like slumber followed by Nature's vigorous resurrection, to this weak glimmer of life. At Osborne and Windsor, or indeed anywhere further away from London, it is different: there the green of the fields is still quite fresh, and makes a pleasing impression.

Near the station[3] we passed through a part of London where great numbers of factory workers live. As the railway embankment was very high, we could look down easily over this forest of chimneys and narrow smoky streets. It is so cramped and filthy here, one little house

---

[1] The Queen went to Osborne 15 March 1855.

[2] Buckingham Palace.

[3] Either Waterloo, the terminus of the London and South Western Railway, or the Queen's private station at Nine Elms.

next to another, that it made me shudder to think of the misery and poverty that pervades these habitations. It made me think of the diary of the English doctor that we read; a little farther off one could see the palaces and proud towers of the rich city. One reads and hears often enough of these contrasts, but the impression they make can only be described by someone who has seen them. I was deeply shocked, and could not take my eyes off the miserable hovels; and hard as I tried to control myself, I could not prevent tears coming to my eyes, which was very noticeable to my three English companions. I could not tell them why I was crying: people here would have thought it very stupid and ridiculous. But luckily I do not have to answer to anyone for my feelings; I tried to compose myself and said nothing, and we sped quickly onwards.

I had so much to think about that the journey to the sea did not seem long. There we boarded the steamer, as I have described to you before; I went with the carriage this time, for we always take turns. It was so cold and windy that I could only satisfy my wish to do a little sketching, before the ship set sail, by warming myself by the fire in the cabin and drawing this. The ship was called the *Medina*. As soon as she began to move I went up on deck, in spite of the wind and rain, for it was so stuffy down below that it was unbearable. The waves were very high. I stood out there, revelling in the atmosphere of an enchanted, fairy-tale world which seemed to rise up towards me out of the waves. It is so magical, the sea; how well I now understand all the tales of crystal palaces and nymphs in the sea; how much poetry lies in those depths! As the shore grew farther and farther away, I felt that I fully understood Salus y Gomez for the first time. I could feel the pain of the poor man as he sees the mast of the only ship fading pitilessly away into the distance. I felt quite well (I had eaten well before the journey and dressed very warmly). At two we arrived at last, and I thanked God I had escaped without seasickness, although I felt dreadfully tired in every limb.

Here on the dear island the sun shone brightly and cheerfully, and everything seemed transformed, now that the dreadful smoke of London was behind us. The house was extremely cold, in spite of all the fires that were burning, and my companions were not at all happy to come here, preferring the liveliness of London; but I rejoiced by myself and for myself. Here one could breathe freely, and when all the work of unpacking was done, I rejoiced to be able to go down to the sea next day. I walked along the shore for three hours; I spent all my free time in the open air, and sketched a little – dear Mother shall have the picture. Once when I was sitting on a ship's timber, drawing, I suddenly heard a voice, which made me jump, and I was shocked to realise that it was my own! Deep in thought, I had begun to sing without realising it. And what do you think I was singing? My own words and music, the inspiration of the moment: I sang out loud, 'Oh! if only the waves of the sea were carrying me home to you!' I could not help smiling at catching myself thus – you can see from this that my homesickness never goes away. But that it should express itself in songs rather than in tears and sighs will not, I am sure, give you cause for concern about my state of mind.

We spent eight[1] lovely days here: that is, half of them were so dreadfully stormy that there was a fearful draught in every room, the wind raged and roared even with the windows shut, the curtains swayed constantly, and the lights flickered in the evening. The house is built to be light and airy, for the summer. The sea looked quite dark, and there were enormous waves; sometimes it was impossible to distinguish between sea and sky, all was the same dark colour, sometimes streaked with the yellowish-white of the foam on the waves. When I went to bed at night I could not help thinking of the poor people who are now at sea. It is so awe-inspiring to see the elements aroused, when one is safe on dry land; how must one feel when one is exposed to them!

We began the return journey[2] on a very cold, rather foggy morning at eight. We went on board ship at once. The sea had taken on yet another, completely different and surprising appearance: the water was very rough, and seemed to be covered with a fine grey veil. The shore too looked quite different in this light. It was so cold that in spite of my coat and fur I wrapped myself up in a thick shawl which belonged to the Prince's Jäger,[3] who had been sent to look after us, together with two men-servants. He was very concerned about us,

[1] 15–23 March 1855.
[2] Frieda is not accompanying the Queen, who did not leave Osborne until 2 p.m.
[3] Prince Albert's personal outdoor servant.

and took some cushions to a place near the engine, where it was a little warmer. So I sat down there, well wrapped up, and enjoyed the glorious sight. The waves were magnificent, often forming curious shapes as the wind whipped them up. Our voyage lasted two and a half hours, during which I felt quite well – which is an extremely pleasing sensation, if one has ever known the dreadful experience of seasickness. The water gradually became calmer and the sky lighter, and it grew a little warmer. Such changes are quite delightful to watch. One had the impression of looking into Nature's workshops, where the view is not impeded by walls and trees, and watching the development of what on land we do not see until it is completed.

When we arrived in the harbour at Southampton, we saw a gigantic steamship[1] – there are very few ships as big – and our boat came so close to it that we could see the passengers on the decks quite easily. The ship set sail before our very eyes: it was a mail packet that carries all the letters and dispatches of the greatest importance to South America and to Britain's Indian possessions. It would certainly be at sea for six months, and then come back again. It is said to be one of the most interesting sea passages one can take, on a ship like that, as it calls at all kinds of important and interesting places. It is for this reason that scientists and other scholars, writers and painters very often travel by these ships, and sometimes rich private individuals do so too, just for pleasure. Of course travellers who want to go to a certain destination cannot travel in them, as they do not follow direct routes; nor can people without means do so, as every comfort is provided and it is therefore very expensive. The people I saw on the deck were all men, mostly young and adventurous-looking.

We did not leave our ship until the steamship had gone. Everyone on deck turned once more towards the land, waving hats. I wondered which of them would come back in six months, if at all, and how? And the thought of entrusting oneself to the elements, against which man can do so little, was a little alarming, but at the same time, precisely because of the mysterious dark fate one would face, there is

1 Probably the Royal Mail. According to the announcements in the *Southampton Advertiser*, the only Royal Mail sailing on 23 March 1855 was the *Atrato*, under Captain Woolley, which 'will leave this day for the West Indies and Pacific. She will have about 50 passengers on board and an average cargo.'

something strangely attractive about it. As a child I often read a story about how Columbus discovered America, when he was said to have shouted out 'Land!' I had no inkling, then, of what endless depths can lie in that single cry. And I have only ever been at sea for a few hours – what must it be when it is for as many months.

From here we went on by train, and arrived in London at three o'clock in the afternoon. What a lot one can learn; I had been travelling continuously for seven[1] hours, and yet I felt quite well. Once I could never have endured that; but if there is anything one becomes practised in here, it is this never-ending gallop back and forth. As my home is so far away, and I shall always feel I am in a foreign country, the journeys are both interesting and instructive for me, apart of course from the many duties they entail, and the real physical exertion they often demand. But on the whole, I never have that real sense of being at home which makes one so happy. If I could choose freely, I would certainly go on a journey each year; but I would never choose to travel constantly.

In London we witnessed another very moving spectacle: a regiment of Guards, nothing but handsome young men, was leaving for the Crimea, and performed a farewell parade in the great courtyard of this magnificent Palace. The whole of the Royal Family was down in the courtyard. I stood exactly above them at a window. There was a band in the centre, playing a fine military march. The men all looked so calm and serious; it is often so, but it gave this scene a much more solemn aspect.[2] When one comes from a small country and modest circumstances and suddenly finds oneself in a post like mine, it is impossible to imagine the effect such things have on one,

[1] The Queen's journey took four hours.

[2] In her Journal for 4 April 1855, Queen Victoria described the scene: 'At 11 went down to meet Albert under the portico, in front of the Hall, in the Quadrangle. George [Duke of Cambridge] was with him and the Colonels of the three regiments, Colonels Wood, Ridley and Upton, also General Bentinck. The children were with me. I advanced to the edge of the portico and then the men began to march by, preceded by the Band, which stationed itself just opposite us. 1st came 400 Grenadiers, Colonel Gordon Drummond (going out in command of the drafts, who sail on the 7th) marching at their head, – then 300 Scotch Fusiliers and lastly the Coldstreams. They marched by in quick time, going out at the opposite entrance, to the one they came in at, and quite close, so that I could observe them well. They marched well and looked typical guardsmen . . . May God speed the brave men and lead them to glory! It is a moving sight, to see them thus ready to go where danger, glory, and maybe death await them. I said to Colonel G. Drummond, 'They are fine men, and I am sure they will prove themselves worthy of the name they bear.'

when one takes the trouble to look at them more closely. In this great country and nation there is such deep seriousness, such great significance pervading everything that when one considers it attentively, the horizon which opens before one is something of which I at least could never have dreamt. Our dear home town and our house seem to me like a puppet play beside it, but I can assure you that it nevertheless has the power to make me happy, like a child in its play-room, so harmlessly happy and gay, knowing of nothing beyond its walls. I shall always long to go back there, to my dear little home; the most magnificent and mighty places I see can never diminish that peaceful house; no, it shines like a star, only brighter and more serene.

Frieda's letter continues with glimpses of the state visit of the Emperor Napoleon III and his wife the Empress Eugénie. This Imperial couple were regarded as parvenus in royal circles. Charles Louis Napoleon Bonaparte (1808–73), nephew and adopted grandson of Napoleon I, had after many adventures and vicissitudes, been elected Prince President of France in 1848. He had staged a coup d'état *in 1851, and had himself proclaimed Emperor of the French in 1852. He failed to win the hand of a princess – Queen Victoria's niece – and married instead the captivating Spaniard Eugénie de Montijo (1826–1920). Two years later a distrustful England found itself in the Crimea with its hereditary enemy as ally. Napoleon III traded on his illustrious name, cherished dreams of new martial glory, and thoroughly alarmed his English allies by announcing in February 1855 his intention to go to the Crimea to take command of the campaign. He was invited to England to be dissuaded.*

The visit was a great success on all counts. The Emperor was talked out of going east; he was well received by the crowds who turned out to see him; and he and his wife established friendly personal relations with their English hosts.

On 15 April, the Queen inspected the rooms which had been prepared for them at Windsor and her Journal described what she saw: '(1) The Rubens Room, beautifully redecorated with very handsome crimson furniture, is the Empress's drawing-room; next to which is – (2) The Empress's bedroom, all crimson satin, with the fine old pictures and very handsome furniture, and a really beautiful bed. The top, with feathers, is the same which used to be in the state bedroom and belonged to George IV's bed, but the bedstead has been enlarged with a green front, on which is embroidered LN and EI, with curtains of violet satin, upon which is placed some beautiful old embroidery. (3) The Empress's dressing-room, also hung with crimson satin and green satin furniture, with a handsome toilet [table]. My gold things are to be put upon it. (4) The Emperor's bedroom, where the Emperor Nicholas [I of Russia] and poor King Louis Philippe slept. The bed and furniture are of green velvet, very handsome; all little details are most carefully attended to, and very handsome. (5) The Zucharelli Room, which is the Emperor's sitting-room. (6) The Van Dyke Room, which looks magnificent, with green and yellow silk curtains and furniture – handsome tables, etc., and the two adjoining Tapestry Rooms, also beautifully done up, are the gentlemen and ladies' waiting rooms.'

The Emperor and Empress arrived at Windsor on Monday, 16 April 1855. From the Queen's account of the visit, it is possible to piece together an idea of what a state visit entailed for the dressers. Beforehand, the Queen was uncharacteristically flustered by what she was to wear, and confessed to having had 'such trouble with my toilette, dresses, bonnets, caps, mantillas etc. etc. of every sort and kind'.* It was not so much that Eugénie was a leader of world fashion, but rather that there were few precedents for such a visit.

The dressers had their work cut out to keep up with events. The Queen received the Emperor and Empress at Windsor in a light-blue flounced dress with shaded trimmings, a lacy shawl and a pearl necklace. An hour or so later, and she appeared at dinner in a yellow dress trimmed with white blonde, opals and her opal diadem. While they dined, Frieda sat in her room across the Quadrangle and wrote her letter. On the Tuesday, after a military review, there was, according to the Queen, 'very little time left for dressing, or indeed for anything', and we may imagine the disciplined flurry as she hastened into a white dress trimmed with convolvuluses and blonde, and the same flowers in her hair, before going down to dinner, a dance in the Waterloo Chamber (delicately renamed the Music Room for the duration), and supper. The evening was not over until half past midnight, so the dressers would have had a late night.

Even if they were tired, they had to be ready for quick changes of plan; on Wednesday a Council of War delayed luncheon, so at the last minute the Queen and Empress agreed, as the Queen put it, 'to dress our heads' – have *their diadems put on – 'and lunch in that way'. After luncheon came 'a great scramble for dressing' in preparation for the installation of the Emperor as a Knight of the Garter. Off with the Garter robes, on with suitable gown, bonnet and cloak for a drive through what was left of the cold April afternoon, and then it was time to dress for dinner and a concert – 'such a scramble always' said the Queen – in a white and gold brocade dress, a diamond diadem, the Koh-i-noor and 'the Indian pearls'.*

On Thursday the entire circus removed to Buckingham Palace (we can only imagine the organisation and packing required of the dressers). For dinner and going to the opera in state that evening the Queen wore a blue and gold dress, her jewels 'a diadem of diamonds, and very large Indian rubies'. All was over for the Queen by twelve, but it would have been much later before Frieda could lay her aching limbs to rest. On Friday things were perhaps a little easier for the dressers: in the morning the Queen, in a white dress with lilac flowers and a white bonnet, went with her guests to the Crystal Palace on Sydenham Hill, and the dressers would have had most of the day to make ready her toilette for the evening, a blue dress, richly trimmed with lace, her rubies, and the two feathers which she wore in her hair. After dinner, according to the Queen, came 'one of our usual concerts: about four hundred people invited'. It was again after midnight before the party broke up. The next morning, Saturday, 21 April, the visitors left, but it was not until Sunday that Frieda found an opportunity to conclude her account which she had begun before their arrival with a tour similar to the one the Queen had made.

———

Windsor

Today I went round the rooms for the Emperor and Empress, which are now quite ready. You cannot imagine such magnificence. There are eight rooms, that is to say great halls by our standards, so wonderfully furnished with satin and velvet, gold and silver, that one can only gaze in astonishment. What is most especially remarkable are the wonderful Gobelins, so well preserved, the faces so expressive – quite exceptional. I have never seen these rooms before, for they are used only for very important guests. One room is full of glorious paintings by Van Dyck, among them the unfortunate Charles I on horseback, life-size; an uncommonly expressive painting. Then a room with nothing but paintings by Rubens. But there really is too much crowded together: one could spend hours just looking at one of these pictures, again and again, and we had barely two hours for all these splendours.

Great triumphal arches have been erected at the station and in the town, and preparations have been made for illuminations. You will read all this in the newspapers. So you may be pleased to think that I too have made my contribution to enhance those festivities: for fourteen days we have had our hands full. Today Napoleon arrived. His entrance was both dignified and splendid. We watched from a tower window as he drove from the station through the densely packed crowds into the beautiful Castle; then we hurried to a window which looked onto the courtyard, and saw him and his wife from quite close by; and finally this evening we saw them all at dinner, from a gallery. The carriage, escorted by the Royal Guard, drove into the courtyard, where it was greeted by the band playing the French national anthem. It was an extraordinarily moving sight, so solemn and fine: the Queen's Guard is such a magnificent sight, all tall, handsome men, with wonderful black horses. When one sees this Imperial couple, so recently married, one can but think – a few years ago, who would have received them? To see all at once before one's eyes the thing which hitherto one had only read about in history books or plays, is a most stirring experience, as if one were living history itself. And even now, sitting in my quiet little room, if I open the curtains I can see the great arched windows ablaze with light, and hear the music faintly. It reminds me so much of all those descriptions in history books of banquets and gatherings of princes in knightly castles.

The Emperor is small, not handsome, but very determined-looking; the Empress has a very noble bearing and a beautiful face. I shall see her from closer later on.

London

I shall end this letter for now, and send you a thousand greetings and many kisses, my dear friends. The illustrious guests have left, the Palace seems dead. You cannot imagine the throngs of people and the bustle of servants running about that there have been these last days.

Buckingham Palace, 22 April

Now you shall have a few more glimpses of the objects of the greatest interest here in the Palace for the last few days, namely the Emperor and Empress. I saw them both often and from very close by. He looks very like the pictures of him that one often sees, even at home, especially the ones taken from Winterhalter's portraits, but he is less good-looking, as he has deep lines on his face which make him look older. His figure is not at all good, as he has a very hollow chest. But his whole bearing and expression convey calm, gravity and vigour: he looks like a man of *great consequence*, although perhaps less prepossessing than his portraits. She is *uncommonly* like her portraits by Winterhalter, although *much* more beautiful, which is not often the case with Winterhalter. She has a charm which cannot be portrayed. Her appearance unites *noble dignity* with *infinite* grace and sweetness. Never in my life have I seen such an enchanting person, except Frau Helferich. Although she is quite different she too has that certain something which no one can fail to be affected by. Unfortunately, however, she looks very frail and delicate, which indeed she is; yet the effect of poor health in her is not to disfigure but rather to transfigure her beauty, as sometimes happens with delicate people. Everyone is delighted with her gentle and sweet nature, which says a great deal for an Empress who is not of royal blood. She has not been seen on horseback here, unfortunately, for she is said to look particularly beautiful on a horse. He rode occasionally, however, and is quite another person on horseback: he cuts a taller and more handsome figure, and sits so calmly on his horse, with a very imposing and majestic air in his uniform which he lacks when in civilian clothes and on foot, for then he seems ordinary and not good-looking, and seen from close by his features are almost gloomy, and his brow furrowed with earnest thought; his eyes at first sight look almost dull and clouded; but when he speaks, on the other hand, his glance is sharp and lively.

You can have no conception of the mass of humanity thronging the streets and parks through which the Emperor drove, and they were standing packed together for hours on end. When we arrived, an hour before the royal paty, we had to drive all the way from the station between the crowds which had been lining the streets since the morning. As they had had to stand for so long without anything to look at, they naturally stared with all their might when at last some carriages appeared, which, even if they contained nothing remarkable, did at least have the distinction of being allowed to drive into the Palace. It amused me greatly to see the faces: I felt as if I were looking at an illustration from the Botz[1] tales. In spite of all the work we had to do, and although our legs ached with fatigue, Sophie and I ran to the best vantage points at every arrival and departure, for the pleasure of seeing the crowds shouting hurrah and waving handkerchiefs. The band played the French national anthem every time the Imperial couple got into or out of their carriage, the Emperor never failing to acknowledge the cheers with a gracious bow.

---

[1] Frieda appears to have rendered phonetically the German pronunciation of 'Boz', the early pseudonym adopted by Charles Dickens.

Letter 4

THE CRYSTAL PALACE
1855

When the Great Exhibition of 1851 came to a close as planned in 1852, the Crystal Palace which housed it, Joseph Paxton's innovatory construction of glass and iron, was dismantled and rebuilt in 200 acres of wooded parkland on Sydenham Hill, the highest spot in south London. It was opened by the Queen to the uplifting strains of the 'Hallelujah Chorus' on 10 June 1854, just a year before Frieda wrote this letter. The Queen had been an ardent supporter of the original, and frequently graced the new venture with her presence, most recently with the Emperor Napoleon and the Empress Eugénie.

The building consisted of a basement floor, a grand central nave, two side aisles, two main galleries, three transepts and two wings. It was half as big again as the original Crystal Palace: 1608 feet long, and the central transept 208 feet high. Its directors boasted of nearly three-quarters of a mile of ground covered with a total of twenty-five acres of glass. Inside was nothing more or less than an astonishing attempt to assemble under one roof all the marvels of the natural and man-made world, to the profit of the minds of the general public and the pockets of the directors. Machinery and carriages could be seen in the basement, all kinds of goods from sealing wax to humane beehives and philosophical instruments (a category which included amongst other items guns, artificial eyes, daguerreotypes and patent trusses) were on display in the upper galleries. In the natural history section, the plants, animals and peoples of the world were exhibited in representations of their natural surroundings, specimen trees and plants having been specially imported.

One of the most important objects of the Crystal Palace, according to the directors, was 'to teach a great practical lesson in art'. For this

69

purpose, copies and casts of the various phases through which art and architecture were deemed to have passed were displayed in twenty- nine separate courts, each devoted to a separate era, which lined the central avenue like boutiques along a shopping mall, so that the curious could wander through the successive courts of civilisation from Nineveh to Birmingham by way of Byzantium and Sheffield.

Appropriate vegetation was placed near each court. At the approach to the Egyptian Court, for instance, were sixteen Egyptian date palms recently imported from Egypt. The directors admitted that these trees owed 'their present unflourishing appearance to the delay that took place in their transmission, on account of the steamer in which they were conveyed having been engaged, on her homeward passage, for the transport of troops.'*

Above the entrance to the Egyptian Court was a hieroglyphic inscription which ran, 'In the 17th year of the reign of Her Majesty, the ruler of the waves, the royal daughter Victoria lady most gracious, the chiefs, architects, sculptors, and painters, erected this palace and gardens with a thousand columns, a thousand decorations, a thousand statues of chiefs and ladies, a thousand trees, a thousand flowers, a thousand birds and beasts, a thousand fountains, and a thousand vases. The architects, and painters and sculptors built this palace as a book for the instruction of the men and women of all countries, regions, and districts. May it be prosperous.'* The aim was to delight, astound and instruct, and Frieda received the impressions of the Crystal Palace in the spirit in which it was conceived.

Osborne, 25 May 1855

To see this sublime monument to the unforgettable Industrial Exhibition in London must truly be counted among those pleasures which remain a rich and lasting memory for everyone, even for those who have little feeling for Art. This huge glass palace has been permanently transferred to a place about two hours' drive from London, for the display of works of art which are intended to instruct and delight for all time, and there is also a small section devoted to the sale of products of art and industry.

As soon as one steps through the main entrance one is so affected, indeed so completely overcome, by the ravishing impression it makes – I could not move a step; it was as if the magnificence of it had suddenly robbed me of my breath and all my senses. My companion said I turned quite pale. The curving glass dome arches upwards, high above one's head; wherever one looks there is shimmering glass, enhanced by the most beautiful plants cascading from innumerable elegant hanging lanterns; these look the size of ordinary lanterns, but as we came nearer we saw that each was as big as a butter keg. The effect of all this is like the most beautiful fairy palace that ever a child's fantasy could create.

Art is indeed the greatest gift of the gods! One is so crushed and humbled by the overwhelming impression made by such a place – and yet how great, how sublime one feels as a human being, for it was in a *human mind* that the idea of this gigantic creation was conceived; *human hands* had the skill to put it into execution and create this temple of sublime art, whose splendour and beauty will delight, edify and uplift millions for hundreds of years to come[1].

Two powerful figures of horsebreakers,[2] on a colossal scale, stand on either side of the entrance, worthy guardians of this palace. The main thoroughfare, apart from innumerable smaller passages, consists of two intersecting galleries, with a fountain at each end and great basins full of beautiful plants. These main galleries are adorned on either side with busts of all the most famous men of history, surrounded with trees and flowers. One quarter shows those of the English nation, one those of Germany, one those of France and one those of Italy and the ancient Roman and Greek peoples. This arrangement is both attractive and interesting, and it has the added advantage of preventing the spectator from seeing very diverse objects at the same time, which would lessen the effect of each; instead, each is slightly concealed from the next.

What astonished me almost more than anything else was the interior of the Alhambra.[3] It is an absolutely faithful copy of that magnificent relic of Moorish art, that is to say, the largest and most

1 The Crystal Palace was destroyed by fire in 1936.
2 Two of the statues by the entrance were colossal equestrian bronze groups of Castor and Pollux by San Giorgio of Milan.
3 Fine Arts Court no. 16 was a representation of various parts of this palace built by the Moorish Kings in the thirteenth century on the citadel above the city of Granada.

beautiful part of the inner rooms. The walls are a wonderful sight, inlaid with gold and coloured stone fragments. The rooms are high, with massive pillars of great beauty. Imagine the impression it makes: you have read descriptions of a wonderful work of art, your imagination has decked it out richly, and then you suddenly find yourself in front of it, astonished that it is so much more magnificent than you could ever have imagined. Most of these lovely rooms open in the centre onto a small courtyard, in the middle of which stands a beautiful marble fountain surrounded by the loveliest flowers. It is the fountain which Chateaubriand[1] described so well: I could almost see the beguiling figures of those lovers before me, and sense the grief they must have felt at the loss of their greatness. For truly, what a people they must have been in their prime, the race which left such rich and beautiful traces of itself behind!

After this one walks through the labyrinthine Temple of the Egyptians,[2] adorned with the strangest pictures and hieroglyphs. *Everything* is perfectly faithfully reproduced, and to scale. I wished so much that our little group, with whom I read the Epicureans, could be there. Everything that Thomas Moore[3] described so beautifully is brought to life here. Colossal gods of stone, painted with the strangest decorations and colours, grin at one, and yet in spite of these strange figures, which are more likely to offend one's sense of beauty, the whole temple makes an extraordinarily peaceful, solemn impression. Judging from the figures alone, one could think oneself in a fools' temple; and yet one has a deep sense of being in a temple dedicated to gods. I cannot account for this; but the whole edifice is pervaded with a sense of calm dignity which compels the spectator to

[1] François-René de Chateaubriand (1768–1848), father of French romanticism. In *Les Aventures du dernier Abencerage* (1826), set a generation after the Moors were driven out of Spain, he tells in limpid prose the story of the return of one of them, the last of the family of the Abencerages. In the ruins of the Moorish Alhambra, beside a fountain stained with the blood of his ancestors, he and Dona Blanca, daughter of the Duke of Santa-Fé, declare their love for one another. Their union is impossible; he is a Muslim, she is a Christian; neither will renounce faith for love. Everyone behaves with the utmost nobility, and nobody wins.

[2] Fine Arts Court no. 13, the Egyptian Court, was approached through an avenue of lions. It exhibited, scaled down, a representative selection from various temples, carvings and tombs, including the Hall of Columns at Karnak.

[3] (1779–1852), who won a European reputation with *Lalla Rookh* (1817) in which the journey of the Indian Princess, Lalla Rookh, to meet her betrothed, the Sultan of Bucharia, in the Vale of Cashmere is the framework for four narrative poems in Eastern settings.

respect the form this religion takes, and to feel how serious it was for those who practised it.

There are also halls and temples from China and India,[1] with figures that are sometimes strange and sometimes beautiful; but the effect of these is more one of interesting and curious objects than of that solemn, sacred awe which comes over one in the enchanting, magnificent Moorish palace, or in the mighty Egyptian temple. Then there are representations of various races of primitive people, displayed with admirable artistry: a thicket in an American jungle, out of which springs a panther, as if intended to give the spectator a fright, pursued by two men who are so wonderfully made that they seem to be alive; a scene showing a piece of sandy desert where a family of natives approaches with a camel, the heat and thirst they are suffering from vividly conveyed by their expressions and attitudes and everything; tribal gatherings such as those described in Chamisso's travel books,[2] showing how they play, and trade beads. Their clothing generally consists of what to our ideas are dirty rags and tatters of strange cloth, very light; a few wear cloaks of a kind, made of animal hides. All these things come from the countries themselves. There are also Indians on an elephant, fighting another elephant. Who could tell how much Art has eavesdropped on Nature here? But the races of mankind are quite wonderful to behold, so very different in expression and attitude. The skin of these people is dark and thick like leather; only a few races have a fine light-brown transparent skin.

Here, then, one can gather impressions of parts of the world one has never seen. I had been told before that the Crystal Palace was of inestimable value to young artists who did not possess the means to travel; that seemed an exaggeration to me, but now I can understand it very well, for one sees the finest and most famous works of art in the world here. There is much from Germany,[3] such as monuments, a doorway and part of the interior of a church in Nuremberg; the entrance to the Cathedral in Mainz, and a mass of other works of art,

1 The official handbook to the Exhibition listed neither of these countries in its maps of the courts. Perhaps Frieda meant the Nineveh and Byzantine Courts.
2 *See* p.29.
3 The small German Medieval Court was devoted to examples of Gothic art and architecture in Germany.

all on the same scale and reproduced in some kind of material of a yellowish colour. There are countless statues and monuments from Italy and Greece; one can hardly take it all in, let alone describe it afterwards.

From ten o'clock in the morning until six o'clock in the evening we walked about in this place. We had something to eat, sitting behind a bush out of which protruded the jaws of a lion. After we had seen everything we possibly could, we climbed up to the gallery to enjoy the view of the whole palace from different sides and heights. A picture of the glass palace which you must all have seen can give you quite a good idea of the galleries. It was a magnificent sight: all the various exhibits seen from different angles and distances, striking one afresh each time. Down below, in the centre, music is performed every day by a German musical society engaged for the purpose. The sound of the music fades very gradually, at a certain distance, becoming fainter and fainter until it is heard no more, which adds a mystical quality to the surroundings. An enormous organ with tremendous volume stands on one of the galleries, and it is also sometimes played. I did not know this, and I was standing quite near it, looking in the other direction, quite absorbed by the lovely view, thinking as I always do on these occasions of home and of all of you, with whom I should so gladly have shared this pleasure, just standing quietly for a few minutes and feeling almost melancholy, when all of a sudden that mighty organ, accompanied by trumpets, struck up the wonderful German chorale 'How Great is The Almighty's Goodness'. What could have been more calculated to make my heart swell and my spirit soar than those solemn, uplifting strains from my homeland! My sadness was soon transformed into courage and strength; I banished all feelings but those of devout joy and gratitude. If only everyone, in moments of heartache and weakness, could inwardly hear a Christian song like this, to give them the strength to bear pain with composure and joy with calm!

There is another section to which a series of statues of famous men form a kind of entrance, and some stand out from the others by their immense size, as for example the famous English statesman Robert Peel, and Rubens, the three Reformers,[1] and many others. It is quite

---

[1] The Handbook to the Crystal Palace listed statues of three German divines, Martin Luther

striking how very many more famous statesmen there are than famous artists in England compared to other nations.

If I tried to tell you about everything, I should never, never reach the end. I hope that this little account will give you a slight impression of it. The Crystal Palace is still being enlarged, and its contents increased: since last year it is said to have been widened considerably, and it is surrounded by extensive and beautiful gardens which are also being added to, and in which one can walk about. Altogether its surroundings are very pretty: low hills and woods and attractive country houses lie on every side. The landscapes here – I mean in country areas – do not have the idyllic, romantic quality of our scenery at home, but rather give an impression of peace, order and comfort.

With that you must be content, dear friends; I have scarcely time to write as much as this.

(1483–1546) 'The Great Reformer', Philipp Melanchthon, (1497–1560), 'Divine and Reformer', and Friedrich Schleiermacher (1768–1834), 'Theologian'.

Letter 5

THE PLEASURES OF OSBORNE
AND THE SIGHTS OF LONDON
1855

From 15 February to 10 July (with the exception of two short visits to Osborne and one to Windsor), Queen, Court and attendants had been in London enjoying, or enduring, the levees, concerts, balls, and other duties and entertainments of the London Season, to which Osborne was such a refreshing contrast and where the Queen was now settled for her usual summer visit of six weeks. For Frieda, and for the other dressers, work here was not so pressing, and she had the time to take up her pen once more.

Osborne, 21 July 1855

What shall I write to my dear friends from here, from this charming island? From here, where there is nothing great or remarkable, but where, wherever the eye turns, it rests upon the wonders of God, and Nature in her beauty speaks with a thousand voices. Yet we poor humans cannot repeat a single one of her words, even if we can understand and feel them. But I am always at one with you in spirit, you shall always know where I am and what I feel, and so I must tell you a little about my life here, which could be called a brief armistice at the moment, for the Season in London is like a fierce battle, which will begin again soon, when we go to Paris. Then there will be still more to tell.

I have already described the palace we live in here, and I can assure you that the impression it makes on me is stronger each time I come. It is delightful to roam about among works of art such as one only imagined in one's dreams of faraway southern lands, and to see gathered together in glorious harmony treasures of art old and new, the like of which one is accustomed to see only occasionally, and only one at a time. Everywhere about one here there is a pleasing sense of harmony which I cannot begin to describe. Every painting, every statue seems destined for exactly the place in which it hangs or stands. I shall never understand how people can grow accustomed to being surrounded by truly beautiful, sublime works of art: however often I walk along the corridors, I can never help feeling a kind of awe as I pass the statues, and I am constantly astonished by the many people who are for ever running past without once feeling or thinking anything. Not all of them love Osborne, either because it is isolated or because it is dull, or because to see it once is enough. But I love it more each time, and when you know that I am in Osborne, my dear friends, you can always be sure that I will be filled with a sense of peace and well-being, even if my homesickness increases here more than at any other place, and my thoughts are always flying to my homeland. But I have a little more free time to draw here, and this beloved art is a great consolation to the soul. I have begun a small book in which there are already many drawings; I collect everything very carefully so as to be able to show it to you when I come home. I want you to be able to imagine yourselves over here with me, and to learn to live with me. I have a nice little room which looks out onto the sea, and from which I can always hear the delightful splashing of the fountain down on the terrace. Near my room a staircase leads up to a balcony in a tower:[1] this is entirely my preserve, as no one else thinks it worth climbing up there. There is a glorious view over the sea from there, and every day when I am on duty and therefore cannot go out, I go up there when the Queen is out for her drive in the evening: I am in the house, and yet I can still enjoy the beauties of Nature. I have placed a little table up there, and have started to paint the view. So you see why I love Osborne. How can solitude hurt me? On the contrary, when I am alone I feel closer to those I love, and to be in a crowd of strange people is merely tedious for me. Apart from my good Sophie I live quite alone, but I am with you in spirit. If the

1 Osborne was laid out so that the Queen and Prince's private apartments, with the dining-room and drawing-room below and the nurseries above, formed a self-contained house, known as the Pavilion, only attached to the much larger service wings by corridors, one on every floor. The Pavilion was finished off with the flag tower that Frieda describes.

weather is very fine, and if I have not much to do, I sometimes go out in the fresh air from seven to eight o'clock in the morning. It is so lovely by the sea at that hour; the water is sometimes so still and clear that it feels quite strange when one has seen it roaring and raging not long before. It is so magical, such a fairy-tale sight, and it is usually only in the early morning that one sees it thus. A fine mist rises, making the faraway hills appear enveloped in fog.

After this moment of sheer pleasure I go back to the house feeling happy and contented, sometimes bringing back a little sketch with me, often to find the others sitting with drowsy faces over their breakfast. I have a splendid appetite, and no one suspects that I have already felt the cool refreshing wind on my face; only the housemaid, who always comes into my room at seven to see if I am awake, shows her astonishment, saying to me in English that the morning is no doubt the best time, but up to now everyone has always preferred to sleep than to go out for walks. Naturally in a house where such late nights are always kept one does not make such an early start in the morning, and in London it would be impossible to get up so early anyway, for there one stays up much too late.

I must tell you something else which is perhaps rather remarkable: I often see the King of the Belgians[1] walking about on the terrace, and sometimes I meet him strolling along a path, and step aside a little to let him pass, for which I receive a friendly, gracious nod of the head. I always think of my dear Mother when that happens – she is always so interested in him. He is already an old man, and stoops a little as he walks; he looks very serious and preoccupied, but seems very pleasant.

Osborne, 26th July

Now that I have been here longer I am getting bolder in my explorations of this place, and am no longer afraid of losing myself, but constantly finding new delights. If one turns away from the shore, which has always been my destination hitherto, one finds oneself in charming rolling country with beautiful green meadows

---

[1] Leopold I (1790–1865), who was at Osborne from 10 to 23 July 1855. He was the Queen's uncle, 'whom I have *ever loved* as a *father*'.*

full of countless herds of sheep, or lush waving cornfields and tall trees a little further away from the sea. One can wander to one's heart's content in the country – at least, if there is time to go out at an hour when the sun is not too hot – but up to now it has always been bearable because it is very windy. I was so happy to climb a hill again, for the first time since last year; even though it was only a molehill I persuaded myself that the air was more invigorating up there. Around the house, it is very flat, for here on the island one has either the sea and its delights or the rolling country. Both can be found together in a very pretty little town which I shall soon take you to. It lies on a small hill which projects out into the sea like a peninsula. It is the sea-bathing resort of Ryde, about four miles away from here. The Queen sent me there with Mary,[1] the Belgian girl whom you already know, to buy a few stone and marble knick-knacks – one can find very pretty ones there – to amuse the princesses,[2] who were ill with scarlet fever. It was a charming drive in a dear little open carriage like the small hunting carriage Herr von Klaubitz has, and it was a beautiful afternoon. At one moment we were climbing a gentle hill; at the next the sea lay before us, and all the way we were able to admire the fresh green of the trimmed hedges along the roads, which are famous for their beauty. Ryde[3] itself is a lively little town in a charming situation, where pretty Englishwomen, looking like shepherdesses in their soft-brimmed bonnets, walk up and down. The sea is particularly beautiful here, which may seem strange to you, since water is always water; but there is a great difference in colour, waves etc., which one must of course see in order to understand. Here one finds stones of a particular type which are most prettily carved, and if it were not one of my principles never to spend money on completely useless things, I could easily have been led astray here and emptied my purse. But when one sees as much as I do, one must leave the buying to others. Nevertheless I bought myself a pretty sketchbook: they are of particularly good quality here, as many painters visit this place. The one I have bought is for painting, and there is already a small painting

1 Mary Ann Andrews.
2 In fact, Princes Arthur and Leopold, and Princess Louise.
3 'The largest and handsomest town and bathing place in the Isle of Wight . . . a modern town and fashionable bathing place'.*

in it that you shall admire one day. How I should like to be able to tell you how enchanting the sea looks in the moonlight. Often in the last few days, on fine moonlit nights, I have stood for a whole hour at the window in the evening, unable to tear myself away from the magnificent picture before me: the sea, so often stormy, was so peaceful; shapes on the shore stood out black against the dark-blue and yet quite translucent water, and I longed to go out and walk down to the shore. But I cannot do that alone at night, and I am happy to be able to see it from afar. I have always loved and admired moonlit landscapes, and I have seen many that were lovely; indeed you and I, dear Elise,[1] managed to copy Calame[2] quite skilfully, and perhaps we even succeeded in expressing peace and calm in our pictures; but that mysterious sense of hidden animation and power which makes the scene seem not dead but quietly sleeping, as if it might awaken at any moment, is something we have *not* succeeded in conveying. Nevertheless I was able to sketch from my window a tower with the moon behind it, and I was very pleased when after half an hour something like a moonlit landscape was laid down on the paper. I thought it really quite effective, and lacked only another admirer besides myself to make my happiness complete.

My dear friends, since I painted you such a dreadful picture of the London fog, when the cheerful sun was still hiding its face from us, and only showed enough of itself, sometimes, for us to feel the lack of it still more, it is my duty to give you a second picture of London as it is now. I am delighted to tell you that I am beginning to like London and to acquire a taste for its pleasures; that is, I should still think it very unpleasant to live here all the time, although if I had horses to ride and a carriage to drive out into the country in, I should like it better.

Imagine, then, the freshest of green foliage, the loveliest of trees, all in the midst of this mighty city; lakes and fountains in the parks, brilliant sunshine, clear pure air, not a trace of smoke, no fog,

---

[1] Not one of Frieda's sisters, indicating that these letters are aimed at a wider circle than Frieda's immediate family.

[2] Alexandre Calame (1810–64), Swiss landscape painter best known for paintings of Alpine scenery and of the ruins of Paestum.

After the Great Exhibition closed, the Crystal Palace was enlarged and moved to this permanent site at Sydenham. The Queen attended its opening in 1854, and two years later presided over the inauguration of the fountains.

Inside the Crystal Palace visitors could wander among the curiosities and wonders of the natural and manmade world.

The Royal Yacht, Victoria and Albert II, *launched in 1855, was fast, modern, and comfortable.*

King Leopold of the Belgians in 1857

The Queen's dining saloon on board the Royal Yacht Victoria and Albert II

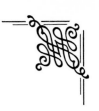

Queen Victoria landing
at Boulogne, 18 August
1855. Napoleon III waits
to greet her. Frieda is
among the crowd of
attendants on the deck of
the royal yacht.

Queen Victoria, the
Prince of Wales, the
Princess Royal and
Prince Albert welcomed
to St Cloud by the
Emperor and Empress.

Entry of Queen Victoria
into Paris; 'no description
can give an idea of the
splendour of the whole
scene', wrote the Queen in
her Journal for 18 August
1855.

The Palace of St Cloud, where the Queen arrived, as she put in her Journal, 'quite bewildered, but enchanted'.

Their Majesties at the Opera, 21 August 1855. Frieda and her brother Ludwig, at th Opéra-Comique on 2 August, would have looked down on a similar scene.

Queen Victoria and the Emperor Napoleon in the Salle des Glaces at Versailles, 25 August 1855. This ball, wrote the Queen in her Journal, was 'quite one of the finest and most magnificent sights we have witnessed'.

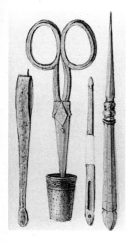

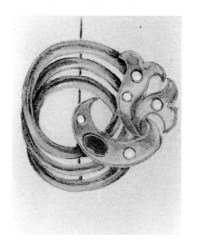

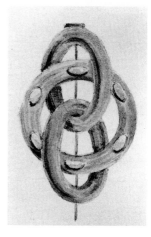

A present from the
Queen at Christmas
1856. 'This is the life-
size portrait of my
golden nécessaire' wrote
Frieda on the back of
her painting, 'the out-
side is of dark leather
... it is very valuable,
also very useful'.

Frieda sent home careful
watercolours of the presents
she was given by the Queen.
At Christmas 1855, she
received this brooch, of three
gold rings bound with a
blue enamel ribbon inset
with five pearls and a
carbuncle; 'the whole, very
massive', she commented.

On her painting of this
gold brooch, Frieda wrote
'From Princess Royal as a
remembrance of the days
at her happy home, given
before she left Windsor'.

Blackgang, Isle of Wight, 7 September 1855, by Frieda, sketched during her well-earned holiday
at Osborne.

Old and New Balmoral, by Frieda, 10 October 1855. A rare view. By the time the Queen returned in 1856, the old castle (to the left) had been demolished.

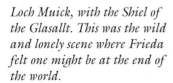

Balmoral Castle, 8 September 1856, by Frieda, who has perhaps included a self portrait in the foreground.

Loch Muick, with the Shiel of the Glasallt. This was the wild and lonely scene where Frieda felt one might be at the end of the world.

The Queen's bedroom at Balmoral; she moved into the new house in September 1855, writing in her journal, 'the house is charming; the rooms delightful; the furniture, paper, everything perfection.'

The Queen's dressing room at Balmoral; simply furnished in comparison with the one at Windsor, but equipped with all the comforts a Queen might need.

The Queen's sitting room at Balmoral.

Queen Victoria dressed for dinner at Balmoral

The Garrawalt (Garbh Allt) Falls which Frieda sketched on 5 September 1856, her second visit to what was for her a sublime and surpassing spectacle.

Scottish farmer's fireplace, sketched by Frieda as being 'especially simple and typical', 18 September 1856.

everything clear and bright. There is an unutterable difference between summer and winter, rain and sunshine, here in London. Even the dark houses look pleasant in summer, for the unpleasant glare of our light-coloured houses at home is absent. The air, always a little damp, keeps trees and grass constantly fresh, in spite of the heat; it is wonderful here in summer. It is only the swarms of people, carriages and riders that I am not yet accustomed to; or I should now enjoy going for walks here much more. I have been to the Tunnel, the Stock Exchange and the City. The City is a truly remarkable place, you cannot imagine what it is like. I was so utterly exhausted by sightseeing and by the noise of the City that when I came home at six o'clock all I could do was to throw myself down in a chair and close my eyes, so as to be able to recover just enough strength to attend upon the Queen at half past seven. A German in the Queen's household, a kind elderly man, accompanied me to the City by the Queen's wish, as she said I must see it once. We boarded a steamer on the Thames not far from the Palace, where these boats go up and down, as the omnibuses are always very crowded. The weather was superb, and we sailed for about an hour down to the famous London Bridge, in the very heart of the City. It was a very interesting trip, with which no doubt few river journeys can be compared, perhaps not for beauty, but certainly for interest. Both river banks are crowded with business premises, warehouses and factories of all kinds. One sees crowds of people hurrying busily to and fro, small boats on the river on which people are working, and beyond the warehouses countless dwellings from the midst of which, here and there, tall steeples rise, most belonging to magnificent churches. The nearer one comes to the City, the more ships there are, and the bigger they become, until as one suddenly comes upon London Bridge, one sees a dense forest of masts. Here are the mighty merchant ships which come in laden from the sea and drop anchor in the river; it is incredible how many there are. We in our dear little land-locked home usually know only by repute the treasures which such ships bring from faraway lands. Or when we see the *Foster Brothers*[1] and find the lamentations of the merchant over his lost ship exaggerated. But I can assure you, my dear

---

[1] By Karl Friedrich Gustav Topfer (1792–1871), who wrote popular comedies. This play in five acts was performed three times at the Hoftheater in Karlsruhe in 1852*.

friends, that it is amazing: it is here that one sees the wealth and greatness of a trading nation, and at the same time one can judge how rich and powerful the nobility and the Court must be in order to hold sway over such wealth, so that in a country and a city where there is so much trade, and where the merchants are rich enough to behave as they please towards whom they please, the aristocracy nevertheless stands above them, and enjoys greater and higher power.

The Tunnel[1] is a most remarkable construction and is worth seeing for that fact alone; if it were not for that one would simply have the impression of walking through an immensely long, vaulted cellar. One climbs down many stairs, to an extraordinary depth, until one reaches the bottom. The passage for carriages is not yet ready. Down there in the vaults, in the corners, poor people sit at small tables lit by gas lamps, selling all kinds of things. As we went past one table an old Jew called out after us, having probably heard us speaking German, *'Mein Herr Sie sind ein deutscher, kaufen Sie mir Etwas ab'*[2] and when we turned round we saw that there was a very dirty piece of paper pinned up with the words *'Hier spricht man deutsch'*. If the wares he offered had not been too disgusting to touch, I should gladly have bought something from him, as a compatriot.

Then we went to the Tower of London,[3] a large and remarkable edifice used in former times as a fortress, before London grew so big. Now part of it is a garrison, and the rest is used to house curiosities, and because of its particular kind of architecture, which is very ancient and fine, it is also shown to visitors. There is a wonderful armoury there, with arms of every kind and of very fine quality, arranged according to the periods in which they were used. Numerous former kings and English lords who distinguished

---

[1] The Thames Tunnel, the first underwater tunnel in the world, built by Isambard Kingdom Brunel, opened as a thoroughfare for foot passengers 25 March 1843. Its twin horseshoe-shaped arches, 1200 feet long, connected at intervals, were originally intended for vehicles, but the money ran out before the carriage ramps could be completed. It was converted into a railway tunnel in the 1860s.

[2] 'Sir, you are German, buy something from me'.

[3] Since William the Conqueror began his fortress palace here, the Tower, from which the king controlled his capital, had been the symbol of the authority and splendour of the monarchy. It was arsenal, treasury, mint, state prison, storehouse of public records, menagerie, jewel house and royal wardrobe. As recently as the 1840s its defences had been strengthened for fear of riot and rebellion, but by now it was, for the first time in its history, more of an antiquarian showplace than an establishment of military importance.

themselves by their courage are represented there, fully armed and on horseback. Also Elizabeth, on horseback, accompanied by two esquires, in the greatest pomp, just as she appeared when she rode out to meet her army returning after a victory. There is also a collection of other objects such as the block and axe with which Anne Boleyn was beheaded,[1] etc. etc. Then there are the priceless Crown Jewels, an immense collection of diamonds, crowns and sceptres of gold and precious stones, which the nation gave the various monarchs for their coronations; I also saw an orb, which one so often sees used on the stage, made of tin. Of course the different crowns each reflect the style of their period, which is very interesting. There are also many priceless vessels which are used only for coronations. And there are numerous prison cells, large and small: those who languished there were mostly people of consequence. Such places always make the saddest and most disagreeable impression on me. One large room, with sealed openings all around it, bearing the names of those who had been immured there filled me with horror.[2] The cruelty of mankind is unbelievable, even if the majority of people are good and gentle. One cannot help but see that there is not and has never been any nation which has showed itself generous and humane towards all its enemies.

Of the Stock Exchange[3] I can only say that it is an enormous building, with endless doors and innumerable people running hither and thither; they give the impression of being merely numbers; they really look like numbers, and the whole place put me in mind of a huge multiplication sum, made up of such a variety of numbers that my head swam at the thought of anyone, let alone myself, having to work it out and then at the end check it all through again – oh! it is a fearful thought, and I eventually began to feel nervous in earnest, and was happy to get outside again. What is so strange is that we could

---

[1] An axe of the Tudor period was for a long time displayed as the instrument of her death; she was in fact executed with a sword.

[2] Frieda may well be referring to the lower storey of the Beauchamp Tower, described in 1842 as having 'several pointed arched recesses originally admitting light into it from narrow embrasures, but these are now blocked up, and windows opened in another part. The walls of this exceedingly interesting place are almost covered with inscriptions, devices, coats of arms, and autographs.'*

[3] In Capel Court, Bartholemew Lane; built 1802 but considerably enlarged between 1852 and 1854.

just walk straight in, and go all over it, past all the numbers working away so zealously, and look at everything. No one sees you; no one pays any attention to you. In all this throng you feel like the only living creature among ciphers.

Yes, my dear friends, as I cannot help repeating to you again and again: for me, these great places have something frightening and disturbing about them. After an expedition like that I am always delighted, amazed, pleased, tired and edified all at once, in a confusion of feelings; but the sight of a single rose, a cloud in the sky, or the peaceful moon and the stars, can give me more real enjoyment, a pleasanter sense of satisfaction. The simple garden of one of our dear beloved little parsonages can make us happier than all these treasures, all this magnificence. We walked around in the City for a long time afterwards, where shop crowds upon shop, people upon people, and horses upon horses, walking or trotting by, or standing still. I can think of nothing more frightful than to have to live here; indeed most of the merchants have their residences outside the town; but there remains a countless mass of those poor workers who are condemned to spend their whole lives in this deafening hubbub.

I also saw St Paul's. I now find it quite natural that the Season here is in summer, and people go into the country in winter. One really should not consider anything strange until one knows all about it.

Letter 6

QUEEN VICTORIA'S STATE VISIT
TO PARIS
1855

After the visit of the Emperor Napoleon to England, the interests of allied solidarity and national pride required Queen Victoria to make a reciprocal journey. In August 1855 she went to Paris. Napoleon III met her at Boulogne with 40,000 troops, and when she arrived at Paris, it seemed as though the whole city had turned out to welcome her. The days that followed were crammed with sightseeing and entertainment. The Queen visited the Exposition des Beaux-Arts, was shown the sights of Paris and Versailles, shivered at the fearful memories of the French Revolution, and discussed, behind the scenes, the conduct of the war. Dazzling entertainments were laid on each evening, culminating in a ball at Versailles, the first since the time of Louis XVI, the design of which was taken from a fête given by Louis XV. All the dressers' stamina and powers of organisation were called upon, but Frieda was buoyed up by the joyful prospect of seeing some of her family again.

Osborne, 29 August 1855

Now, my dear friends, I shall describe a journey to you that was full of such beauty and pleasure, as well as toil and stress, that I shall probably never be able to bring it alive to anyone who was not there to experience it. How I wish, as I write this, that I could make you truly feel what I felt so vividly. Of course what mattered most was to see my beloved brother again, and my dear Aunt, and Herr Müller and Rachel – that was what made it so hard for me to leave Paris, and I have not got over it yet. It revived so many memories of the home that I love, that it has made me feel as sad as I

85

did during my first days at Windsor. But this feeling will pass, while the joys of the journey will remain with me always. I will not plague you with descriptions of festivities, for they can be read about in all the newspapers. But you shall travel with me, see with my eyes, share my feelings, and exclaim with me those words that still echo in my mind: '*La belle France!*'

Yes, France is a beautiful, happy land. Everyone we met was so gay, so friendly. People, landscapes, even the objects one sees about one – everything seems made for happiness. One feels so stimulated: the stiff, cold Englishman, just as much as the good-natured German, cannot help but love it, this land where every heart is full of joy and sunshine. And yet I would not wish to live in France, nor could I; I do not think I should be happy. Everything gives one a sense of impermanence, everything seems to be for the moment only. '*Il faut s'amuser autant que possible!*' a cheerful Frenchman said to me, and that is how they all live. It is pleasant and agreeable to be a visitor in France, but I prefer by far to live among the calm English, from whom one may expect stiffness and lack of consideration but never dishonesty, which is why one feels so safe and secure among them. In France one need expect no unfriendliness, yet one feels no confidence, one finds in general no reliability. The French are charming, agreeable, warm and sympathetic, but the German conscientiousness is lacking. The English are admirably steadfast, serious and firm, but they have not the German good nature. You may be surprised that after so short a stay in both countries I have such decided opinions about them. But in circumstances such as mine one takes everything in at an extraordinary speed; one can feel the pulse-beat of the nation; when one sits up by the coachman one gets to know the horses quicker than if one only sees them galloping by, however many times.

At the English Court, for example, at grand ceremonies, the old English bodyguard[1] with their long pikes, stiff collars and pigtails stand there solemn and unmoving, like the representatives of a past age, as guardians of a great Royal House that has stood firm for centuries and will endure for centuries to come, while in the great halls of France's palaces the delightful Imperial Guards lie idly about,

---

[1] Frieda almost certainly means the Yeomen of the Guard, bodyguards to the sovereign since 1485.

so handsome, and so beautifully dressed that they reminded me when I went through the anterooms of the young ensign in *The Glass of Water*;[1] or in the *Marquise von Vilette*.[2] They are like the glittering ornaments of a glittering Imperial throne. One can gain such insight into the history of nations if one only observes the customs and manners of their Courts with a little attentiveness; they are so different in England and France, just as the people themselves are so different from each other. How extraordinarily unlike each other are the expressions on the faces of these two peoples! Here in England everything has a measured, straightforward air, even to the point of stiffness; while over there in France it is free, fiery, uncontrolled, even to the point of a complete lack of constraint. How much climatic conditions affect character and mood! The sky in France has a far more southerly aspect; the air was so warm, indeed hot, and yet so pure and light, that one remained fresh and cheerful in spite of the great heat; we were all amazed at how much more one can endure there than here; we never had more than four or five hours of sleep and we were on our feet the whole day, and yet at every free moment we went off to see something, which was often quite exhausting too. Here the air in winter is so foggy, in summer so oppressively heavy, the sky lowers so densely and impenetrably over one that it makes one's head heavy and oppresses one's spirits. The quietest people in the house here who came to France with us became quite lively and jovial over there.

I would compare the conditions and the way of life in these two countries to a ride in two different kinds of carriage. Life in England is like a journey in an immensely heavy, solid travelling coach, which rolls ceaselessly on at a measured pace towards its goal: one is utterly safe inside, regardless of the weather outside. If the sun should shine brightly outside, one might well feel too cramped and enclosed in this coach, too restricted and uncomfortable; or one might burn with impatience to reach the goal – but alas! complaints are of no avail, the

---

[1] By the French dramatist Eugène Scribe (1791–1861). A comedy in five acts, performed once at the Hoftheater at Karlsruhe, in 1852.

[2] A play by the prolific 'Franz Fels', the pseudonym of the actress, director and playwright, Charlotte Birch-Pfeiffer (1800–68).

coach goes steadily and heavily onward, and either one gives in to necessity, and in the end finds it comfortable, or one becomes gloomy and melancholy. In France, on the other hand, one sits in an elegant open caleche, very dainty but not solidly built; it rushes gaily along at a lightning pace, wonderful scenes flash by with the speed of thought; as long as the sun shines one thinks oneself in paradise. But one is only too conscious that this airy conveyance cannot survive any storm, and if one happens on a mountain or a cliff, one longs for the heavy old coach, and realises with shame that because one was put out of sorts by the many discomforts, one had forgotten the quality that outweighs all others – *safety*! Our German life, however, I would compare with a ride in a simple little country wagon. It may not be as strong as the English one, but it is *solid enough* to roll unharmed over many a stone, and serves us excellently in our beautiful mountains. It may not be as pretty and elegant as the French one, but it allows us to enjoy the warmth of the sun and the view all around *just as well*. If a shower of rain should fall, we have inherited enough resistance from our forebears not to suffer too much from it. I am firmly convinced that if any of you, my dear ones, goes to Paris, like me you will carry away warm, delightful memories, and the shorter one's stay there, the more one loves it, because it welcomes one so warmly and gaily that one expects to find everything one loves there, although the time is too short to be sure of what one would really find. *One cannot but love it*. Goethe's words 'One can esteem it, trust it, but not rest on its bosom' apply best to England. But now, at last, to the journey.

Three days before our departure, the magnificent ship[1] we were to travel in was already lying at anchor off Osborne. From all the windows one could see it looking expectantly towards us. In the house there was endless packing and preparation.[2] No previous

---

[1] The new royal yacht, *Victoria and Albert*. The Queen had tried her out for the first time on 11 July, 'a most magnificent and enormous vessel. One feels quite lost in her!' The yacht was state of the art, capable of going 'full four miles an hour faster than anything else',* which gave the Admiralty, arranging the ships to escort her to France, a new headache: 'we will make as good a show as we can. The real difficulty is finding an escort to go *with* Her Majesty as the yacht is so much faster than anything else we have.'*

[2] 'Much troubled with questions of toilettes, and other arrangements for Paris', wrote the Queen in her Journal for 11 August, and again, two days before leaving, 'All, preoccupation and bustle for our great journey'.

88

journey had aroused such interest in everyone as this one. The servants in the house who were going were delighted, and had learned a few words from one of their number who knew some French; when we climbed into the carriage, the servant who closed the door called after us '*Bon voyage, Mesdames!*' We could have died laughing. We left on the 17th, at five in the evening; Mary and I were travelling; Sophie was already in Paris with the luggage.[1] The Queen came on board at seven o'clock. Meanwhile we unpacked, and prepared everything for the evening toilette, for dinner was to be served on board. The ship has three decks: the lowest one is quite below the water, without any daylight, and the luggage and everything that is needed is stored there. There are also rooms for the servants and sailors. The second deck is half below water level and has small round windows high up through which about as much air and light come in as on the steamers you know, in the first class, and here we live. When all the princes and princesses travel the youngest ones also sleep here, as there is only room for five children above. Where Sophie and I sleep there is a large room in the middle with a table and a sofa, and round this room there are doors which lead into little bedrooms. In each of these there is just enough room for a sofa which turns into a bed at night, a little table and a chair. The upper deck is the Queen's and it has large rooms with big windows; that is, a drawing-room, bedroom and dressing-room, dining-room etc. etc., the Prince's and the children's rooms, and our wardrobe room, everything beautifully and splendidly furnished. All the furniture is fixed down and the tables have little iron railings round them to prevent things falling off when the sea is very rough. Looking out of a window from here and seeing the waves foaming and roaring is a most impressive sight. On the deck there is a large room with glass walls all round, just as if someone had placed a great glass dome there; it is delightfully pretty, with a sofa and every comfort, and it is for the Royal Family, so that they can stay up on deck in all weathers and see everything. The ship is so big that only half of it is used by the Queen

---

[1] The dressers' coach, with Sophie, Cart, other attendants, and a police inspector, was sent from Osborne to London and one to Paris via Folkestone. Three vans were sent direct from Osborne by sea to Boulogne.* Sophie, and the others travelling with the dressers' coach, had passports; Frieda, as one of those 'actually in attendance on the Queen' did not.*

and her servants; the other half is occupied by the lords and ladies, the
naval officers, the doctor, and the various members of the suite with
their servants.[1] Then there are little hidden passages constructed
everywhere, where the servants who have to bring or take anything
away can go through, so that one does not notice any comings or
goings at all. It is a masterpiece, and has a most remarkable engine –
one is not aware of any smell at all, as one usually is on a ship. The
sailors are always dressed in fresh white and blue uniforms, quite
enchanting.

After we had prepared everything I went up on deck, where I
beheld an indescribably delightful scene: I saw the sun going down in
the most glorious sunset I have ever seen. The fiery sphere seemed to
lower itself majestically into the sea, and it seemed as if the shining
silvery waves slowly and gradually engulfed it. The weather was very
clear and fine. Then the Queen arrived, and my work began exactly as
usual, only it felt so strange to be on the water.

'At four o'clock in the morning we shall sail, the sea is so calm and
fair, no one will be ill, we can go to bed without worrying' – such was
the general verdict. But I thought quite otherwise, and acted like a
dying man making his will. I kept saying to myself, 'You are still well,
so arrange all your affairs now.' When everyone was in bed, around
midnight, I packed everything that was no longer needed as quickly
as possible, and arranged everything necessary for the next morning
as best I could. Then I went to bed, but I could not sleep, for the
memory of Calais[2] came more and more vividly back to me. At four
o'clock I felt a sudden violent jolt, upon which I got up, dressed

[1] Four members of the Royal Family were travelling: Queen Victoria, Prince Albert, the
Princess Royal and the Prince of Wales. There were thirteen ladies and gentlemen of the suite, or
Household: the Marchioness of Ely and Lady Churchill (Ladies of the Bedchamber), the Hon.
Mary Bulteel (Maid of Honour), the Marquis of Breadalbane (Lord Chamberlain), the Earl of
Clarendon (Secretary of State for Foreign Affairs), the Marquess of Abercorn (Groom of the
Stole to the Prince), Lord Alfred Paget (Clerk Marshal), General the Hon. C. Grey (Equerry-in-
Waiting and Secretary to the Prince), Colonel the Hon. C. Phipps (Keeper of the Privy Purse),
Colonel Biddulph (Master of the Household), Sir James Clark (Physician to the Queen), Miss
Hildyard (Governess to the Princess Royal) and Mr Gibbs (Tutor to the Prince of Wales). It is
not so easy to come to a figure for the servants, some of whom had gone ahead. The French were
expecting: 2 pages, 1 hairdresser, 2 valets for Prince Albert, 1 Jäger, 2 wardrobe men, 1 valet for
the Prince of Wales, 1 messenger, 2 dressers to Her Majesty, 1 wardrobe maid, 1, 1 dresser to the
Princess Royal, 1 housemaid, 2 police inspectors, 3 footmen and 2 'tapissiers'. Servants for the
suite consisted of 3 ladies' maids, 3 valets and 5 footmen.*
[2] Frieda is probably referring to her journey to England the previous winter.

myself completely, for I was still afraid that soon I would not be able to do anything at all, and lay down again, summoning up all my strength and composure. I was afraid that I would be ill in the first quarter of an hour, as I had been before, but imagine! I fell peacefully asleep and woke two hours later feeling quite well! I went upstairs, drank some tea, and dressed the Queen. But while I was doing this I felt rather dizzy. The ship was moving very little, the weather was glorious, but it did not last long, and around ten o'clock I began to feel as wretched as could be. I was the only one on the whole ship who felt ill. When the Queen heard about it she sent Sir James[1] to give me something, but he laughed heartily when he saw me lying on the sofa with a white face and trembling limbs, and said there was no reason to be ill and I would cheer up again in Paris.

When we were in sight of Boulogne we stopped for about an hour[2] and had breakfast, and then everyone got into their Court dress: all the gentlemen, the Prince at their head, wore splendid uniforms, and the Queen changed completely,[3] which Mary saw to: she was as fit as a fiddle. In this half-hour I recovered sufficiently to be able to gather up my bits and pieces and throw them into my suitcases in the greatest disorder. Then I put on a better hat and good gloves, and *everyone* went up on deck. I felt quite well now, apart from a little dizziness. Then the ship began to move again, and sailed ahead at top speed. As soon as we were spotted, cannons thundered on all sides. The sky was deep blue, the sea like a mirror. The closer we came, the more beautiful and wonderful was the scene which met our eyes.

Boulogne is picturesquely situated at the foot of rocky hills, on which, as far as the eye could see, soldiers were drawn up, and were firing muskets and cannon. The houses were decorated with flags and flowers, and there were crowds everywhere. A long way out to sea, on both sides as we sailed by, large and small ships, decorated with bunting, were in position, covered right up to the topmost mast-heads with smartly dressed sailors and soldiers, who greeted us with music and cheering. In the harbour into which we sailed there are

---

[1] Sir James Clark (1788–1870), the Queen's doctor.
[2] To wait for the tide.
[3] For a description of what she wore for the journey and entry into Paris, *see* Introduction, p.17. Gentlemen at Court wore uniform on state and formal occasions.

high walls on both sides which reach out into the sea, and which are probably used for trading ships. These walls were now completely covered with people waving handkerchiefs and shouting; it looked quite amazing, they seemed to be standing on the water. The enthusiasm of the lively French must be the *non plus ultra*[1] of vivacity. We moved ever more slowly towards the place where we were to land, and where the Emperor stood, bareheaded, surrounded by his General Staff, bowing three times towards our ship, which the Queen reciprocated. Everyone on board removed their headgear, and then, after the *enormous* noise of shouting and firing which had gone before, there followed a moment of solemn, ceremonial silence. It seemed as if Nature itself, and everything, had to draw breath, in order to take up the jubilant cheering again with renewed energy. I shall never forget this arrival in all my life. The historic importance of this royal visit gave the jubilation a certain dignity, a gravity which one sensed behind it, and which filled even me with a sense of my own role, for I was after all taking part in this too, and was certainly no useless appendage to this visit.

When we stopped, a little gangway was quickly thrown across, onto which, from one side, the Emperor stepped up, and from the other the Queen stepped down. When they reached the middle they held out their hands to each other and kissed each other; we were standing quite close by, and it was a moment of solemn suspense. Behind the Queen and the Emperor, the Prince with the two children[2] on either side of him walked down, followed by the Household. There were of course innumerable people in attendance on the Queen as well as on the members of the Household on board, and for all these, and the luggage too, to get to the railway *after* the Queen, would have taken some time even with the greatest haste, and it is well known that emperors and kings (sometimes other people too) only make others wait, and never wait themselves. It had been arranged that half an hour after the Queen another train would leave, also an express, to take everyone else. As everything here is done strictly according to rank, I as the first of the Queen's servants was the

---

[1] *ne plus ultra*, or, thus far and no further.
[2] The Princess Royal was fourteen, the Prince of Wales thirteen. This visit made a profound impression on both.

one to follow the last lord of the suite down onto the gangway. Mary followed me, then came one of the Prince's valets, who had the task of looking after us, for there was such a dreadful throng of carriages, soldiers, horses and people etc. etc. that one could hardly believe it. All this made my head swim, I could only see where I had to go and nothing else, but how great was my astonishment when halfway across the bridge a strange man seized my arm in a firm but friendly grasp, and called out gallantly, *'Les deux dames de la reine!'* Before I had time to recover from my surprise I was sitting beside him in an open carriage. Mary and our escort had followed us and were sitting opposite us, and now we flew along, through soldiers, music, triumphal arches, amid the incessant cheering of the crowds, following the royal carriages, to the railway. There, on high platforms, arranged in a pretty circle under garlands of flowers, stood countless beautiful ladies, who greeted the Queen with bowing and waving of handkerchiefs and throwing of flowers. But all this happened so quickly that one could only remember afterwards what one had seen. When we left our carriage we had to go through a hall that was likewise thronged with people, who like a divided river closed in at once behind the Queen in dense masses, so that we could hardly force our way through. I held tightly onto the arm of my escort, the two others following in our footsteps. The former kept calling out loudly, *'place pour les dames de la reine!'* upon which, for a moment, a narrow gap would appear which we pressed through; and then we found ourselves sitting in an elegant carriage, on a sofa with a little table in front of it on which refreshments were laid out. In an instant we were off (the ride and all this lasted no more than fifteen to twenty minutes). Only now, when we were safely sitting down, did the unknown gentleman introduce himself. He is a very remarkable, interesting man, who accompanies the Emperor everywhere, and who had been captured with him in Boulogne, as I was told later. He is now at Court, in charge of all the servants, and is said to have great power, which is certainly the impression given by his unusual personality.[1] The Emperor had brought him with him to get us into

[1] Frieda, it appears, is describing Charles Thélin, discreet, faithful and immensely capable, who had been with Louis Napoleon since 1811, when Louis Napoleon was three. It was reported that Louis Napoleon's mother, Queen Hortense, had exhorted the valet on her deathbed to look after her son. In 1840 Louis Napoleon planned a Napoleonic *coup* from

the train so that we should be there if the Queen needed us, to which he gallantly added that the ladies must also see the fine reception and everything. He showed us now a small door in our carriage, which resembled a small room; this door led into the Emperor's saloon, which was in the same carriage, and here, close to us, were the Queen and the Emperor. He (the stranger) is always in this side compartment in case the Emperor needs him. He told us very civilly that he had decided to keep the ladies to himself in his compartment, because in this way we would have the best view of everything. We expressed our lively appreciation of his kindness, and made ourselves as comfortable as we could. So our first step on French soil had begun with an act of kindness, and had we had time enough we could have received many acts of kindness; meanwhile we profited from this one as much as we could.

After we had gone a little way, I felt quite well and indeed very cheerful and delighted to see the crowds which were everywhere. They often provided the funniest sights. At every station we stopped for a little, so that the good people should not in vain have robbed woods and gardens, and put on their Sunday best. Everywhere there were soldiers, bands, throngs of people: '*Vive la Reine, vive l'Empereur*! – so many open mouths shouted at us that I nearly died of laughter at some of the grimaces they made to shout even louder. Such enthusiasm – no, it defies imagination, if one has not seen it oneself! Those French soldiers with their brown faces, black hair and eyes and bold expressions! The women also played an important part – they were everywhere, from babes in arms to matrons, waving and bowing ceaselessly. Of course the royal party always stood up and showed themselves at the window and thanked the crowds warmly. I peeped out of my window all the time, and saw and heard as much as the short time allowed, but always long enough to be able to take it all in, and fix it in my mind during the journey to the next station, where

London, where Thélin was at the centre of operations. The attempt failed on the beaches of Boulogne. The conspirators were captured, together with, it was said, a large sum of money, 1000 English-made muskets, and a live eagle. Louis Napoleon was imprisoned at Ham. Thélin obtained an unwise government's permission to remain with him, and was free to come and go from the prison. In 1846 the valet played an essential part in his master's escape. Louis Napoleon walked out of the prison disguised as a workman; Thélin met him outside in a hired carriage. Six years later the prisoner was Emperor. Thélin survived the fall of the Second Empire and retired to 'a charming villa, almost buried with flowers, at le Vesinet'.*

the same scene, only in different colours, would present itself to our eyes.

In Amiens, however, the rejoicings took on a more solemn, dignified character. After the first cheer there was complete silence; then a fine band played 'God save the Queen'. On a large dais, under a canopy of flowers, stood a select band of ladies, while a little lower and further forward stood all the clergy in their vestments, with the Bishop of Amiens in their centre, also in his ceremonial robes. He opened the door of the Queen's carriage, whereupon she and her suite got out for a moment, and the Bishop presented an address. This was a very striking and solemn scene, and seemed to me (a very profane comparison) like a drop of good wine after one has eaten a quantity of sweet things. Of course I watched closely and found it most interesting, as you can well imagine. Our French companion, on the other hand, did not think this so natural and said smilingly, '*Vous êtes encore très jeune, Mademoiselle, et je ne crois pas qu'il y a longtemps que vous êtes à la cour, des choses comme cela ne peuve* [sic] *plus m'amuser.*' I hope, however, that I shall not be sated with such things as quickly as he.

From there the journey continued in the same way until we reached Paris, where we were received by a cannonade which made the train shake. Here too, with the help of our attentive guide, we were soon in a carriage. He said we should be there ten minutes before the Queen, so as to draw breath for a moment, for we should be needed at once. We drove very fast through side-streets onto the boulevards, where everything was beautifully decorated, with soldiers and crowds of people lining the streets densely on either side. Of course no carriages were allowed there, one had to drive around by side-streets; but even here our guide had taken care that we should be lucky: thanks to a card that he showed, the crowd soon made way for us. They had already been standing there for hours without anything to look at, and when at last something came all eyes were upon it, and curious Frenchmen thrust their heads right into our carriage, one calling out '*Voilà des petites Anglaises!*' We told the Queen about it afterwards and she laughed heartily, and said she thought that calling me a '*petite Anglaise*' was the funniest thing she had ever heard. It was already twilight, but we could still admire the beauty of the decorations, and in some places torches were already lit. The road, for our journey of about one and a half hours, was filled all the way with people: sometimes there were girls in white dresses, flags, flowers etc.; in short, it was a delight to drive along through it all. It was so exciting, and it kept us going, for you will not be surprised to hear that we were tired out.

Towards nine o'clock we arrived at St Cloud,[1] and the Queen came soon after us. Sophie, cheerful and rested, came out to meet us, and she had prepared everything for the Queen's toilette. She had arrived on Thursday evening, so we only had to see to the toilette, and then our day was over.[2] I went to bed at once. I tried hard to put my many impressions into some sort of order in my mind, for I did not want to forget anything, although it would have been a relief to my overburdened head and heart to throw part of its cargo overboard to sink into the sea of oblivion. But I did not want to do this, and I stretched my powers of perception like elastic threads as far as I could so that there was room for everything, even at the risk of tearing the muscles of my brain.

At last I fell asleep, and woke next morning happy and cheerful, and not at all tired. I felt as if I were breathing the air of home when I opened my window, in front of which three gigantic fountains played merrily, while under the trees nearby the handsome zouaves[3] and soldiers of the guard lay about smoking, and occasionally blowing a horn, just as if they were playing at tin soldiers, for the sheer fun of it, not as soldiers usually behave when they carry the trappings of a rigid discipline with them. We were all so cheerful, each smiling at the other, that it almost seemed to me that a note from the magic flute

[1] South-west of Paris, one of the five Imperial residences, which had once been the palace of the Dukes of Orléans. The château was designed by Jules-Hardouin Mansart and Le Nôtre laid out the park. St Cloud was bought by Marie Antoinette in 1785. During the Revolution it became the property of the state. It was Napoleon I's favourite official residence. In 1810 the civil ceremony of his marriage to Princess Marie Louise of Austria took place here. St Cloud was gutted by fire during the Prussian occupation of Paris in 1870 and later demolished.
[2] The Queen, 'quite bewildered but enchanted'* with Paris and her reception, dressed for dinner and did not get to bed until midnight, when Sophie must have been on duty. In spite of all the organisation, and the luggage being sent on ahead, many things had still not arrived, including the evening dress of two of the Queen's ladies, who were therefore unable to appear at dinner – to their secret, exhausted relief.
[3] French light infantry, originally recruited from the Algerian Kabyle tribe of Zouaoua, who served exclusively in Algeria until 1854. They were famous for their dash and hardiness and their showy 'oriental' uniforms.

had touched our ears and put us into this unusual mood.[1] Now we began unpacking; and in the afternoon we drove to Versailles. This was the quietest day: the festivities were not to begin until Monday, so we rested.

We rode in a charming little open hunting carriage pulled by four horses that were so swift and plucky that they got us there in half an hour, although it usually takes an hour. Two of them were ridden by postilions, cracking their whips so dreadfully that it drew the attention of the crowds of people on the road to us, which amused us greatly. The people stared at us all, and drew their own conclusions as to who we might be, for the postilions were wearing Imperial livery. We were *of course English*; but in fact of the six of us only one was an Englishman. That was probably the freest, gayest day, for even if for me the best moment only came later, with *the reunion*,[2] by then we were in such a whirl with so much work to do that it was not at all a *free* enjoyment. The gardens at Versailles are wonderful, and such immense fountains! And although anywhere else the sight of trees clipped so exactly to the same size and standing in such straight avenues makes a displeasing impression in contrast with Nature in its free and uncontrolled form, yet at Versailles the gardens are so magnificent and the fountains so beautiful that the wonderful artistry of it quite reconciles one to the human hand that has dared to tame nature. Enormous quantities of water spring with gigantic force up into the sky out of the jaws of animals that are themselves true works of art. Our time was too short to see the inside of the palace, otherwise we could not have enjoyed anything properly. I indulged in my favourite pastime of watching the variety of faces that we passed, trying to judge from the expressions a little of the national character. Crowds of people were strolling about, and enjoyment of Sunday leisure could be read on every face. Every lady was on the arm of her gallant, and on every face happiness and satisfaction; on every

---

[1] The Queen had been touched by the music too, and wrote of that Sunday morning: 'While dressing, I stopped to look at the *Cent-Gardes*, very like our Lifeguards – magnificent men of six feet and upwards – riding by; and then hearing a charming sort of fanfare, I ran to another window, and saw a body of Zouaves marching up, preceded by buglers. They look so handsome, and walk so lightly.'*

[2] With her family.

forehead I seemed to see the words 'Gather ye rosebuds while ye may'.[1]

We went back to St Cloud with much gaiety and good cheer; and the next day I had to go on duty to the Palais de l'Elysée,[2] where the Queen was receiving the *corps diplomatique*. I drove there with Mr Löhlein, whom you know, the German, in a two-seated cabriolet (on the way I read a letter that I had received from home three hours before, but had not even been able to open, let alone read!). It was so amusing to drive through the streets, for wherever the Queen went, the crowd followed. We arrived there at twelve, but the Queen was not coming until two,[3] and it did not take me long to prepare everything that was needed. So I used the remainder of the time to look over this charming little palace. It has a pretty little garden, and it is splendidly furnished, with some handsome paintings and statues. And as a curiosity, the bed in which Napoleon I slept. I do not know whether it was because I had seen the bed, or because there is a good picture of Napoleon there, but this was where I could best imagine the living Napoleon. I had some very pretty rooms to wait in, which had been prepared for the Queen. As nothing was quite ready yet, and the palace was alive with the bustle of servants, I had an opportunity of making some very interesting observations about the way in which the servants work at the French Court, which is so fundamentally different from the English one.[4] A talkative old

1 Frieda's actual words are *Pflücket die Rosen so lange sie blühn*, a phrase which has proverbial status in German. It probably derives from the verse *'Pflücket die Rose/Eh' sie verblüht'*, by Johann Usteri (1763–1827), which itself echoes Robert Herrick's equally proverbial line.

2 Built 1718, subsequently much enlarged and altered. Previous occupants had included the Marquise de Pompadour, the Empress Josephine, and Napoleon I, who signed his second abdication here in 1815. His nephew used it while President of the Second Republic, before moving to the Tuileries as Napoleon III. The Queen thought it 'very pretty, but not neatly fitted up – except one or two rooms – and is small'.*

3 The Queen had spent the morning at the Exposition des Beaux-Arts (London having put on the Great Exhibition, Paris now followed suit). In the afternoon, the Queen received the *corps diplomatique* (a formal occasion, requiring formal dress; Prince Albert, for instance, putting on his uniform), afterwards she drove back to St Cloud, via a little sightseeing at the Sainte Chapelle and Notre-Dame.

4 The Queen's ladies in waiting were not at all impressed with French servants: 'those who were not actually told off for any particular duty were most disobliging and uncivil to the maids for instance, leaving them to drag the boxes if the footmen happened to be out of the way – "a great contrast" said the maids, and at dinner . . . they did not seem to know their business as ours do, for instance you constantly heard behind your chair a great scuffle of five or six over something, and an authoritative *"Imbécile!"*, which seemed to denote that all was not going on precisely as smoothly as could be wished.'*

steward, who had been with the Emperor in Strasbourg, and to whom I talked for a long time, also gave me the opportunity of many a penetrating glance into that remarkable life, so that I can only say I wish Georg could have been in my place, for such things are a good key to an understanding of history. Such personalities are like pictures in our mind's eye, but they begin to come to life if we but speak to one living person who was involved.

By five o'clock we had finished and drove back to St Cloud, after I had been brought a quantity of things to eat which would have suited a gourmet better than me, and a bottle of champagne from the Imperial breakfast, for the servant said, *'Je suppose qu'il vous faut quelque chose à manger, Madame.'*

I will say nothing of all the countless things to see to each evening, and of all the running up and downstairs, often ten times in half an hour, which in any other air than the cheerful atmosphere of St Cloud would undoubtedly have left one quite breathless, for this letter is quite long enough already; only the pleasant things shall be mentioned. For just as delicate flowers cannot bear any harsh wind, so the loveliest and noblest blossom of my life's happiness, friendship, shall not be touched by any cold frost.

On Tuesday the 21st I met Ludwig:[1] Mother will tell you about that. I went with him to the Louvre. What shall I tell you about that? Time was short, so that I could not hold fast to any single impression that I can call a pleasure. But at least I have an idea of what it means to have been in the Louvre. I could never before have grasped the idea that so many works of art existed in the whole world, let alone crowded into that one single building. The Louvre is a world in itself, of whose existence one is convinced the moment one has been there, but which one can only get to know and understand through long and frequent visits. Just as you, my dear ones, in little Karlsruhe, know that there is a great wide world outside, but one in which you would have to travel about to get to know and understand it.

The next day I stayed in all day: everyone else was away,[2] and I had

---

[1] Ludwig Arnold (1831–1908), Frieda's brother. The Queen was spending the day at Versailles, among the ghosts of the *ancien régime*, where 'all was most interesting, instructive, and melancholy'.*

[2] The Queen spent the morning at the Exposition des Beaux-Arts, lunched at the Tuileries, saw the private and state apartments there, visited the British Embassy, and drove incognito

things to do, so I took the opportunity as well of looking round the inside of the Palais de St Cloud. It is really quite delightful, particularly because of its lovely views over Paris. Then I found a brief hour or so to spend alone with Ludwig, which proved to be the only time I was able to spend quietly with him, although from now on he came every day. Days at St Cloud always seemed to go on for ever, one saw and heard so much; and yet it was all over so quickly. We rarely got to bed before two or three in the morning: at midnight there was often as much going on as at midday at home. The longer it lasted, the more dazzling the festivities became, the more work there was to do, so for instance we had to dress the Queen at the Tuileries[1] on two evenings, which meant that we had to pack up *everything*, large and small – and that is more than you think – each time, and send it there. We ourselves followed. On one of these days I had an hour on the way to go into the Exposition des Beaux-Arts. Here too I can't speak of real enjoyment, only of getting some idea, yet some of the fine paintings have remained vividly enough in my memory to have made a lasting pleasant impression. The whole exhibition is magnificent, and you must get someone who has seen it himself to tell you about it, for it is really worth the trouble! As for me, I am only a little bird – perhaps a sparrow – on a little secret perch under the wings of a golden eagle flying out into the great wide world, watching everything with its two eyes, but firmly attached by an invisible thread stretching from its heart to its little nest called Karlsruhe. And so all the impressions it receives have their echo there!

The several hours I spent in the beautiful and historic Tuileries gave me one of the most interesting experiences I had in France. The splendour and beauty of the interior is beyond imagination. For the

round the streets of Paris, arriving back at St Cloud at seven, with just time to rest a little before dressing in 'a light full white organdie dress with diamonds and blue flowers',* for a dinner party for eighty people and a performance in the theatre in St Cloud of the comedy *Un Fils de Famille* by Jean-François Bayard and Charles Desnoyer de Biéville.

1 On Thursday, 23 August for a ball at the Hôtel de Ville, and on Friday, 24 August before the Opéra-Comique. The Tuileries, the Renaissance palace of Catherine de Medici, took its name from the site of the tile-kilns on which it was built. It was a palace of grandeur and violence. Louis XVI and Marie Antoinette were kept virtual prisoners here. In 1792, 600 Swiss Guards were massacred here and the royal apartments sacked by the mob. In 1848 the insurgents attacked the Tuileries, King Louis Philippe and his family fled, and the palace was sacked again. It had, however, been Napoleon I's principal residence, so Napoleon III completely redecorated it and made it his official residence in Paris.

Queen they had prepared the rooms usually occupied by the Empress, which no one is ever allowed to visit, and it is impossible to convey how imposing and yet how luxurious they are. There were quantities of huge candelabra of heavy gold, in the form of sculptured groups, in our dressing-room, each of which one would have liked to study for hours, and that is how it was everywhere.[1] We arrived early enough to be able to look around, for on such occasions the inevitable *waiting about*, usually so tiresome, stood us for once in good stead. I saw the window from which on that night of terror the king fired.[2] I looked down onto Paris, where just now the people were flocking towards the palace again, and although they were coming for a pleasant reason now, it still helped bring alive for me that horrifying scene, which I could not help thinking of. The place had such an overpowering effect on me that I thought I could see people with white bandages among the crowd, and when we walked, later, through a veritable labyrinth of corridors, great and small, which were mostly quiet and empty, except when a window in a nearby room was open, and one could hear the shouting and cheering of the people down below, I could vividly imagine what it must be like in a royal palace at such a moment, when everyone is fleeing and hurrying away. But soon these sad thoughts were to vanish, when we came back to our rooms, where the beautiful view onto an empty square was enhanced by a peaceful sunset.

Hardly had I had time to enjoy this from a little balcony, when a military band set itself up on the lawn below me, and after little more than ten minutes our mistress came, to be greeted by the most delightful music. Endless shouts of '*Vive la Reine!*' rang out, intended to entice her onto the balcony. But she had been on view all day long,

---

[1] The Queen picked out quite different aspects of the rooms: 'The Empress's bedroom is a beautiful room, white and gold, with blue satin furniture. Next to it, the last of the suite, is her dressing room, where I dressed – a pretty small room; but opening into the other with folding doors. There was a picture of her mother, and in a frame some beautiful long flaxen curls, which the Emperor told us were his, when a little boy. He said that they had been cut off, and that his godmother the Empress Josephine saved them, put them into this frame, and there they are, quite safe.'*

[2] The Tuileries adjoined the Louvre, where in 1572 Catherine de Medici persuaded her son Charles IX to order the massacre of St Bartholemew, in which thousands of Huguenots were slaughtered. Frieda must have been looking across to the window, which Queen Victoria was shown that afternoon, from which the king was popularly supposed to have fired on the victims.

and still had to appear at the ball at the Hôtel de Ville an hour later, where of course a thousand eyes[1] and as many spy-glasses would be directed at her. She had to have a little rest, and the enthusiastic crowds meanwhile had something by way of a substitute when Sophie, Mary and I showed ourselves on a little balcony at one side for a while. Or to put it better, we went out to see how a hot-blooded people behaves on such joyful occasions. It was a most fascinating sight, enhanced by the lovely music that was being played, and although we were more exhausted than I can say by the heat, we never stopped enjoying ourselves. When the Queen and the Emperor eventually went to the ball and I threw myself into an armchair protesting that I could not move a muscle, this provoked as hearty laughter as if I had said I wanted to dance. And the proof of it is that when we had finished packing at eleven o'clock at night and had sent off our baggage, and then eaten our supper, we gladly accepted the suggestion of the gentlemen with us that we should drive over the Elysée to see the cafés chantants, which was a roundabout way to St Cloud.[2]

There is something attractive and genuinely French about these cafés chantants[3] on a fine summer night. We got out of our carriage for a quarter of an hour to look. It is rather like the nights when the museum garden is illuminated, and as if, on the slope, instead of a band there were a tent of flowers, in which a few ladies in ball gowns sit and take turns to sing. Of course the liveliness and enjoyment of the crowds give the whole scene most of its charm, as the singers themselves are said to be prettier than their voices in general. We had been offered tickets for the theatre and the opera in the evening, by

[1] This is not hyperbole but understatement; according to the Queen 'seven or nine thousand' people had been invited. During the afternoon the Queen had spent three and a half hours in the Louvre. She arrived at the Tuileries at seven, rested a little, wrote, 'was coiffée', had 'a nice quiet vertrauliches [cosy] dinner with the Emperor' and then dressed for the ball. 'I had on my diamond diadem, with the Koh-i-noor in it, a white net dress embroidered with gold and trimmed with red geraniums, and (as were all my evening dresses) very full. It was very much admired by the Emperor and by the ladies. The Emperor asked if it was English; I said, No, it had been made on purpose in Paris.'* According to the Court Circular for 24 August, the geraniums were embroidered.
[2] The dressers obviously did not expect the Queen to return to the Tuileries, but she did and there, 'took off my diadem which Lady Ely carried back, and we changed carriages, and were at St Cloud by half past twelve'* For the Queen to have mentioned one of her Ladies in Waiting being thus encumbered suggests that it was out of the ordinary.
[3] Cafés providing evening entertainment by artistes.

the kindness of the Empress,[1] but we could never accept them for lack of time. But on Saturday[2] evening, when we were again at the Tuileries, we took a small box for four at the Opéra-Comique, which the royal party was also attending. Our box was opposite them but a little higher, so that we could see them very well, which of course did not matter to me; but one of the *femmes de chambre de la reine* that night was Herr Ludwig Arnold, and for him it was interesting. Two of our gentlemen went with us. I can only say of the opera[3] that it was well sung, for in reality I was too tired to pay attention, and my chief pleasure was in being able to take Ludwig with me and to be with him. Sophie had asked the gentleman who offered us the box whether my brother might go instead of her, which of course French gallantry prompted him most kindly to allow, happy that at least one of us wanted to see their beautiful theatres, whose praises they were full of. I had only gone for Ludwig's sake, and had no need to regret it either, for it gave him much pleasure to drive there in comfort with me from the Tuileries, through the closed-off streets, for no other carriages were allowed this way, to the overcrowded theatre, where people were fighting for seats. In a box near us, in the interval, the speculative occupant was charging people a few francs for the privilege of looking down at the heroine of the day for a moment.

On the way back to St Cloud I slept soundly, and we arrived just ten minutes before the Queen, just in time for me to rub my eyes, go to her room, and undress her, for I was on duty. She had luckily stopped to take some refreshments and so arrived a little late. Sophie had nevertheless waited up in case I did not arrive in time.

---

[1] A routine courtesy; servants of royalty visiting the English court would be provided with theatre tickets.

[2] A slip of the pen. The Queen was at the Opéra-Comique (opera with a spoken dialogue and usually with a happy ending) on Friday evening. During the afternoon she had visited the tomb of Napoleon at the Invalides. In the painting of this occasion by E. M. Ward, in which she took a great interest, she is depicted wearing a silk dress of leaf green, white lace at the collar and its three flounces trimmed with black lace; over it is a pink, fringed wrap. Her bonnet – one of those less than perfect specimens – is veiled in a lacy cloud, trimmed with daisies at her ear, and fastened with a huge silk bow under her chin. In her white gloved hand is another froth of lace, her handkerchief.

[3] *Haydée* by Daniel François Esprit Auber (1782–1871). First produced 1847. The Queen wrote of the occasion: 'to the Opéra-Comique, not in state, though we were recognised. We were in the Emperor's private box, which is on the stage . . .The first act was over when we arrived. After the opera, before the curtain dropped, *God save the Queen* was sung, and I was obliged to show myself, and was loudly cheered.'*

I have not seen the Industrial Exhibition,[1] for I was a little unlucky with my free days, which were usually ruined by some special party which robbed me of my freedom. Yet I am more than satisfied with everything I saw, for I had not expected *anything* for myself, but took everything that came as a lovely, unhoped-for gift, without spoiling my own enjoyment by grieving over what I did not see.

I have told you the essentials, up to the return journey, although a lot of curious, amusing things also happened. But they are better fitted for the spoken word than my halting pen. The journey home set a worthy crown on the whole experience. Our work reached its climax with an endless flurry of packing and saying goodbye, which likewise surpassed anything that had gone before, and which for me was mixed, by no means pleasantly, with melancholy feelings at the thought of leaving the Continent, feelings which had to be suppressed.

We drove with the Frenchman (who now accompanied us, with the Emperor, to Boulogne) to the station,[2] taking a shorter way, so that we arrived first, and took our seats in the Imperial carriage as before. Around the carriage stood a crowd of gentlemen covered with decorations, only notabilities of course, who were to receive the Queen here. The station was excessively full of people. Then a small, fat, unprepossessing-looking gentleman with a large star on his chest came over to me and addressed a few questions to me in English, presumably just to show off his knowledge of the language. I answered in English, but he noticed that I was not English and began to speak French; I likewise answered in French, but here too I could not express myself with French softness, whereupon he said, 'Are you German, then?' I said yes, and then he asked whether I had been with the Queen long. I said, only a few months, at which he screwed his face up into a grin and said, like a tradesman, that I was surely especially fortunate to have been there for so little and yet to be able to come on such a remarkable journey. He then took his leave, and my companion told me that I had had the honour of speaking to Baron Rothschild.[3]

---

[1] Connected with the Exposition des Beaux-Arts in the Champs-Elysées.

[2] The Queen left Paris on Monday 27 August.

[3] Baron James Rothschild (1792–1868), the banker, who was involved in important financial dealings with the French government.

At all the stations we were given more or less the same reception as on our journey to Paris, if possible with even more noise; or perhaps my ears had been affected, for my head buzzed and rang all the time with '*Vive la Reine, vive l'Empereur!*', and sometimes '*vive le Prince Albert!*' too. I watched the different faces again, on which joy and enthusiasm expressed themselves in the most varied fashion; but I could not be as cheerful as I had been when we arrived. I had to suppress a painful ache which tormented me constantly at the thought of not seeing any of the people from home any more. I had said goodbye to Ludwig the evening before, and told him not to come back the next morning because I felt that I must save all my strength for my work. Now the thought that I had not seen him for one more moment gave me pain, and I looked around constantly, hoping to spot him in the throngs round the station, but in vain. Then I could not help thinking that he had certainly been there, only I had not seen him. As if at one blow all the merriment of the past days vanished, I could not be happy, I was completely downcast, and there is probably nothing more calculated to increase a mood of gloom than travelling for hours in a railway carriage with nothing to do. One needs a light-hearted love of travelling and eager anticipation of one's goal in order to make it bearable. At last I fell comfortably asleep from heat and fatigue, and was awakened by cannon fire; we were in Boulogne. Now all personal feelings had to be put aside, and I was forced to take part in the general good cheer. For what we were now to see was one of the finest and most admirable sights of all. The sea was a long way out, for it was ebbtide, and on this great sandy expanse, which a few hours later was covered by the waves, thousands of soldiers were drawn up, their weapons gleaming in the sun, which turned the sea and everything to gold. So amazing, so completely different was this from anything we had seen up to now, that one was quite carried away by it.

We at once drove off through another throng of people and into the nearby 'Hôtel de l'Empereur'.[1] A large, handsome hotel which the Emperor had rented for the whole of the summer. After a rest of no more than ten minutes the royal party drove out to the Review.[2] By

---

[1] According to Queen Victoria, this was the Hôtel du Pavillon.

[2] According to the Queen, 'on the sands immediately below the hotel . . . were assembled all the troops of the camp, 36,000 infantry, besides two regiments of cavalry, *Lanciers*, and *Dragons*, and the *Gendarmerie*.'*

this you can see what kind of person a king has to be: I am perfectly certain that every one of you would have gladly sat down or rested on the sofa for a moment after an unbroken journey from nine o'clock in the morning until six o'clock in the evening, in the most dreadful heat. The Queen did no more than to change the dustiest part of her costume, very quickly, and then got straight back into the carriage, quite fresh and cheerful. I have *never* yet seen her tired; she is always alert and ready. On the other hand, however, this also makes our task very difficult, because at every moment *everything* must always be there and unpacked, and hardly has one arrived when everything is already needed. But now there began a stir and a bustle such as I had never before seen. The Emperor's own servants were in the hotel, but they were not like those at St Cloud, very many of whom spoke English. Here only French was spoken. Our servants now had to bring a mass of luggage in and put it in the various rooms: no one could understand anyone else, and yet it all had to be done with the greatest speed. There was such a scurrying and hurrying about in the broad corridors that it could have been either ridiculous or terrifying. Whenever our servants could not make out what to do they always said *'femmes de chambre de la reine'* – that was their last resort, they would come running to us, and we had to tell them what to do. It came to the point where even when we had retired to our rooms to change and refresh ourselves a little, we were constantly and most inconveniently disturbed by the cry from the corridor, *'Où sont les femmes de chambre de la reine?'* It did not take us long to arrange what we needed for the toilette, which we had to see to here this time; then we drank a glass of seltzer water with champagne, and felt wonderfully strengthened and rested. From the Queen's rooms we could easily see the whole area where the great Review was being held, and the ships which were manoeuvring at sea, not far away from us. So we watched this gigantic spectacle, which was favoured by the most beautiful weather. The sun sank slowly down towards the sea, directly opposite us, and the colour of the light changed constantly, so that the clear, momentarily still surface of the sea reflected the most magical play of colours. In contrast to the calm of the sea all was life and movement on shore. It is still a mystery to me how no accidents happened, for there were people, carriages, horses and everything, all

mingling together in the greatest confusion, right up to the hotel
itself, so that the soldiers had the greatest difficulty in keeping the way
open for those going in and out. One often saw a horse's head
suddenly rising above all the human heads around. The French have
an enviable talent for moving about in dense crowds, and feeling
quite at ease the while. And at the same time they are so lively and
good-natured that they barely take any notice of any blow they might
receive, let alone try to return it. In this appalling crush I noticed not a
single person trying to make room for himself with his fists, as one
often sees at home; they always maintain a certain courtesy towards
each other, from the lowliest workman up, which is very pleasant to
see and which quite removes the frightening aspect that such throngs
always take on when the police have to clear a way through by force.
In the thickest crush I only ever heard them calling, *'place, Messieurs,
place'*. People often complain about the rudeness of our officials, but
we are no doubt partly to blame, just as the children who complain
about their teachers are usually the most unruly ones. I can only praise
the way in which those fiery Frenchmen, even in moments of the
greatest enthusiasm and exaltation, never forget to be polite and
considerate. I was most agreeably struck by this, because one could
see that it was not a case of each individual having come to get what
amusement he could, but rather of the whole population being there
together to see and hear together. They were as one, not a gathering
of individuals. Of course with all this there was cannon fire too,
rending the air. Meanwhile twilight had fallen and it was over; but we
could not go on board until eleven o'clock at night, at high tide, for
the ship was lying a long way out to sea, and because of its draught it
could not come in to shore at ebbtide.

Hardly had the Queen gone in to dinner[1] when I heard the
everlasting call for the *femmes de chambre de la reine* once again. I went
out, and a Frenchman very politely gave me a most inconvenient
order from the Emperor: I was to have all the Queen's luggage
brought down in ten minutes, as it had to be taken over to the ship in
small boats, which would take more than an hour, so that when the
fine ship came sailing proudly in this evening, all covered with lights,

[1] The Queen returned at eight, dressed for dinner, and dined at about twenty minutes past;
a tribute to the dressers' powers of organisation.

no boxes and packing cases should be visible. So I hastily packed everything up – and here I cannot resist saying that *nothing* could surpass an English royal servant: on such occasions they are so quick, so obliging and at the same time so quiet, in helping one. Hardly had the last suitcase gone, when another Frenchman appeared and invited us to come and eat. My amazement was to reach its height now: as the building was not equipped for such enormous numbers of guests, a huge hall with three large tables had been arranged for all the servants. At the first table we who were with the Queen sat with a few Frenchmen to do the honours; at the second were the servants of the lords and ladies, and at the third the English and French servants all together. Dinner had already begun half an hour ago, and when we entered glasses were just being filled with champagne, which flows like water in the Emperor's household. There was another shout of '*vive la Reine!*', which almost burst my eardrums. I can't tell you what a sight it was – it was like Wallenstein's camp,[1] but not unpleasant, as one might expect; no, everyone was full of such good cheer, and even at their most jubilant the English, like the French, are never uncontrolled in their behaviour if ladies are in the room. The footmen at the Imperial Court are the most ridiculous figures I have ever seen. They wear large white knitted gloves, just like undertakers at home, and oddly enough they are the only Frenchmen I have ever seen who are slow and lethargic. As there were not many of them there, they had to run to and fro with their roasts and their bottles, which made the most comical spectacle. I ate and drank a little, but I could hardly manage it for the convulsive twitching of my laughter muscles, which were so often and so irresistibly tickled by some funny sight or word that reached my ears, that I could not stop myself laughing out loud. But no one saw or heard anything that anyone else was doing or saying, for the drinking of toasts never stopped: 'England and France', '*Vivat*' and so forth. When I had satisfied my appetite I went quietly out and left the company to its celebrations. I had left a servant waiting outside the Queen's rooms to call me if she needed me, and I sent him down, thinking that there was still a little time for him to

[1] Frieda is apparently referring to the first of Schiller's trilogy of plays dramatising the life of Albrecht von Wallenstein (1583–1634), a general in the Thirty Years War, in which Schiller sets the scene for his hero's ultimate tragedy by depicting the motley elements that make up his camp.

celebrate our departure from France with his brother servants. I sat down in front of an open window; it was about ten o'clock. A silver moon was shining brightly over the sea, which was coming closer and closer with a gentle murmuring sound. Down below on the shore preparations were being made for the illuminations, and already blue and red lights flickered now and again. Everything was bathed in a delightful glow of light; the quiet night, the gentle moon lent everything a peaceful enchantment which was wonderful after the tumult and bustle of the day. It is after such days as this that one feels the healing stillness of night. With its soft pressure it closes tired eyelids, and its irresistible power stills the restless activity of the day. Utter silence reigned around me; in the huge hotel both high and low were all at dinner, and the corridors, so full of life a short while before, were deserted. So I had a delightful half-hour of peace. The view of the sea from Boulogne is indescribably beautiful.

Then the bustle resumed,[1] until we had embarked; and what pleased me particularly was the friendly, fraternal way in which the French servants shook the hands of ours and invited them to come back soon. The Emperor accompanied the Queen on board; we had had to drive the short distance there between flaring torches and links,[2] which was a fine sight. The Emperor remained on board and we sailed slowly away. It was wonderful: the illuminated town lay like a fiery garland around the sea, on which, stretching away into the distance, lay ships lit with different-coloured Bengali lights[3], and firing rockets up in to the sky, while on the quayside an enormous firework display was set off. It surpasses the power of human imagination, the sight of fire floating on water like this, and on such a scale. We were all on deck. The illuminations were so brilliant that one could recognise every object from far away. This went on for almost a full hour, while our ship sailed slowly and majestically away. Then all became quieter and quieter, and we stopped. A small boat came to fetch the Emperor and his few servants and take them ashore. All was done quietly and everyone stood still and the sailors doffed their caps. But as soon as the boat pushed off from our ship, a farewell cheer was raised; a whole army of rockets was let off at once, with a

---

[1] At about eleven, wrote the Queen, 'we went upstairs to put on our shawls and bonnets.'*
[2] Torches made of tow and pitch.
[3] Fireworks.

roar and a hiss; and then silence fell. *It was all over!*

It was two o'clock before I went to my cabin, where I passed a few miserable hours; although I was not really ill I felt unbearably sick. We flew like an arrow before the favourable wind, and hardly had day broken when we were told we were nearly at Osborne. And at eight o'clock we arrived. It is certainly remarkable to travel so fast.

Of course we were all tired, and the change of scene was so great that it was like waking from a dream: one felt confused and did not know how to behave now that everything was back on the old course, for it was as if one were still caught in the dream. When I got out of the carriage which brought us to the house I could not but wish that I should not drive any more for a while, for it is quite extraordinary how many carriages I have already bumped about in, in my eight months here. Now that it is quiet I often – and gladly – think back over this epoch in my life, for an epoch is what this journey will always remain for me. What is so agreeable is that not a single unpleasant occurrence spoiled it; the weather was so exceptionally fine, everything went as well as one could wish. In our department too nothing untoward had happened, and not a single member of the party came home dissatisified.

Finally, my dear friends, say '*Vive la belle France!*' with me; and I wish with all my heart that heaven will one day grant you a few happy days on French soil too! The next account you will receive will be of this place, the divine Isle of Wight. But not until we have moved to our winter quarters at Windsor shall I be able to talk to you again, for in six days I am going to Scotland. There, it will not be the sense of history which dominates, as in France, nor the idyll of this place, but fresh, vigorous Romanticism. Until then, farewell!

Always, in true love, your

Frieda

Letter 7

THE ISLE OF WIGHT
1855

There was little let-up for the dressers in the royal routine. Two days after coming home to Osborne, the Queen was busy 'Unpacking and distributing presents, and now, all the bother of selecting things and packing for Scotland'.* The Court left Osborne for Balmoral on 5 September. Now, at last, there was rest for Frieda; she did not go with the Queen, but stayed on alone at Osborne until 18 September. We are fortunate that she had this respite; her description of the visit to Paris is one of the longest of her letters because she had the time to write up her experiences while they were still fresh in her mind.

Writing was not all Frieda did while she was alone. Letter 7, although dated November, describes her activities between 5 and 18 September. This fortnight seems to have been her annual leave: Osborne was the natural place for Frieda, who was happiest there, to spend her holiday, and it was also the time of year when, with the Queen at Balmoral among the walking boots and the Stuart tartans, and without any grand functions, the pressure on the dressers was less intense. Marianne Skerrett, for instance, contemplating a journey the Queen wished the old dresser to make, felt herself most easily spared in the autumn: 'when the Queen can do without me, she does and I am not so much wanted then during the five weeks they are gone to Scotland.'*

Ready as ever with an apt quotation, Frieda furnished her letter with an epigraph, the first two verses of 'Herbstlich sonnige Tage' by the lyric poet Emanuel Geibel (1815–84), whose poems were so popular as to be almost folk-songs.

Sunny days of Autumn
Granted me for pleasure,
The heart breathes you welcome
With a gentler measure.

Hovering Time is revealed
In blessed rest and calm!
Each painful wound is healed
With its tender balm.

Windsor Castle, 22 November 1855

*W*hy do those clear autumn days lately passed at Osborne come into my mind so vividly, today of all days? Why today, when not a single ray of sunlight pierces the damp cold fog, and one could almost doubt the existence of the bright sun itself, vanished for so long? Who can answer this 'Why?' that suddenly conjures up a particular scene, often quite distant, before one's mind's eye? This autumnal scene reminds me now that I have not told you about a time that I enjoyed, and so you shall hear something about it at once, my dear friends.

I had been left behind at Osborne for fourteen days, without Sophie, without my usual occupation, and I was at leisure to live quite as I pleased, to a degree that I had never known. This was very pleasant, but certainly not in the way I had expected, or as you may have imagined it, you who have never woken up in the morning and gone to bed at night without exchanging a single word with anyone really close to you in spirit. So now I roamed about on the sea-shore for a few hours each day, watching the waves and admiring the incomparable beauty of the changing light mirrored by the sea, as the cloud shadows passed over it, and the countless little shells cast up by the sea. The time generally passed so quickly for me, I became so familiar with the smallest secrets of Nature, my feeling for it became so acute that I saw life and movement everywhere, in every blade of grass, in every grain of sand, for I was always alone, and all was quiet around me, yet not desolate or empty. I never felt lonely.

One morning at nine o'clock we found a comfortable carriage for four standing before the door to take us to see the wildest part of the island. The housekeeper[1] at Osborne, a dear, sweet old lady of whom I am very fond, and who is so kind towards her fellow creatures that one could take her for a German – she, Mary (whom you know) and I were the three ladies in the party, while one of the gentlemen in the house was invited as our cavalier. He was a middle-aged, middle-sized man, whose portrait one could paint for a book of natural history, and label it 'An Englishman', so typical are his looks. Quite apart from this, he is a man whom I like very much, and who possesses all the good qualities which could be wished for in a companion in a country outing – straightforward, knowledgeable, cheerful, courteous without standing on ceremony etc. etc.

Our goal was Blackgang, which means what its name implies, for it is a place particularly favoured by smugglers, and it is said that in the old days whole bands of them used to frequent the place. Nowadays there is an inn nearby where, since it has become fashionable (or rather, since the railway has made this fashion possible) for both the healthy and the sick to have a change of air in summer, families go to stay throughout the season. We were favoured with good weather for our drive there, which was very charming and rural. We stopped to look at an old church in an isolated spot: its ancient ivy-covered walls and its air of solitude struck a solemn note in that smiling landscape. Nearby stood a fine parsonage; not like those at home with their little kitchen gardens, neat lawns, jasmine or hazelnut bowers sheltering a love-seat for the curate and the rosy-cheeked pastor's daughter; but with a big park, which gave an impression of wealth rather than of romance. I wondered whether, in this outwardly quiet house, there might be living one of that band of German girls who have left their homes full of illusions, or with aching hearts, to become governesses in England, only to be disappointed or unhappy, unless they can summon pious resignation and strong will enough not to think their lot a pitiable one. I could not have resisted calling, and saying 'I have come to greet you in this foreign land'. It is mostly parsons' families which have German governesses. But nobody appeared and nothing moved.

[1] A large number of permanent staff lived at Osborne. Mrs Mathes the housekeeper retired in 1856.*

We drove on, through pleasant rolling country, until we suddenly found ourselves on the sea-shore, or rather on a high cliff road from which we could look down onto the sea far below, where the land dropped steeply away beside us. In a few seconds we had reached the head of the cliffs, and found ourselves at a friendly house; but only our horses and coachman were to seek shelter there. As for us, there was a servant behind us on the carriage with an enormous basket from which we were to take our refreshment in the open air. For a few moments we were struck dumb with amazement and delight, which gave way to cheerful merriment. You cannot imagine how beautiful and unspoilt the sea-shore is here. We were standing at the top of an immense cliff, which falls away very steeply; tortuous little paths cut out of the rock wind downwards, but the descent is very difficult; at the bottom, at ebbtide, there is an expanse as wide as a street where one can walk about on the most wonderful sand, which seems to consist entirely of tiny little pebbles of exactly the same size. As far as the eye can see, there is nothing but sea and sky, except to the right where three tall snow-white points jut out of the sea. These are the Needles, chalk cliffs. After we had gazed our fill, and I had made a sketch,[1] we sat down on the highest point, where meanwhile the servant had laid a table-cloth on the ground, and spread out the riches of our picnic basket upon it. The food tasted wonderful; and afterwards we climbed down to the beach, an experience which was delightful for me, terrifying for Mary and exceedingly difficult for the old lady. It was marvellous to reach the foot of the cliff: the beach was so soft and warm, unlike anything I have ever seen. We were on part of the sea-bed, for at midnight when the tide comes in this is all covered by the sea, which rises far up the cliffs. Strangers have sometimes been unable to climb up fast enough, the tide comes in so rapidly. We lay down on the beautiful warm sand (some of which I have brought away with me),[2] with a sweet breeze wafting over us. I could neither speak nor think; I was held fast by some magical force, and could do nothing but gaze out into the sea and the waves. All along the shore there were groups of families sitting on the beach,

---

[1] Frieda inscribed her sketch 'Blackgang Isle of Wight 7 September 1855'.
[2] Frieda spent the following winter painting little boxes with appropriate emblems for each of her family and friends, which she sent home filled with this sand from Blackgang.

men, women and children gazing into the waves. This sea air is said to be very strengthening; families come here to spend a few weeks, and when it is fine they climb down to the beach every day and spend the whole day there, taking food with them, and only coming back up again in the evening, at tea-time. The sea air is said to be particularly beneficial to children. When one sees the English like this, one can begin to understand their calm, seemingly cold natures, which have much to do with the climate. It has such a wonderful effect on one; one can watch the waves the whole day long and do nothing else. And indeed even the waves are beautiful here: they glide so silently and slowly up to the beach, on fine days. Often the water creeps slowly up almost to one's feet, and then in some strange way the next moment the sand (or rather the little pebbles) is quite dry and warm. Blackgang is well known for the beauty of the sea.

We left our elderly companion here, and went for a walk with the gentleman, far along the shore, looking at the wonderful way in which the massive cliffs had been hollowed out smoothly by the waves. I brought back a few smooth stones which I use as paperweights. How Georg would have loved rummaging around there to find hand-warmers for Mother! We stayed here on the sea-shore for almost two hours. When the sea is stormy they say it is terrifying here, as one can well imagine. One could be terrified by the sight of these precipitous cliffs; but that indescribable spirit that is so much one and the same in its origin and yet so different in its manifestations always pervades Nature like a silent, peaceful presence, and makes the starkest contrasts seem familiar. Many young couples from London choose this place for their honeymoon, for which I must admit I think it is almost too beautiful; these glories should be left to sober souls – after all, to lovers, everywhere is paradise. They ought indeed to go to the less beautiful places. All the same, my dear friends, I should think it very suitable if one of you came here for your honeymoon – certainly a very unselfish wish!'

We climbed up again now; and I bought from a poor woman in a hut two beautiful shells which I shall send home one day, but to which of you I do not know. Whoever is good until they arrive shall have them, dear children.

We drove on for half an hour to a most delightful little inn where we had tea, and then set off for home. The evening was fine and clear, and we were happy and contented. We talked little, absorbed by the sight of the sunset. My thoughts were at home. Every joy and every sorrow is hallowed for me by thoughts of home.

Another pretty excursion I made was to the ruins of Carisbrooke, where the unlucky King Charles[1] was a prisoner, and from which he made an unsuccessful attempt to escape. It is only a short way there, and an easy route, until one reaches a small hill, at the top of which one is rewarded by a wonderful view. This castle was one of the biggest and most famous in England. Some parts of it are still habitable, but most of it is ruined. As a whole – the site, the architecture etc. – it is very fine and impressive, a remarkable relic of the age of chivalry in England. We were shown an old chapel, deep dungeons and a well of tremendous depth, reaching down to the very bottom of the hill, as well as the window through which the poor king made his attempted escape. Then I wandered among the ancient walls for as long as time permitted, constantly discovering new delights in the landscape and interesting relics of the Middle Ages. I had a strong desire to stay longer to sketch, but I was only allowed a quarter of an hour; we had to be back in time for a meal. I am very much attracted by these remnants of a strong, manly age (the darker side – the barbarity and tyranny – are easily forgotten when one has not seen them; one is influenced only by the beauty one can see). A ruin like that, in such a pleasant, cheerful setting, always seems to me like a venerable old man in the company of light-hearted youth. He gives a note of solemnity to their merriment, just as a great castle imposes a deep and serious significance on the joyous blossoming of the surrounding landscape.

Our way home took us through the little town of Newport, which you can find on the map. Close to Carisbrooke is a little place where many foreigners go to stay each summer.

A third expedition, by water, was to the great seaport of Portsmouth, which of course I have already mentioned a few times. But I had never been into the town. Now I was to see and admire the

---

[1] Charles I escaped to Carisbrooke Castle in November 1647, hoping to find a secret sympathiser in the Governor, Colonel Hammond. The king was held prisoner here until his removal to Hurst Castle in December 1648.

mighty shipyards.[1] A man was ordered to show us over everything. When I entered the biggest of the workshops, teeming with life and movement all around me, I became quite dizzy at the thought of the endless calculations of the human brain needed to work it all out. I looked at everything very attentively and tried to understand it as best I could; and as long as I could see it, it was very clear to me. But now as I cannot see it, I am incapable of telling you anything about it beyond the fact that it is *enormous*, and extremely interesting and instructive to see.[2] What struck me favourably was that the workmen looked strong and lively, whereas in most factories it is the opposite, which is unpleasant to see. The sea air is said to have an uncommonly invigorating effect on those whom it suits. Just as fishes stay fresh in salt, so it often seems to me that the salt air has the same effect on the seaside people; they remain so pink and fresh-looking and usually have a healthy common sense, courage and strength.

The enormous bakery[3] where *all the biscuits* for the English Navy are baked interested me most particularly. Only a few people are needed to produce in an amazingly short time an immense quantity of biscuits. The world-shaking power of steam works unceasingly here too, turning the raw wheat into biscuit dough with great rapidity in a most remarkable way. Baker's boys slide it into ovens which are kept permanently hot by the same power, and from which the finished biscuits soon emerge. We looked over the whole building, which is immense, and even went into the vast stores where the salted meat for

[1] A rare privilege, which makes this a rare account. From the eighteenth century until late in the nineteenth the Admiralty were extremely sensitive about any civil visitors to HM Dockyards, and no articles, drawings, publications or photographs from civil sources were allowed.

[2] This was a period of great works in building better harbours, equipped with some of the most up-to-date-technology. At Portsmouth, in Brunel's mechanical factory, steam-powered machinery turned out 140,000 blocks for the Crimean War. The scale of everything was indeed enormous: the Rope House (1096 feet) was the longest storehouse in Europe; the Cable and Chain Test House was 600 feet long. There was plenty to impress: the large Mast Pond, the boat repair sheds, the covered slipways and the huge basins for 'rigging out', the vast steam-powered saw mills, numerous large storehouses and the large new iron foundry.

[3] In the Royal Clarence Victualling Yard at Gosport, close to the royal station. Steam-driven machinery had been in operation in the bakery since 1831. There were nine ovens capable, at an unofficial estimate, of producing 10,000 biscuits per hour or 10 tons of biscuits per day. Baking usually took place during the winter months in a vain attempt to avoid weevil infestation. In September 1855 the Royal Navy was supplying the army in the Crimea, which may account for this summer baking. Gosport was in fact one of several victualling yards producing the 113.15 million biscuits it is estimated that the Royal Navy would have required in 1855.*

the Navy is kept.[1] The scale is enormous. Then we went on board the famous warship *Victory*, on which Nelson fell. It lies anchored in Portsmouth now, and is used as a school for sea cadets. One half is for the young men who want to be naval officers, the other for those who will be ordinary seamen. The German Prince Victor of Hohenlohe[2] was there for a few years. We looked over the ship from top to bottom: it is very big, and the cannon and everything is in war order, for the boys to learn from. On the deck is the place where Nelson fell, marked with a silver plaque bearing his name. Over the main entrance to the cabins Nelson's last words[3] are engraved: 'England expects that every man will do his duty'. Down below in a small cabin where he was brought after being wounded, he died, and everything has been left untouched; and *anyone* can see it *at any time*. England's greatness evidently lies in her sense of nationhood. The young men all look so cheerful and well, that it is a joy to see them; even in the lowest cabin boy in ragged clothes one sees a certain pride; his glance seems to say 'I belong to a great nation'. What could we Germans not be, with our passionate hearts, our assiduous hands and our enlightened heads, if we had only half this national pride!

With love, Your Frieda

---

[1] The nearby cattle-pens and curing facilities could process not more than 100 animals at a time. Other victualling yards also supplied salted meat for the sailor's daily one-pound ration.

[2] Prince Victor of Hohenlohe Langenburg (1833–91), a younger son of the Queen's half-sister; pursued a successful career in the Royal Navy, and then achieved some distinction as a sculptor.

[3] Nelson's last general signal to his fleet before the Battle of Trafalgar, 21 October 1805.

Letter 8

JOURNEY TO SCOTLAND
1855

Queen Victoria and Prince Albert discovered the Highlands of Scotland in 1842. The grand, austere scenery, so complete an escape from their southern life, which seemed tame and confined in comparison, the opportunities for sport, and the rugged directness and natural manner of the Highlanders clad in their picturesque plaids and tartans, all deeply impressed the royal couple. They returned in 1844 and 1847, each time more surely ensnared. In 1848 they leased Balmoral, a sporting estate with a small castle on Deeside, which they bought in 1852. Prince Albert, just as he had at Osborne, immediately began to plan improvements and alterations. A completely new castle was built. The Queen laid the foundation stone on 28 September 1853; the next year she could see the new house was well advanced; and by 1855, while Frieda was at Osborne on her well- earned holiday, the Queen was finally sleeping under the new roof and enthusing in her Journal: 'the house is charming; the rooms delightful; the furniture, paper, everything perfection'.* The old house was being used for gentlemen of the suite, servants and offices, and the two houses were connected by a long wooden passage.

The rest of the Court being in Scotland, Frieda had to make her own way to Balmoral. Her account of the journey gives an insight into the physical realities consequent upon the sovereign, whose constitutional role was by no means passive, choosing to reign from a distance of some 500 miles from the seat of government.

Royal visitors to Balmoral, such as the young Prince Frederick William of Prussia, coming to press his suit for the Princess Royal, were advised by Queen Victoria that her 'forest retreat', was normally a two days' journey from London, involving a train journey of twelve *hours to Edinburgh and then another day's travel, half of it by rail, via Aberdeen to Banchory, whence Fritz could be fetched by post horses.* Arduous enough, but not such an endurance test as Frieda was set.*

Balmoral, September 1855

A nd now, my dear friends, you shall hear how I came here, so far, so very far away from you. It was no trifling matter, this journey. I left Osborne on the morning of September 19th, accompanied by a servant who looked after my luggage, and crossed the water to Southampton, and from thence to London, the same way you have often travelled with me. I arrived there at three o'clock and drove to the Palace, which looked empty and uninhabited.

The next morning I was fetched at eight o'clock by the Messenger[1] (the man who takes the Ministers' papers to the Queen), in whose company I travelled without stopping until the next morning at eight o'clock. He was an extremely pleasant, kind man, who took pains to make the journey as comfortable as possible for me. The Queen had sent a message that he was to bring me and take good care of me. We sat in a small compartment by ourselves, and the weather was quite splendid. It was an express train:[2] they travel incredibly fast in England, and stop only rarely, and then only for two minutes, except once at six o'clock in the evening for ten minutes. I tried to gain an impression of the different regions we were passing through, but until two in the afternoon there was nothing particularly remarkable to see – green meadows, little streams, isolated cottages, herds of sheep and cattle, all alternated with each other in the bright sunlight, and so a constant succession of cheerful country scenes passed rapidly before my eyes. But although it was much the same as what one sees at home, its general character was nevertheless different: one sees no villages like ours, only scattered farms, and wherever a few houses cluster together the industrial state is at once in evidence, for one can

---

[1] Three men were always on duty in London in case papers suddenly needed to be sent to the Queen; routine journeys were also made.
[2] On 20 September 1855 the Privy Purse paid 'Miss Arnold's fare by express train to Balmoral', £4 19s. 9d.*

be sure of seeing at least one gigantic black chimney, if the sun is not entirely blotted out by them. In the same way shipbuilding rears it head everywhere, for even the smallest stretch of water has its little ship. We passed Manchester and various other important towns. We missed Edinburgh, as we were taking the shortest possible route. As the English never forget to eat, a complete meal had been packed for us, which we consumed with much enjoyment during the journey. One could not get out anywhere. But towards two o'clock I began to find the endless shaking and rattling very tedious, and I felt very tired. My companion gathered together various cushions from the carriage and made a comfortable couch for me. I lay down and felt so comfortable that I stayed there the rest of the way. Towards three o'clock the country began to be mountainous, and very beautiful in places. What is most particularly remarkable about this journey is the enormous tunnels, some of them several miles long, and so cleverly and curiously constructed that I constantly wished the various engineers of our acquaintance could be in my place. There were always lamps burning in the railway carriages, because one is so often and so long in darkness.

A magnificent sunset enhanced the landscape which we were now flying through, and which was becoming more and more beautiful. It gradually grew dark, and my eyes and head felt heavier and heavier. We got out of the train for ten minutes and had a cup of tea, and then I tried to sleep, but with little success, for all too often a jolt or a sudden noise shook me awake. Here I cannot neglect to say a word in praise of the organisation of the English railways. All this long way, with such short stops at such frequent intervals, I *never* saw, at any station, the rushing about, the noise, the running after luggage that one sees for instance at home in Baden, not to mention in *France*! The calm and order here is admirable – there stand the policemen,[1] those *true* models of men, who never make disagreeable faces, never talk or run, but all the while stand there, and wherever they are there is always calm and order. This makes it easy to understand why one sees Englishwomen travelling alone in Germany, which always surprises us so much. Here one can leave everything, even the most valuable

[1] Frieda writes '*Polisman*'; she may have mistaken the uniform of the railway guards.

things, in one's carriage and go off where one likes. The policeman stand at every carriage door and allow only the people who got out of the carriage to get into it. My companion asked me whether he might wake me, if I should be asleep when we passed Gretna Green. I of course agreed, for after all it was a good thing to know the place, *just in case*.[1] It was fairly dark, and I looked suspiciously out and saw a little light glowing in the smithy (*The Fair Maid of Perth* by Walter Scott).[2] It stirred many a thought, both solemn and light-hearted, in my mind; until I fell asleep again. One learns to appreciate a bed that stands still when one's poor limbs are being constantly thrown back and forth.

Around midnight we were supposed to arrive at a very curious place where practically all the coal for England and Scotland is prepared: they make coke out of the raw coal. It is like a large town consisting entirely of burning towers. These are nothing more nor less than round ovens, open at the top, out of which blazing flames rise upwards. In the darkness this made a magnificent spectacle: the atmosphere was thick and black with smoke, in the midst of which countless huge flames burned. In this ocean of smoke and flames every now and then one saw quantities of people working: they were quite black. It was extraordinary. The train travelled quite slowly here, so that one could have a good look at everything. Not far away there were many houses, for it is a sizeable place, called Newcastle. London is bright in comparison. How can anyone live here? No, it is fearful how much smoke and fog there is in this country.

Now I begin to feel more and more uncomfortable, and I was dreadfully tired, but it was a fine night and not cold. Of course I sat there quietly and kept my fatigue to myself; there was no reason to add to the worries of my anxious companion, who could do nothing about it anyway. Which later, as I happened to hear, won me much

[1] Eloping lovers crossing the border from England and reaching Gretna Green, could be legally married without licence, banns, or priest; all they had to do was make a declaration of their willingness to marry before witnesses, usually a blacksmith, landlord, or toll-keeper. Local people complained that the railway had resulted in a large increase in these 'anvil' marriages but by an act of 1856 such marriages became only possible after one of the couple had been resident in Scotland for at least twenty-one days.

[2] Published in 1828, was not translated into German. Set in the fourteenth century among feuds and counterfeuds in Perth. After much bloodshed the hand of Catherine Glover, the eponymous heroine, is finally won by the sturdy armourer, Henry Smith.

credit, for the Messenger told the people in the house that he had never known a lady bear the exhaustion of the journey with so much stamina. The good man seems to have been a little nervous, and perhaps thought he would have a lot of trouble with me, for he knew what it meant to travel like that.[1]

At two o'clock we stopped, and now we were obliged to continue our journey through the mountains by post-chaise. We were in Perth. A small, light carriage with two strong horses was already waiting for us, and so we got in immediately. The carriage was only half closed, so as to be lighter and travel faster. The night was dark and growing ever colder the further we travelled into the mountains. I was so enveloped in coats and woollen blankets that I could hardly move. My companion now did the same for himself, and it was not long before I could see the necessity of it, for an icy-cold morning wind was blowing from the mountains. As dawn began to break, I was so surprised that I forced my eyes open, although they kept closing again. It was the sleep that would sometimes come over one during a lecture by Hundeshagen, in spite of all one's interest in the subject. We travelled very fast, and changed horses every hour: they were always waiting for us at little posthouses, which appeared every eight to twelve miles along the road, so that we barely stopped at all. One saw nothing but high, high, bare mountains and a little sky, which gradually became more visible, through a light mist. The valley was very narrow and closed all the way; whenever we turned a corner, there it was again, enclosed by more mountains. Massive, rocky mountainsides rose all around us, one behind the other, in all directions. An indescribable, eerie silence reigned everywhere; not a living soul, not a single house, nothing at all, for as much as twenty or thirty miles, except for the little posthouses. On the mountains, which were mostly covered with heather, there were sometimes whole flocks of partridges,[2] running about quite tamely. On all these bare mountains one can see the rock formation very well: there is nothing but rock, partly overgrown with moss, partly with heather.

[1] Speed was of the essence on affairs of state. The badge of office of the Queen's Messengers was a silver greyhound.

[2] Anyone following Frieda's route is more likely to see grouse. The word Frieda uses is '*Feldhühner*', normally translated as partridge, but again, Frieda may have mistaken the uniform.

The colouring of these mountains is wonderful. Brown and mauve in the most diverse shades are mostly the ground colours, but there are often streaks of yellow and green. The dawning day coloured the landscape violet; the sky was fiery red in places; it was going to be another beautiful day.

For thirty miles there was not a single tree to be seen; we were still driving along a narrow valley, and if we seemed to come to the end of one, it was only to enter another. Everything was deathly still and empty. I had never had such an impression of wilderness, and yet of such wonderful beauty. It was very cold. The road was so narrow that two carriages could not pass each other, and often we were scarcely a hand's breadth from a precipice. When I asked what happened when two carriages met the postilion laughed, and said it was rare enough for one carriage to come here, and as for two, that never happened. The road through Edinburgh is rather more used, although even that is not much, for travelling in these Highlands is too expensive to be very common.[1] My limbs felt as if they were broken; I was so utterly exhausted that I was sure I would not be able to stand up any more; and then we came to a steep mountain called the Devil's Elbow,[2] where we had to drive very slowly. It was six o'clock in the morning, and a most refreshing morning breeze was blowing from the mountains. I climbed out and walked, on the arm of my companion, slowly up the hill, which made me feel quite cheerful and brave, for it was at least a change. There was a little clear brook running down the hill, prattling merrily along beside us. Just imagine, my dear friends, being so alone in the world, looking down over innumerable mountains and rocks, with not a soul to be seen far and wide, not a living thing. And this shortly after returning from a journey where one was almost besieged by crowds of people! Now I know what the word isolation means. Being alone in one's room, and that kind of solitude which we often find so painful, seemed to me now like an illness of the mind with the same name as that exhilarating,

---

[1] The going rate was £4 4s. per pair of horses, including post boys and expenses.* Compare this with the cost of Frieda's ticket from London to Perth. This route across the mountains, less than a third of the distance of the alternative route via Aberdeen and Banchory, took Frieda and her companion through Blairgowrie and the Spittal of Glenshee, over the Pass of Glenshee and through Braemar.

[2] Strictly speaking, more of a pass than a mountain, at the head of Glenshee.

magnificent stillness of the mountains, in the freedom of Nature untouched by the hand of man. This feeling of isolation strengthens and uplifts, one feels at one with Nature, one is overwhelmed by the feeling of an immeasurable whole, there is no sense of separation or of being separated here. Oh! if only I could use the magic coat of our German fairy-tales to transport you all, whom I love so dearly, into this wilderness! If only I could tell you how holy, how venerable almost, Nature seems where man has scarcely trod. One feels as if the hand of God had just created it. On all these mountains there are no paths, the people hardly ever walk on them; one must find one's own path. It is very dangerous climbing these lonely mountains, for when one reaches the top the air is so thin it makes the weary traveller sleepy, and if he sits down and falls asleep he never wakes again, but freezes to death even in the middle of the summer, for it is very, very cold in the night. And not a soul may come that way for weeks, and often months. Many travellers have already met their deaths in this way. The brother of a girl in the house here died like that while out walking.

We walked for about half an hour. The sky changed colour constantly, until finally a delicate red covered almost the whole sky, so that the mountains looked quite black against it except here and there where they were lit up by a reddish glow. It was the most beautiful dawning of an autumn day that one could imagine. Like a sweet child woken from sleep, who at first opens his eyes wide and looks around him in surprise, until he recognises his surroundings, and a happy, rosy-cheeked smile spreads over his face. Thus the new day awoke, at first casting a sudden vivid glow over the landscape, which then turned rapidly into a soft, pleasant shimmer. Ah! and that sublime stillness, that endless peace. I am not sure, my darlings, that I would not have expired completely with delight if I had not been so tired, and I was overcome with a most unpleasant fit of shivering caused by a sleepless night and an empty stomach.

We climbed back into the carriage and now sped along again. Soon a few trees came into sight, slender birches and firs, but they were very thin and not very tall, until we suddenly turned a corner, and our road ran along the banks of a cheerful mountain stream. It was the Dee, which from now on increased in size, and accompanied us all the way to Balmoral, past which it flows. This pretty river is so clear, so lovely; its bed is strewn with large stones, sometimes even massive rocks, over which it leaps undaunted onwards, forming many a delightful little waterfall. Now the country began to look more inhabited: one sometimes saw a flock of sheep on the mountains – here all the animals stay out on the mountains at night. And now some of the mountains had trees growing on them: there were pines, very thin, pointed fir trees, and birches. Here and there a few farmhouses stood by the river, and soon larger, landowner's houses came into view, each a few miles from its neighbours. Here was life and activity again, for although we saw no one, traces of human occupations were visible on all sides, and this transformed that solemn feeling that the wilderness gave me into one of comfort and good cheer. In spite of my profound absorption with the beauty of the scene, the thought of the cup of coffee which would soon be warming me was not unwelcome, prosaic though it was, and I do not know whether it was this expectation about to be fulfilled, or something else, but my strength returned and I felt much less tired.

At last we saw Balmoral! Inwardly I jumped for joy; and soon I was climbing out of the carriage. Two servants who were standing at the gate received me with expressions of condolence, they felt so sorry for me after the exhausting journey. But I was perfectly cheerful and happy, and asked them to show me my room, assuring them that I really was not so very tired. And in fact it was astonishing to find, after I had changed and drunk some coffee, that I was fresh and hardly tired at all.

Balmoral Castle

The charming, gentle mountain river Dee flows through a narrow valley, and on its banks lies Balmoral, lonely and quiet. As a hunting-seat, it is very simply built in the style that is now customary in Scotland, which is not distinguished by anything in particular except that the windows are not in a row or symmetrical but higher or lower than each other, quite irregular, which naturally means that the rooms inside often lie on different levels and one often has to go up or down a few steps into the different rooms. The house is built of the stone of which most of the rocky mountainsides consist, a pretty grey stone[1] of which I shall send you a piece one day. The window-frames and doors are of unpainted wood, with very pretty carved decoration – the corridors are adorned with countless large antlers from the stags killed by the Royal Family. Stuffed birds and rare kinds of stones found in this region are the ornaments in the corridors here, and of their kind they can well stand comparison with the works of art that draw the eye in the corridors of Osborne and Windsor. Instead of the magnificent oil paintings there, here the walls are decorated with fine engravings in simple wooden frames. In the Royal Family's own sitting-rooms are portraits of the Royal Family, and in the salons hunting and animal pictures of all kinds. The furniture is of plain wood, tastefully made, and instead of the golden door-handles and bell-pulls, here they are of a kind of pewter with the letters V and A cast in them like this ⅄ , which has a pleasing effect. The upholstery of the furniture and likewise the curtains in the sitting-rooms are of glazed chintz, with a light-grey background and the Scottish thistle in purple and green printed on it, which looks very good. In the salons this is poplin, with the Royal or Balmoral check, table-covers and carpets all of the same design. So everywhere one looks there is the most beautiful harmony, which gives one a very pleasant feeling; the wall-lights are silver antlers, guns or game-bags, and if one's pen needs dipping, one must look for ink in the back of a hound or a boar – who could describe all these little things, which if they are well chosen enhance a castle so well? The irregularity of the windows has the advantage that most of them look out at precisely the best viewpoints, so that as well as the daylight a bright, clear glow shines in, a reflection of the quiet peace of the mountains. The contrast between the extravagant splendour of Windsor and the wealth of art treasures in Osborne and this lovely country hunting-seat is like a modern, elegant town house at home in comparison with a simple, country pastor's house with its white walls and homely, cosy rooms. It gave me such a feeling of happiness to climb a wooden staircase without a carpet again! What surrounded me here was more like what I had left behind and love.[2] Balmoral is arranged in the simplest and

[1] Granite from Glen Gelder.
[2] Frieda is responding to the architectural idiom of her homeland. There are strong

noblest taste, which does its builders the greatest credit; here again one can see so plainly and so well that the only harmony is *true* beauty. Nor is there anything there which offends the eye or the feelings, which means more than one might fleetingly think. If one should – after an expedition into the wild, still mountains, where one feels so small and yet so big, where the greatness of Nature overcomes one, so that all works of human hand and mind seem mere trumpery –if one should then walk into a magnificent palace, where everything spoke of the might and power and wealth of individual dynasties, how easy it would be for the question to arise in one's mind: what is the meaning of all the vain display, of all this splendour reserved for the few? Whereas in Paris or London the proud splendour of a Court seems like the pillars of a great Nation, 'in Scotland's moors and mountains' all this looks like a mere puppet show. But if one steps out of the freshness of Nature into this simple, tasteful hunting-lodge one is enveloped in a feeling of pleasant well-being; one is still among the mountains and yet one has a comfortable place to rest from one's exertions. One can go into Balmoral from a Highlander's hut without feeling the painfully marked contrast which of course certainly exists between poverty's hut and a royal castle. The whole shows an extremely fine, delicate and therefore simply *good* taste. Without disfiguring Nature, gardens have been laid out in the immediate surroundings of the Castle, and a little farther off good roads, so that even in bad weather one can go out walking or driving.

Georg asks whether I have seen the Highlanders in their national costume? Yes, indeed, I have even seen them dancing, or rather hopping and jumping, their national dances. Every year the Queen gives the Highlanders a ball; near the Castle is a building[1] specially erected for it, consisting of a single enormous hall – wooden floor and wooden walls, round them wooden benches, in the middle of which are some which are slightly raised and covered with carpets, for the Royal Family. The walls are decorated with flowers and heather, the

resemblances in style and atmosphere between Balmoral and the Rosenau, the country retreat of the Dukes of Coburg, where Prince Albert was born and spent the happiest days of his childhood.

[1] The Iron Ballroom, looking like a cottage orné, in fact a prefabricated shed of corrugated iron, with two doors, eight windows and a ventilator resembling an ornamental chimney. Designed by Edward T. Bellhouse and Co. of the Eagle Foundry in Manchester, seen by Prince Albert at the Great Exhibition, and put up at Balmoral in 1851.* In 1856 the ballroom in the new castle came into use.

lighting is suitably arranged – the temperature at the beginning is icy cold, but then rises in an unbelievably short time to a heat that, mixed with clouds of dust, transports us into a tropical summer. A striking proof of the warmth of a people. The Queen, with all the children and the Prince, and the Duchess of Kent, accompanied by her retinue, appears, and they take their places, likewise the whole Household. The Scots from the whole district are invited and often come from many miles away. The bagpipes begin to play, and now begins such a hopping and running about that one bursts out laughing when one sees it for the first time. The couples move with tremendous agility, always in a small space, like quadrilles. In the middle the Princes and Princesses dance, in Scottish costume, even the smallest of them, who look very sweet. The Queen wears a Scottish sash over her shoulder. The Prince is in Scottish costume; they both watched. A few handsome young Scots danced the sword dance alone; it was wonderful and very graceful: swords were laid in a cross on the ground and they danced between them. The Royal Family stayed until eleven o'clock,[1] and the rest of the company until four. Then, thoroughly warmed up, they went off home over the mountains in the cold morning air.

Now I have been here for fourteen days, and have grown truly fond of these lovely mountains. We have had the most beautiful weather almost all the time, although it has been bitterly cold in the morning and evening. I have been on several longish expeditions by carriage, to get to know the area, and I have climbed many mountains on foot. Let me tell you something about it. First, there is a light Scottish carriage, in which one can travel fast through the mountains. Four people sit very high up on this, two facing backwards and two forwards, back to back with each other. One of the front ones drives, and this is usually Herr Löhlein,[2] our ever cheerful compatriot. Next to him sits Sophie or I, whoever is free, and at the back anyone else

---

[1] The Queen described the evening in her Journal for 28 September 1855: 'I and the girls were all in dress Stuart satin dresses, with Royal Stuart scarves . . . after dinner we went to the Iron Ballroom where there was a Gillies Dance. All our children there. Three officers with the detachment of the 93rd 79th Highlanders stationed at Ballater, and 18 of the men who had been in the Crimea, came. It was very gay and our children each danced two or three times, and we were quite astounded at Louise [aged seven] dancing her reels so very well. Fritz was much pleased with Vicky's dancing and appearance. She was most anxious, the moment she got into the ballroom, to sit near Fritz, which I managed for her. We remained till ½ p. 12.'

[2] *See*. p. 33.

from the house whom we ask. It is a small shooting carriage, which we are allowed to use whenever it is not needed. Sometimes we have it for a long time, sometimes very little, it depends. There is no more amusing way of riding about in beautiful country than in a little carriage like this; for one can see everything and enjoy the fresh air from all sides, which is sometimes a cold wind, but it is very refreshing and healthy, if like us one always has a waterproof and a woollen rug over one's knees. So this is how I went one day down a very narrow valley to a waterfall, which was wonderfully pretty. The waterfalls here are not very high – I have seen several of them already – but they rush down in such wild torrents over the rocks that it is a joy to see them. At one of them we set up camp, and had a cold luncheon, which we enjoyed immensely. The ground was covered with quantities of boulders, large and small, between which rose slender birches and firs. From every seam, indeed every tiny crack in the rock, soft moss or pretty little heather flowers stretch out their little heads. Here too one is always alone, not a soul to be seen, although one often sees stags and does running about, quite unafraid, as they are very rarely hunted in this area. That was a lovely warm day, and the light was glorious.

Another trip, to a narrow mountain pass by Ballater,[1] showed me the mountains in their grey rain-colours, which was no less beautiful. It was a dull afternoon, such that one could be sure it would be raining by evening; but here the rain does not do one any harm. Everyone here goes out walking or driving even when it rains, for it is usually a fine drizzle, and sometimes it stops suddenly, and then one has the most beautiful views. Even the Queen has not a single closed carriage here; in all weathers she goes out in a light open caleche. We drove a few miles along the edge of the river, which was full and flowing very rapidly. Many of the roads had high mountains on either side, which sometimes lay in such deep shadow that they looked quite black and gloomy, and sometimes were bathed in brilliant sunshine. A little way off we saw a colossal rock, split down the middle. Nature formed this pass, and man has made a perfectly passable road through

---

[1] The Pass of Ballater.

it. We drove through: the rock is so thick that it takes a quarter of an hour to traverse. The rock is split apart in the most indescribably strange way, into a multitude of jagged points. The inside of the stone is of the most delicate pink and grey colour, and pieces of rock still fall down, so that in winter and spring when there is snow on the mountains its weight pushes stones down and the road is very dangerous. In many places there are openings in the rock, out of which pour small rivulets of clear water, which seem to announce that there is life within the rock, and only its outside is so stiff and hard. Since I saw these mountains I understand many of the things Walchner[1] said; now I can easily imagine the interior of the earth is fiery and liquid, which always seemed incredible to me when Walchner explained it. But once one has seen a terrain as wild as this, and had this vivid sense of life in its depths, one understands completely what he meant. In the same way one can easily imagine the gigantic upheavals on the earth's surface that Walchner also frequently spoke of: for when one sees these stones lying there in such confusion, it looks exactly as if some immeasurable force had once shaken these mountains, leaving them lying as they are now. My dear, beloved friends, I beg you never to let yourselves be led astray by that narrow-minded attitude which is so prevalent even among the best people, and which considers anything apparently recondite to be unworthy of attention. I have heard it said recently that one cannot understand Walchner or Eisenlohr[2] without a thorough knowledge of the subject, and that it is useless to listen to their lectures otherwise. Certainly there is some truth in this, and often when I had listened to Walchner for an hour my desire to hear something about science was satisfied, but I understood little, and after a while I seldom thought about it any more. But now, when I see something that I have heard about before, all the words I seemed to have forgotten come rushing back into my head and I begin to understand what I had heard before. If one only has a lively interest in something, one absorbs everything, even what seems to be most unnecessary. Nothing is lost, nothing is

[1] Frieda is probably referring to Friedrich Augustus Walchner (1799–1865), the German scientist and writer, a prominent exponent of the theory of vulcanism.

[2] Wilhelm Eisenlohr (1799–1872), Professor of Physics in the Polytechnic Institute at Karlsruhe 1840–65. His chief work was 'Lehrbuch der Physik'. In 1863 he was a witness at the christening of Frieda's daughter.

unnecessary except giving in to mental sloth. Who could ever have imagined that I should learn to understand these 'quieter forces of nature', as Walchner expressed it, in the Scottish Highlands?

Back, then, to that overcast day. We drove through the pass and back through a little Scottish town, Ballater, which is charmingly situated on the edge of the mountains. What they call a town here is a few houses, a church, a posting inn, a general store, a tailor, a cobbler and above all a butcher; for where we live there is never any meat to be had when the Queen is not there. Think how difficult it must be to run such a large household with all its needs, great and small, in such a remote place as this.[1] The road we drove along was beautiful, I cannot describe it to you. Rocks, mountains, copses succeeded each other in constantly changing light, for the sky and mountains looked grey, but the sun was trying to break through, and so sky and land were lit with shafts of glowing colour, now here, now there, until finally a grey veil covered everything thickly, giving the landscape such a ghostly aspect that little mountain dwarfs might have come slipping out of the rock crevices without surprising me in the least. It became dark and gloomy and began to rain hard; but we drove on for over an hour in the open carriage, which was not uncomfortable at all, for we were quite covered with waterproofs, even over our heads. It was beautiful to see how the sky and mountains gradually became one, until night covered all. Arriving home, one threw off one's coat, drank a cup of tea, told one's dear friend Sophie all about the expedition, and dressed one's mistress, just as skilfully as if one had been out for a drive in the sun.

We went on another, similar expedition, to a waterfall[2] beside which all other waterfalls pale into insignificance. I thought I had seen the most beautiful things here, but I have never seen anything like this! It had been raining hard for a day and a night, after which, the day which brought me to the waterfall in the little hunting carriage dawned fine and clear. I shall say nothing of the journey there and back: it was through the lovely mountains. Once there, a

[1] In 1855 Marr and Milne supplied Balmoral with 6468 lb of beef, 650 lb of veal and 68 lb of lamb; Robertson supplied 6039 lb of beef. The total 'animal food' consumed was 13,225 lb and the total number of 'diets', or separate meals, for the six weeks of September and October 1855 came to 5937.*

[2] Falls of Garrawalt, in the Ballochbuie Forest.

spectacle awaited us that surpassed everything. From a height about a third as high as the Turmberg,[1] the water rushes down in steps of differing sizes, forming at each level a pool of unfathomable depth. One waterfall crashes down onto the next with huge force and a mighty roar, sometimes steeply, sometimes more gradually, over colossal rocks. The water was particularly high because of the rain before – can you imagine it? (but no, you cannot). It poured down from a mighty cliff, out of which fresh young firs and birches sprouted upwards here and there. At the very top a dizzying bridge crosses the waterfall, so high that with the waterfall rushing downwards beneath one one has a magnificent view over the mountains all around. It is a picture that remains in one's mind as something so sublime and so indescribable that one cannot compare it to anything. A fine autumn evening rendered our journey home inexpressibly delightful; the sky was a fiery red, behind the mountains. We began to sing for pure joy, each in his own language – there were Germans, a Frenchman and an Englishwoman – imagine how lovely, how harmonious we sounded!

Another expedition, by a lake high up and deep, deep into the mountains, I must also describe to you. Altnaguithasaich is a little hunting-lodge near the lake, which belongs to the Queen – it is very small, like a cabin. The lake is called Loch Muick, that is, black lake.[2] It was a clear, fairly warm autumn day when we set off, before luncheon, a little after eleven. We had to take furs and coats, in spite of the mild weather, so cold were we told it would be. We drove for two hours, deeper and deeper into the wilderness, always climbing higher into the mountains. All was utter silence and solitude; we were among a range of the most beautiful mountains, covered with pretty heather, and above them a sky that was so clear and fine that it was a joy to see. The air became increasingly thin and cold, but we were so well wrapped up that only our noses peeped out, and we felt quite snug and happy. The roads are of course very bad and uneven, and the little carriage often flew up so high over stones that one had to hold on tight all the time so as not to bounce out like a ball. All of a sudden a broad black expanse became visible between the mountains: it was

---

1 A hill near Karlsruhe.
2 Loch Muick means lake of the pigs; Dubh Loch, or Black Lake, lies further to the west.

the lake! A few fir trees came into view next, and the little house was hidden behind these. We went inside and warmed ourselves, that is to say, from within, with a true Scottish drink called Whisky: it is the strongest spirits that can be distilled, and one has to drink it in the thin air, in order not to fall ill. How could I drink it, when a mere drop of such a thing makes me dizzy; but I drank a little glass of it, and it rolled down my throat like fire, but warmed me so agreeably from within that I shall never again think ill of the poor washerwomen who drink schnapps on a winter night! We walked by the lake, and it was then that we really felt the benefit of our inner warmth, for it was as cold as I suppose Russia must be. I was quite overwhelmed by the beauty of the lake. It takes over an hour to walk the length of it, and it is unfathomably deep. The water is quite black, coal black. It has no shore, for on both sides the cliffs drop steeply down into it. At the far end it is closed, and it is open only at the near end, which is very narrow. Along one side a narrow path has been cut recently, with great difficulty, into the rock, so that on one side one looks straight down into the water, and on the other up onto the mountain. At the far end is a little cabin where a keeper[1] lives with his wife and an angelic little girl: this was our goal. The keeper stays at Balmoral as long as the Queen is there, in order to go out hunting with the Prince. So this woman, with her child, is alone for six weeks, and sees not a soul – she might be at the end of the world. She and her child could die and no one would know anything about it. Her husband had been away for four weeks, and we were the first people she had seen since. She never has any news of her husband. She is cheerful and contented in her little room with the child, cooks an oatmeal broth every day, sits by the hearth and weaves nets. We sat by her fire to eat our midday meal, for which our male companions never forget to obtain copious provisions from the royal kitchen. We gave the woman a roast chicken and all kinds of other things, with which she was highly delighted. I made two little sketches of the lake which I particularly treasure because it was so extraordinarily beautiful beside this black lake. One was literally out of this world. The little four-year-old girl, shy at first, ended by smiling so candidly with her blue eyes that it

---

[1] Charles Duncan.

made quite a curious impression on me: what kind of thoughts, impressions, feelings will a girl brought up like this have one day? What we experience, hear and see with and among other people is the stuff of our thoughts and feelings, or at least forms them. Impressions of joy or pain, after all, come mostly from other people, or through them. This child sees only the lake, the sky and the mountains; she hears only her mother, she does not know that there is a world full of hopes and disappointments. In the winter they are often completely snowed in fooughts, impressions, feelings will a girl brought up like this have one day? What we experience, hear and see with and among os in a little room without light, without anything that we have learnt to know and want! The dear little girl made me think of a flower, growing up without wishes and without pain.

We walked back along the narrow, picturesque path, in the loveliest evening light, which flooded the mountains with glorious colours; but the lake remained dark and still like a black mirror. Yet there is said to be such life in its depths that one is in mortal danger if one tries to cross it, for the water is often violently disturbed from the depths. Have you read *The Lady of the Lake*?[1] It might have happened there! What shall I say of our journey home? It is truly beyond my powers to describe such beauties of Nature as vividly as I should wish. The sun had gone down, the dusk spread its veil slowly over the earth. I sat high up on our little carriage, and as we drove along over the mountains one felt so close to the sky that one almost expected to feel the damp, cool veil of night falling over one. Then the beloved evening star appeared, and soon a host of little stars. We drove silently on, and arrived home without mishap. I had brought back the most beautiful, vivid impressions, two little sketches, and a face beaming with pleasure, all of which I at once inflicted on the good Sophie, who had been there the week before and had also come back delighted and enthusiastic.

I had also been on many walks, long and short, mostly alone.

[1] Sir Walter Scott's most popular narrative poem, published in 1810 and translated into German in 1819. Set among the warring clans under King James V (1513–42). The action opens when a hunter (who turns out to be the king himself) benighted among the wild and lonely scenery of Loch Katrine, meets fair Ellen Douglas anxiously awaiting the return of her outlawed father to his island stronghold. It was an accepted fancy at Balmoral that Loch Muick was a suitable setting for the poem; after an early expedition on the lake the Queen quoted a passage from it in her Journal (16 September 1850).

Heavy boots and a blue cape (like the Englishwomen in Baden), with one's skirt hitched up high, and a mighty stick in one's hand – that is how one goes out walking here. Several times I climbed a hill just beside the Castle, quite alone, and looked out over the endless mountains, which filled me with a feeling I had never had before. It was not the excitement or admiration one feels at the splendours of Paris or in the Crystal Palace; it was not that blissful light-heartedness that fills one at the contemplation of an idyllic landscape like the Lichtenthal,[1] nor even the spell cast over one by the sea at Osborne. No, these hills seem rather to speak of a majestic calm, of an unconstrained freedom, one feels so strong, so elevated, so free. The further beneath us the hurly-burly of humanity lies, the more insignificant its cares seem to us. 'On the mountains is freedom'[2] etc. etc. I shall have to finish my tale, my dears, for true joys can have no end of themselves! One could go on describing the beauties of Nature in such a place for ever, for wherever we turn our eyes, both physical and spiritual, Nature shows us something new and different.

Just a little more about our journey back from Scotland. The Royal Family and the entire Household left in one morning. We travelled by Edinburgh. A multitude of luggage of all sizes stood at every door by eight o'clock; all were ready for the journey, climbed into the carriages and were off, on a fine clear autumn morning. We changed horses often,[3] and drove to Aberdeen,[4] where we arrived at eleven o'clock. From there we sped off to Edinburgh in a special train. In the mountains many of the people had gathered from far afield to see their Queen leaving, after her presence had enlivened the quiet valleys for a few weeks. We travelled at tremendous speed; it was incredible. At two o'clock we stopped for twenty minutes at a place where a meal

---

[1] A village in a valley south-east of Baden Baden which Frieda must have known well. Baden Baden was only a day's journey from Karlsruhe.

[2] Schiller.

[3] The Queen's migrations to and from Balmoral put a great strain on local resources. In September, to bring Queen and Court from Aboyne over the three stages to Balmoral the number of horses ordered for each stage had been forty-six: '10 fours and 3 pairs'; a total requirement of 138. All forty-six had to be ready and waiting at each stage, as Her Majesty's carriages could not be kept waiting for 'return horses'. The Post Master James Ross complained that it was 'impossible to get the requisite number without taking a third of the horses from 40 to 50 miles from the different stages' which meant paying them three days' hire. He went on to point out that 'Railways lately made in Aberdeenshire have rendered Post horses very scarce – it is with difficulty that so many trustworthy horses can be got'.*

[4] Frieda is mistaken; the royal train was waiting at Banchory.

had been prepared for us; then we continued to Edinburgh. Unfortunately it was nearly eight o'clock and dark when we arrived at this curious old city.[1]

I have heard much-travelled people say that Edinburgh is the most beautiful city one could wish to see. I tried to see what I could by the light of the street-lamps, which was quite good. I have never seen such old, strangely built streets! We drove to the famous old palace of the Scottish kings, Holyrood.[2] It has a melancholy and sinister air, but it is very impressive. When we had finished our duties I asked to be shown round the Palace, which is immense. There are panelled walls everywhere, and sumptuous apartments, but it does not strike one as a place to live in.[3] The many little staircases and hiding-places seem to tell one uncanny stories from a time when tyranny and despotism reigned. Everything is so solemn and quiet; it fascinates one, but one would not want to stay there long. Nevertheless we were not at all pleased to leave again so soon, at eight o'clock next morning. We would have liked to see the sights of Edinburgh. Last of all I was taken to the oldest part of the castle, where Maria Stuart's rooms remain unchanged, just as they were when she lived there. They are shown to visitors, but no one is ever allowed there at night; only we were shown them because of the Queen. They are extremely old, and very remarkable. We went into the small room in which the unlucky Queen dined with Rizzio at night, and we climbed down the little narrow winding staircase which the murderer Darnley came up. We saw the place where he was murdered and where they laid his body.[4] It was very eerie, and since seeing it I am filled with horror and

[1] The Queen left Balmoral on 16 October 1855; her account of the day in her Journal reads: 'We breakfasted before 8, then walked out and about the house. I felt very sad as we drove away in the sociable, with the 2 girls, – the others, having all gone on in the heavy carriages . . . Got into the travelling carriage at Ballater and at 1 o'clock got to Banchory, stopping at Stonehaven for a little luncheon . . . At ½ p. 6 we reached Holyrood, which looked rather gloomy.'

[2] The Abbey of Holyrood, out of which the palace grew, was founded in 1128. Building of a royal residence began in 1501, and parts of the building completed by James V between 1529 and 1532 still remain incorporated in the fabric of the palace which was begun but never finished under Charles II.

[3] Holyrood was never more than a staging post for Queen Victoria on her way to and from Balmoral. She first stayed in 1850, and every year until 1861 broke her journey here. In 1862, after the death of Prince Albert, she made the journey overnight in the train for the first time and did not return to Holyrood until August 1872. She stayed here again in 1876, 1881 and 1886.

[4] On Saturday, 9 March 1566 Mary Queen of Scots' Italian secretary and favourite, David

aversion for the luckless Mary, although Schiller[1] had made me like her, and I was inclined to take her side against proud Elizabeth. Although I shall never forgive the latter for her action, and although I shall never condemn poor Mary, in England one learns to value Elizabeth highly, while in Holyrood Palace one learns to fear and pity Mary. The deed was done in her bedroom – is it not frightful! It is only when one sees the place that one really feels the horror of it. What must her dreams have been in this room?! which she continued to live in afterwards. The next morning I had another glimpse of the city as we drove through it. It is so strange and attractive that it was sad not to be able to stay. The second day passed like the first, without interruption – but now we were tired of travelling. We stopped again once, to eat, and there was always music and noise at the stations.[2] There were three of us in our travelling carriage, fastened on to the train. I read, slept, ate and drank alternately throughout the day, and reflected on my last days in Scotland, compared them with my past, and thought about the veiled future! It would have been quite tolerable if we had not been so tired. At nine we arrived at Windsor, all yawning, and we slept well!

Rizzio, was dragged from her presence in a supper room to the Outer Chamber of her apartments and brutally murdered by Lord Darnley, the Queen's second husband, and other conspirators. Rizzio was the victim of a jealous husband and a struggle for power.

[1] Schiller's five-act tragedy *Maria Stuart* was first performed in 1800. Schiller sacrificed historical accuracy to psychological drama. In the words of Thomas Carlyle, 'We are forced to pardon and love the heroine, she is beautiful, and miserable, and lofty-minded; and her crimes, however dark, have been expiated by long years of weeping and woe . . . Elizabeth is selfish, heartless, envious; she violates no law, but she has no virtue and she lives triumphant: her arid, artificial character serves by contrast to heighten our sympathy with her warm-hearted, forlorn and ill-fated rival.'*

[2] 'many people out', noted the Queen in her Journal for 17 October 1855. The royal train was reported to consist of: engine and tender, break, first-class carriage for servants, first-class carriage for pages and other attendants, family carriages for ladies of the suite, blue saloon for the princesses, royal saloon, blue saloon for the princes, family carriage for gentlemen of the suite, first-class carriage for the directors of the railway and the press, and two carriage trucks.*

Letter 9

'A CHANGING PICTURE', LONDON AND WINDSOR

1856

The Queen's annual programme varied very little. After Balmoral, she spent the winter at Windsor, and about the middle of February, would move to Buckingham Palace. By the time Frieda was writing this letter, in February 1856, she had been with the Queen for a over a year and there was little that was new to her in the annual royal round. In her letters, more systematically composed than their fresh delivery at first suggests, Frieda was careful not to repeat herself, and here she widens her net to draw in accounts of what she sees outside the Palace walls and to compare aspects of English and German life.

Buckingham Palace, February 1856

*L*ondon at this time presents a changing picture, varying from cheerful, warm spring weather to the dirtiest, coldest, dampest winter weather, which only someone who has lived in England and experienced this humid atmosphere can grasp. Today, for instance, it is mild and pleasant, the parks are fresh and green and full of gaiety and liveliness. The season is not yet far enough advanced for the crowds in the parks to be as large as they will be later. I have got accustomed to crowds now and they do not seem so enormous to me any more. I have been for a walk, and I wished all the while from the bottom of my heart that I had one of my loved ones with me. One sees and hears so much here in London that one longs for someone with whom to see and watch everything – two eyes are not enough – and with whom to walk, so as not to feel so keenly, 'I am alone'. I enjoyed watching the handsome Englishwomen riding in Hyde Park. Near the broad roads for the riders are pretty gardens arranged for walking, for those not in possession of a noble steed and thus obliged to seek air and exercise modestly on foot; for that is the only reason for an Englishman to go for a walk. They do not go to admire trees or flowers or even stars, for that serves no useful purpose. And so I too walked up and down like them, for half an hour in each direction, and at the end of it I had to admit that English horses and Englishwomen are indeed beautiful. The former are doubtless perfect; but the latter, in general, have something merely picturesque about them, better to look at than to possess. When one sees a German woman or young girl, her whole being expresses life and activity; one feels she is always doing, thinking, learning something; she has an energetic nature that quickly finds itself occupation wherever it is. Even the type of German nature most prone to dreaming is active, if only in the world of the imagination. But once one has seen one of these beautiful Englishwomen and observed how enchanting her features are, to stay in her company a little longer is almost invariably to ask, 'What am I to do with her now?' The most elegant and distinguished behaviour among these ladies consists in doing absolutely nothing; they lack any inner impulse towards activity; they can but ride, drive, walk about, go to the theatre or into society, get dressed and undressed, just to while the day away. The word 'work' is very vulgar; when one sees such pictures of beauty and charm and observes their expressions closely, one feels that activity driven by inner impulse is the only thing which, in the end, gives people the pleasant, contented expression that one sees at home on practically every young girl's face – faces that are perhaps not always pretty, but always fresh-looking. The fine, well-formed features of the ladies here all too frequently have an expression of calm which easily becomes coldness or severity, while their fiery eyes betray all too often a passionate temperament. There are few people here like our middle class at home: this description is of the upper classes. In the lower, working classes here the women and girls are totally ignorant, they are brought up too much for practical work to have time to think of anything higher; they are uncultured in the extreme, although there are also beautiful or very attractive faces among them. But in whatever class, their figures are

usually poor. The exalted idea that people in Germany have of the
education of English women quite disappears here. It is perfectly true
that one finds ladies who have received an outstanding academic
education here, as perhaps in no other country, but they are the
exceptions. At home education is something much more universal,
and thus knowledge and learning are much more the common
heritage. Just as here these treasures of the mind are heaped in
profusion in one place or another, at home they have become
fragmented and distributed everywhere; even if at home one rarely
finds such fine and perfectly educated ladies, it is equally rare to find
one who is completely ignorant, taking into account the circumstances and class, of course.

I have quite wandered away from my walk, and I wanted to tell you
about another odd and striking thing in London: it is that even a long
way away from busy streets, where one's ears almost burst, one still
hears the constant dull roar of the distant traffic, the whole day long
and all through the night; and that even in the finest weather a veil of
smoke and fog hangs over the houses – you cannot even begin to
imagine what it is like. These two things together oppress one's mind
and feelings and always leave a melancholy impression. One never
hears anyone singing or whistling in the streets, or showing any other
signs of happiness or good cheer. How different from Paris! Only
frightful-looking dirty men, women and children sing or play fiddles
or organs in the street, with hoarse voices, to earn their bread. People
do not sing in the air of London because they feel happy, like birds;
the children have to sing to get money. These singers always have the
most dismal effect on me. The only cheerful people are the Italians,
with their organs, on which they often play quite pretty tunes. They
have their districts, where they stop in front of each house and play a
piece, which they contrive in such a way that they come to each house
once a week, and they are given a penny. As I was coming home today
I ran into a troupe of ragged children who were singing, to the
accompaniment of a flute, an English translation of the old German
song 'Du, du liegst mir im Herzen'. I was very moved to hear the dear
old German lullaby; I slowed down to hear more of it, and would
gladly have given the poor children something, but I am strictly
forbidden ever to give anyone in the street anything. Ladies may

never do that. Once when I expressed pity for an old beggar-man in the street, I was told that these people make themselves sickly, old, blind and lame by day, and by night eat and drink in underground dwellings, live very merrily from their begging, and are in fact young and healthy people. But I cannot help pitying them all the same, if not for their maladies, at least for their spiritual misery.

Tomorrow we may have such cold, gloomy weather that the air seems to be made up of a mixture of little drops of water and particles of coal dust. It is this mixture in which one moves here, so that the ground is a black morass. With it there often comes a strong wind, blowing the flames from every hearth out into the room, and filling everything with smoke. Then flee if you can for a breath of air that does not stick in your throat!

When the weather improves I shall stir myself and visit a few of the sights. So far I have seen a beautiful Panorama of the Battle of the Alma,[1] and another of the Swiss Alps. They are in a round hall, very big and beautifully painted. The spectator stands in the middle of this hall on a platform. The lighting is very ingeniously arranged, and the whole effect is very pretty and pleasing to look at. I have also been to a theatre, the Olympic,[2] which is small and pleasant. They performed a mediocre comedy that amused me mostly for the language; then a traditional pantomime, which is what the Queen had sent us to see. It was sheer nonsense, really, but so original and so genuinely English that we were highly amused. Watching the audience in the theatre like that always counts for as much of my enjoyment as the performance itself; for anyone who pays can get in, there is no distinction as to rank, only as to money, and all that matters is where one goes with a hat and where without one. If one but thinks of London, this giant city, one can well imagine what mixture the audience is. Such toilettes! I often could not help laughing. Then again those beautiful, charming ladies. We are always in the Dress Circle, in the first row; this time there was a German Jewish family

[1] An early victory in the Crimea, September 1854. Panoramas, hugely popular, dated from the late-eighteenth century when Robert Baker devised a system of painting scenery on a cylindrical surface, using curving lines of perspective which looked correct when viewed from the central platform.

[2] 6–10 Wych Street, Strand. Specialised in comedy, farce and melodrama.

behind me, who certainly did not imagine that I was listening to their comments in German.

Two days before we left Windsor for London, I went for one more delightful drive in the Park,[1] as it were to say goodbye to our dear winter home. It is too big and sprawling for one to be able to explore all its beauties on foot, for there is an hour's walk before one gets into the Park itself. So without my friend Herr Meyer,[2] who often takes me out for drives, I should never have been able to get to know how beautiful it is. This time Virginia Water was our goal: it is one of the loveliest areas of the Park. The weather was clear, sunny and mild, although it was February. Isolated spring days like this often occur suddenly in the middle of winter here, as if heaven-sent; and if one can escape outside, one revels in them like an unexpected gift; if one cannot, then of course the fog which lies impenetrably over everything again the next day oppresses one all the more.

First we drove for about an hour, deep into the most thickly wooded part, where on either side of the road whole herds of stags and does roamed about, quite tame. There were farms and keepers' cottages at intervals all the way. From time to time, wherever a pretty view, an attractive path or something else interesting came into sight, we got out and walked for a little. Soon we were at our destination. Virginia Water is a lake, very long and fairly wide, about half an hour's walk from end to end. Its shores are most beautiful, and even at this season they looked fresh and green. One result of the damp air in England is that the grass stays green throughout the winter, which makes a most comforting impression, and is the only thing which takes away a little of the gloomy aspect of the damp fog and the grey sky. The lake is surrounded by laurel bushes in profusion, and they too have that wonderful freshness in this country that one surely finds nowhere else but in the South. Little summer-houses of different styles, sometimes quite hidden, stand at intervals along the shore. Previous kings used to spend most of the summer in Windsor, and

1 Windsor Great Park. The Queen took up residence at Buckingham Palace on 11 February.
2 Since Frieda's Herr Meyer seems to have had ready access to horses and carriages, this is almost certainly Wilhelm Meyer, who accompanied Prince Albert to England as Stallmeister, or Riding Master. He supervised the riding of the royal children, and bought and schooled horses for the use of the Queen and the Prince. He retired in 1867. His retirement present was a carriage and horses.

Virginia Water was the scene of many amusements of a rich and royal kind, as also of those more peaceful, idyllic pleasures which are necessary even to the over-indulged tastes of kings who can have everything. There is perhaps no place so fit for such pleasures as Windsor Park. It is so big that in some parts of it one feels quite cut off from the world, and yet near enough to allow a king whose fancy for solitude lasted but a short time to escape from it with little delay. George IV[1] particularly loved this Park; he even went to live sometimes for a few weeks in a little house hidden deep among the trees, not quite alone, of course, but with his special favourites only. Various monuments and places which events in English history have made famous give the Park, with all its freshness and natural beauty, a deeper significance, which never fails to leave an impression on the visitor. The English are unsurpassed in the art of laying out parks. Theirs are too grand and broad in scale to have the stiffness of artificial pleasure-grounds; they know how to arrange them in such a way they do not seem to have subdued Nature, but rather to have made it possible to enjoy her beauties with ease and comfort. But in other countries, where industry is not the principal source of income, there could never be such enormous tracts of land lying idle, or kept only for pleasure. I am not speaking of this Park, which belongs to the Crown; many private families have enormous parks.

All the roads here are especially well kept and pleasing to the eye. But riding and driving here is also quite different from what it is in Germany or France. The horses are so beautiful, the coachmen so reliable – this is something one cannot but enjoy in England. With *means*, one can live comfortably in England; but only rarely is life *'gemütlich'* in our German way. Once one understands the English and their language, one finds that the whole difference between the types of family life in our two countries is summed up in these two words. *'Gemütlichkeit'* often asks no more than a wooden bench and a bowl of potatoes or hot soup; but to be *'comfortable'* one needs an armchair, a cheerful fireside and roast beef; *'Gemütlichkeit'* comes

---

[1] In his later years the king spent much of his time in his favourite summer retreat, Royal Lodge, a cottage orné. He had embellished lake and park with Roman ruins (real; imported from Leptis Magna in North Africa), a Gothic belvedere, a Chinese fishing temple, and the colossal bronze statue of George III.

*The Queen after a drawing room, 11 May 1854. Her train was
of green and white brocaded silk, trimmed with white tulle and blonde
and alternate bunches of violets and pink and white may blossoms.
Her wreath was also of violets and may.*

*The Queen in the dashing military tunic of
which she confessed herself 'not a little proud'
and which even* The Times *was moved to
call 'a piquant and graceful costume'.*

*Mr Meyer. Drives with him allowed Frieda
to see far more than she could ever have on
foot.*

Buckingham Palace from Piccadilly, June 1856. Homesick Frieda felt, if anything, more lonely in the crowded park than she did when alone in her room at the Palace.

A London street on Sunday morning. Frieda was as appalled by the poverty and squalor of London as she was overwhelmed by its size and grandeur.

On the night of 29 May 1856, the whole of London was illuminated by the fireworks celebrating peace.

Guards passing Buckingham Palace on their return from the Crimea, 9 July 1856; Frieda's could have been one of the faces at the windows above the Queen's balcony.

The Queen's sitting room in the Pavilion, Aldershot.

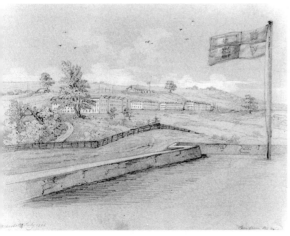

A privileged viewpoint from behind the royal standard; Frieda sketched what she saw from the window of the Royal Pavilion at Aldershot on 18 July 1856.

Queen Victoria at Aldershot, reviewing her troops on horseback.

Queen Victoria distributing the first Victoria Crosses in Hyde Park, 26 June 1857.

Queen Victoria at Aldershot, 17 July 1856; an idealized likeness of the Queen, but a clear picture of the dress, bonnet, 'visite', and parasol the dressers would typically have laid out for a public engagement.

The tableau 'Luna in her car accompanied by the stars personified' impressed not only Frieda, but all who saw it, and the Queen included this watercolour by Egron Lundgren in her Theatrical Album

Inauguration of the Peace Trophy and Scutari Monument at the Crystal Palace with (inset) one of the angels by Marochetti, which Frieda so admired.

The marriage of the Princess Royal, 25 January 1858. Much of the preparations for the wedding dresses and the bride's trousseau devolved upon the Queen's dressers.

Mrs Waetzig, who before her marriage was Frieda's colleague, Lydia Greatorex the wardrobe maid.

Monsieur Nestor Tirard, the Queen's hairdresser, who concluded that being responsible for three women and a horse wa too much for one man.

The Shiel of Altnaguithasaich, the Queen's mountain retreat, where Frieda listened in awe to the soughing of the wind and the roaring of the stags.

Holyrood Chapel, by Frieda, dated 29 August 1856. To draw this Frieda would have been standing in the window of the room now known as the King's Closet, two doors away from the Queen's bedroom, which suggests that the King's Closet was being used as the Wardrobe.

Frieda, about 1860, after her marriage to Ernst Müller. The child is probably her daughter Victoria, to whom the Queen was godmother.

Frieda in her old age.

only from within, from a true, happy, contented German heart. Comfort is defined chiefly by outward things: if these are present in abundance, there is indeed no one who can make himself as comfortable as an Englishman, who thinks of *himself*, without any petty scruples.

Three hours later our excursion was over. I was left with only one wish: to be able one day to stay longer in many of the places we had seen, so as to draw them. But this wish will probably remain unfulfilled, because we only go to Windsor in winter, and then even in the finest weather one cannot sit outside. Farewell. Farewell, my friends, farewell!

Letter 10

THE LONDON
SEASON
1856

This letter covers the period April to August 1856 while the Court was in London for the Season. Although the Crimean War was over, and the peace had been signed in March, matters military still dominated the Queen's public life. Her levees were crowded with officers returned, often wounded, from the Crimea, and the celebrations for the peace continued throughout the summer. The Queen took an intense interest in the returning troops, and one 'Great military day' followed swiftly upon another.

A poet once gave his autobiography the title:
This too was a young life

But I, my friends, give you as an introduction to these few
   pages:
This too was a Season in London

How many millions of people spend a lifetime, how many but a season, in a great city! We may read and hear about magnificent Seasons like this, but we cannot really have any idea of it unless we have lived through it. Do not expect any insight into this tumult, no explanation of the rich promise of this word 'Season', for my part in this world is even smaller than that of the poet, who lived only one young life among the millions and billions which are lived and dreamt through. And yet I can say something about it, because I tried my best to capture some of the sounds which drifted over to me from far off, and to gather them into a brief cadence, if not a harmonious melody. The Season in London, for many people, is like a shining star which pierces through the thick fog of winter, and in the beau monde it is the goal to which all hearts aspire, just as men who know only the joys that come from God alone smile at the approaching sunlight of spring. The richest and most distinguished gentlemen plot how they will make the most dazzling display and give the costliest banquets. Mothers speculate on the beauty and wealth of their daughters; these languishing, melancholy beauties pin their hopes on finding the heart or the man of consequence on whom they will be allowed to pour out their passionate feelings, or on whose arm they can go into society as fashionable ladies, beautiful, but cold as ice. The sons often squander health and wealth in wanton enjoyment of their youth: they ride, drive and drink themselves half to death. Tradesmen speculate, craftsmen hope for work and profit, artists exhibit the work of the past winter, which they have usually spent in France or Italy, for profitable sale; celebrated musicians hope to be received in exalted circles, poor workmen hope for good earnings, and rogues and pickpockets of all kinds rejoice in a season of rich pickings.

These, my dears, are only very commonplace things which no doubt everyone knows about, for how could I, or would I want to, penetrate depths that only powerful minds can and should investigate. But I know that even if you have already heard the same thing a hundred times before, you will still be glad to hear from me, and to know what part I have played in all this magnificence. The thought comes unbidden to mind: how many will be leaving this great city satisfied, and how many disappointed, when at last they flee, half-dead, to lonely watering-places, as it is the elegant and fashionable thing to do? Indeed, although I take no part in all the pleasures and festivities, I am surely fashionable too, for of one thing I am sure, and that is that I shall thank God if I can leave the city behind me and still have a clear head and be able to stand upright. From early in the morning until late at night there are endless preparations to make and adornments for parties to help with, and my poor brain has to know weeks ahead on which day this or that ball, or this or that concert takes place, without my own feet ever dancing a step, or my own ears ever discerning a note of the beautiful music they play! But that sounds gloomy or sad, and yet it is not! Whether it is that human desires and aspirations always reach out towards what is far away, or that the past has such an indescribable power over one, I want none of it all. What I would most like would be to hear the dear old St Cecilia Society singing again. I approached the Season, that is to say the outer world, without expectations, hopes or wishes. Anyone in a position like mine has long given up having any will of his own, or any plans, and learns not to expect anything from outside. Yet I am rich in hopes, richer in wishes, and certainly not lacking in joys! and have a stronger, firmer will than I could ever have believed possible; but all this related to *my* world, to my heart and soul, which will always be my own preserve, whatever happens outside.

Thus it was that your old, faithful friend, who had learnt to feel perfectly happy and at home in little Karlsruhe, surrounded by all of you, came to London for the Season. There was endless, endless hard work and exertion for me which I neither can nor wish to describe, and of which I will say only that I wished from the bottom of my heart that one of you could one day know what it was like! But I was always ready, as soon as there was the smallest glimmer of a chance for me to snatch some little pleasure for myself, for my very own self – I was always ready to grasp it at once, and so I gained something from it after all. You will be amazed, my dears, but I too have done the Season, in my way, and am *very well content*. At every pleasant moment I thought of you, and wished you were with me.

At the beginning I went a few times to the theatre, about which there is nothing in particular to say, except that it amused me very much; if one does not go frequently, and get to know the actors and the traditions, it cannot really be called truly enjoyable, but only amusing. There is so much to look at around one, and so much to amaze one, that it is impossible to devote one's entire attention to the play. In all I went four times, each time to a different theatre. *The Winter's Tale* by Shakespeare was without doubt the most outstanding play I saw; Kean played admirably. There are tableaux in it which are quite unrivalled. The sunrise is entrancing; a fiery sphere contains Jupiter on his chariot, drawn by white horses, illuminated in a most magical way. The sun is so huge that horses and all are quite life-sized. Then the moon rises, in a scene that imprints itself indelibly on the mind. Graceful veiled figures with bowed heads and wonderful sparkling stars on their foreheads can be seen within the moon's sphere. The whole piece could better be described as an artistic performance in groups and tableaux than what we are accustomed to call a play or a tragedy.

————

This production at the Princess's Theatre was the theatrical sensation of the season. The actor-manager, Charles Kean, who himself played Leontes, had set the play in classical Greece. The scenery was drawn from representations of actual Greek architecture, such as the Temple of Minerva and the Theatre at Syracuse, and the costumes were taken from those depicted on Greek vases. No doubt Frieda would have been delighted had she known that the costume for Florizel was based on a figure of Paris on a vase in the collection at Karlsruhe. Classical and modern proprieties were observed; and unruly anachronisms like references to Christian burial or the Russian Emperor and other 'prominent incongruities' were expunged from the text;* Kean's productions have been criticised for over-elaborate staging, but his contemporaries were delighted, none more so than the Queen and her husband, who went to the opening night: 'one was led from one more splendid scene to another, really bewildering, from its wonderful beauty . . . Albert was in ecstasies, for really the whole mise en scène, the beautiful and numerous changes of scenery, the splendid and strictly correct antique costumes – the excellent grouping of every scene, the care with which every trifle was attended to, – made it a wonderful performance. There was appropriate music, composed by a Mr Hatton. Parts were touching beyond belief, and we came back deeply impressed and enchanted.'* The Queen went again three times.

The sunrise, which came at the opening of Act IV, was particularly admired. Frieda's remarks are clarified by the description of the tableau given by the Morning Herald *on 1 May 1856: 'Clouds now descend and fill the stage, leading on to a classical allegory representing the course of Time. As these clouds disperse Selene, or Luna, is discovered in her car, accompanied by the stars (personified), and gradually sinking into the ocean. Time then appears, surmounting the globe, and speaks the lines with which Shakespeare connects the two epochs of his play. As Time descends Phoebus rises with surpassing brilliancy in the chariot of the Sun encircled by a blaze of light which fills every portion of the theatre. The group appears to be suggested by that in the centre of Flaxman's shield of Achilles. The horses are modelled with a life and fire which would have done honour to Baron Marochetti himself. The statue-like grace of Apollo as he stood in the car reining his impetuous steeds, impressed a universal conviction that this figure also was artificial; but the living reality was conveyed in the most startling manner, when, at the full height of his ascent he suddenly raised his right arm to lash a restive courser. The effect was unprecedented, and baffles description.'*

————

As soon as a brief instant of free time appeared, I hurried out into the park or into some of the less busy streets. There is always something to see that is new and therefore attractive, even if the groups and tableaux in the streets of London do not always flatter one's sense of beauty. The organ-grinders are always my particular favourites, a very poor compliment to my musical sense, as sometimes the notes are ear-splitting; but sometimes they are quite pretty too. I am always glad to hear them, they have something so like home about them that when I made a determined effort to find out what exactly it was that they reminded me of, I could not explain it as anything but happy memories of fairs in my childhood. You may well laugh at this, but it shows that nothing in life is too poor and mean to be of use one day, or to bring happiness. The old so-called '*Schnurranten*'[1] on the Spitalplatz[2] could never have suspected that the effect they had on one of the merry long-legged children who usually followed them about, armed with a copper kreuzer,[3] would be so profound that when those legs were considerably longer and the said child had reached quite a respectable age, she would be taking solitary walks in the unending streets of London and still feeling a melancholy but joyful emotion at those familiar sounds!

With the advancing Season, I had ceased to choose the grandeur of Hyde Park for my walks. It is too full of people. Carriage after carriage, countless ladies and gentlemen on horseback, pedestrians, baby carriages etc. etc. make up an alarmingly lively population, so that one feels lonely and lost if one walks quite alone among them.

1 Street musicians.
2 A public square in Karlsruhe.
3 Small change; a copper coin the equivalent of a groat or a farthing.

Not that it is at all noticed here if a lady goes out walking alone, but I tried twice to go in there and came back feeling very low and melancholy. The loneliness one feels in a cheerful swarm of people enjoying themselves is certainly much worse than if one is quite alone in a small room. In the spring I went there frequently and happily; then it was only moderately full, and I thoroughly enjoyed myself watching the lovely lady riders, who often arouse one's admiration. Now I direct my steps more often towards St James's and Green Parks, where no carriages are allowed, so that all the children and their nurses go onto the lawns. It is very pretty there and I often enjoy myself watching the sweet, happy children, and wish I knew a few, so that I could play with them. But you can have no idea of how completely, here in England and in such a big city as this, the thread that binds together humanity in general, down to the children, is severed. The nursemaids sit in little groups with the children on the grass at their feet, but apart from each other: there is no playing together. Of course nobody knows anyone else, and it is too dangerous in London to come into the slightest contact with anyone unknown, as one can never tell whether he is heathen or Turk.

One day we suddenly heard that the Queen might be going away for a whole day, and taking only one of the wardrobe maids – what luck! Before our mistress said anything to us herself, which did not happen until shortly before the said day, good Sophie and I hovered in constant fear and hope as to whether it was true or not. It is so ridiculous, and now that I speak of it I cannot help laughing, what great value a single day can have: the very air one breathes seems to change at the thought of being *free*, one almost believes one has wings; never in my life have I walked so lightly as on that day – I never felt tired, and I was full of that happiness – oh such happiness – that I used to feel as a child after I had successfully reached the end of my French lesson and was allowed to run down into the Spitalplatz with a piece of cake in my hand. But now just imagine the endless discussions about what we should do if it were true? Of course we had to choose the best and most intelligent plan.

Neither of us had been into the City this year, and that is where we decided to go. Mr Cart[1] was to accompany us. We went in an omnibus as far as the Bank. It was a fine morning, and still only ten o'clock. All was movement and life around us, and on every side people hurried about their business. That morning they seemed to us livelier and more cheerful than people here usually are in the streets: this, I realised later, was however only a reflection of our own cheerfulness. We went into the Bank:[2] Mr Cart happened to have some business there. Everything is perfectly quiet inside; there are desks arranged in a circle and marked with letters, at which the employees stand, the accountants and clerks. Business is transacted there in a hushed and ordered atmosphere. Mr Cart explained it to us. The establishment is arranged in such a way that even a lady on her own can conduct her financial affairs in this great Bank of England without running the risk of making a mistake.

From there we set out on foot to the enormously tall column[3] built as a monument to the great fire which devastated London. It stands right in the heart of the City. As the weather was so unusually fine and clear our path through the side-streets was perfectly clean. Walking through the streets of London is an extremely difficult procedure even in the driest weather, for the countless carriages and coal wagons always make it dreadfully dirty. That is of course why one so rarely sees any really elegant women on foot, and that only in certain streets. On the other hand, there are female figures and children dressed in dirty rags such as one can scarcely imagine. It was an amusing sport to make one's way through these streets: one had to overcome all kinds of minor dangers, whether in crossing the slippery road without being run over by a horse, or escaping a shower of mud from a wheel rolling by, or trying not to become separated from one's companion, or simply not to be pushed. I always find something repellent in being touched by such filthy creatures, even if it is only the hem of my dress.

Mr Cart is a man who is completely at home in London, and knows every corner of it, besides which he is a very careful man. We stayed

1 See note on p. 51.

2 Bank of England; at this period, the buildings were those of Sir John Soane.

3 The Monument, at Monument and Fish Hill Street, EC2, erected to commemorate the Great Fire of London of 1966, was built by Christopher Wren 1671–7. Two hundred and two feet high, surmounted by a gilt-bronze flaming urn. Panels at the base bear descriptions of the fire in Latin and an allegorical representation of Charles II coming to the rescue of the city.

close on either side of him, and so got through several narrow streets safe and sound, into broader streets that were just as busy but immeasurably easier to walk in than the others. The bustle and activity of the crowds, with their serious businessmen's expressions, is most entertaining for the cheerful spectator. We climbed the column, which is very, very high, and the day being so extremely clear, as I said before, we could see over part of the City, into the distance where the roofs gradually disappeared in the smoky air. The dense forest of masts belonging to the merchant ships in the harbour was an extraordinary sight.

After we had climbed down, we crossed the famous London Bridge,[1] on which the crowds, the filth, the noise and the bustle were indescribable! As it was, we had to shout at the tops of our voices in these streets to make ourselves heard, there is such a noise all around. Indeed people scarcely talk at all in the streets; everyone hurries about his business without a word. In a few of the main streets there are magnificent shops; they may not be quite as daintily and attractively arranged as the French ones, but most of them outdo by far in splendour and richness those in the Parisian boulevards.

Scarcely has one crossed the bridge to the other side of the river when all seems deathly quiet; the noise sounds like a dull hum growing farther and farther off; the streets are still and deserted – relatively speaking, of course, not like Stephanienstrasse[2] in Karlsruhe. I think if anyone who lived in the City were suddenly transported there he would be terrified and think himself in a town inhabited by ghosts who went about their business invisibly and in silence.[3]

Here we visited the huge and famous brewery of Barclay and Perkins.[4] It was a place that interested us less on account of what it produced than for the enormous scale of it. This day was intended to

[1] Frieda passed across the five stone arches of the structure built by Sir John Rennie and opened by William IV and Queen Adelaide in 1831. Replaced 1967–79, sold, and re-erected at Lake Havasu City, Arizona.

[2] The street where the Arnold family lived.

[3] Visitors did indeed think so; as William Howitt, who visited Karlsruhe in 1842, expressed it, 'There is everywhere a feeling of silence and loneliness; of a want of life and action, that makes you long to be gone, and that with a feeling of pity for those who must pass their dreamy life there.'*

[4] Barclay, Perkins & Co., in Southwark, one of London's leading breweries and one of the sights of London. In 1850 the buildings extended over ten acres, the machinery included two steam engines. The store-cellars housed 126 vats, some containing 4000 barrels, and about 160 horses were used to convey the beer to different parts of London.*

give us a glimpse of business life, as far as possible. The buildings
which go to make it up are like a small town, and the number of beer
barrels is incalculable. I have forgotten how many thousand measures
of beer are brewed daily; I shall only tell you that the containers in
which the beer is cooled are so vast that after we had climbed a small
stepladder we found ourselves looking into a sea of beer; the smell
was overpowering. I wonder what a crowd of German students
would feel, confronted by one of these containers! Everything is
driven by machines, in the most wonderful way. I could never stop
wishing that just one of my friends, who also find pleasure and
interest in the product itself, were with me. I wished particularly that
Georg were at my side; it would have made the German Professor
open his eyes wide! It was half past one, and as there was half an
hour's drive to Buckingham Palace we took a hansom cab and drove
home, well content, hungry and tired.

The afternoon was set aside for pleasures of quite another kind, for
we wanted to see a watercolour exhibition by a Mr Simpson,[1] who
had been in the Crimea and had brought about forty of the most
wonderful sketches back; these were all on exhibition. They are
painted with a lightness and beauty that astonished me. Using only a
very few colour tones, and often very few brush strokes, he has
created pictures which hold one's attention in thrall, even if one
knows nothing of the subject, which in itself is often quite
insignificant. Others are more elaborate. All the figures in the
landscapes are portraits. All the pictures show views of the Crimea,
scenes from battles or in the encampments. The various places where
fallen officers lie buried, or which are significant for other reasons, are

[1] William Simpson (1823–99). Painter, illustrator and engraver, sent to the Crimea by
Messrs Colnaghi to make sketches, and became known as 'Crimean Simpson'. 'It was quite a new
thing,' he later wrote, 'to have an artist at the seat of war depicting events as they took place.' He
claimed the highest degree of accuracy for these paintings, and would consult the officers present
at the event; one painting, which he submitted to Lord Raglan, being met with a very cold
reception until His Lordship was made more conspicuous at the front of his men. His paintings
were sent home in Lord Raglan's bag. In London they were submitted to the Duke of Newcastle,
who was War Minister, and then sent to the Queen for inspection. Two volumes of lithographs
were published, and the originals went on show at P. & D. Colnaghi, 13–14 Pall Mall East.
  While Simpson was in the Crimea, he was commissioned by the Queen to paint the scene of
Balaclava, with the Guards' camp. When he met her he was most impressed by her knowledge of
Sebastopol 'more than anyone I found at home knew'.
  He later travelled in India, Kashmir and Tibet, joined the *Illustrated London News* in 1866, and
visited China, Russia and Afghanistan.*

of the greatest interest for everyone who followed this war, but still more so for those who took part in it themselves or had relatives who were involved. Many of these pictures have been engraved, and apparently sell very well. We stayed there for three hours, and then returned to Buckingham Palace, well satisfied with our day, arriving an hour before our mistress. We used this hour to rest a little, for the evening brought further pleasures of the Season of another kind. After this wonderful day, the experiences of which remained our chief topic of conversation for a long time, for they were associated in our minds with so many funny little details, so typical of this country, which alas none of you can understand – after this day, as I was saying, there followed a series of days which contained more troubles than joys. Often I did not go to bed until it was growing light in the morning, and I slept all too little. I often expected my long limbs to refuse to carry me up and down the countless stairs any more; but moral strength and self-will can work wonders; and by the grace of God my courage did not fail me. Apart from a few lonely hours in my room I was always cheerful and good-tempered, and often made jokes or laughed about our running about and tidying and God knows what. Remember, dear friends: there is nothing more ridiculous and unworthy of a stout heart than a dismal, irritable face when one has a moral or physical burden to bear, and it makes it much heavier. I have had many an example of this before me here, and have acquired a hearty dislike of allowing one's burdens to be visible to others' eyes. It gives one no relief to do so, and one makes oneself ridiculous and disagreeable without realising it.

Sophie and I rarely had a chance to talk during this time, that is, to gossip after our usual fashion, and discuss our own affairs. We always had work to do together, or if one of us had a free hour, we certainly never missed the chance to slip out: we have become extraordinarily skilful at that. I would hurry out into the Park, or sometimes I went to see the two families I have grown so fond of, the Meyers and the Nickels; I always returned in good spirits from them, having heard and seen much which gave me matter for thought and comparison. Sophie also visited her friends from time to time, and then the next day whenever we were working together we would tell each other everything down to the last detail, with that girlish thoroughness which always amazed and impressed Georg in me and my girl friends: he would say, 'Girls can gossip about *anything*', or Ludwig would call it 'idle chatter'. Well, it did us a great deal of good, and we said to each other every time we had some such experience, that it was really a very good and agreeable thing that we were in London. In this way our toil was forgotten in no time, and we tried to remember and hold fast to all the good things, which I did with the greatest ease.

Once the Queen went away for half a day, and Sophie and I went together to visit a cemetery a long way out of town. I had never seen an English God's Acre. A wonderfully moving sense of peace reigned there; it was kept like a beautiful garden, with fresh flowers; the monuments were mostly simple, although there were also some imposing ones. It was Brompton Cemetery.[1] What is chiefly responsible for the peaceful impression is the deep silence, in contrast to the continual noise and bustle of the city. For us, who had not been so far away from the Palace for almost three weeks, and never far enough to escape the thunderous and unceasing rumble of carriages, it made a particularly pleasant impression. Unfortunately we could only stay for half an hour: it would have done us so much good to spend some time walking in this quiet place, in the pure fresh air – it was a beautiful day, and the cemetery lies on very high ground. But we had to leave as it was a long way home. When we had a few free hours together another time, we went to Regent Street and looked at the shops, which are magnificent beyond belief; beside this street Paris looks like a dear dainty little doll's house.

We now had the prospect of fleeing from the joys of the Season for three weeks, as we were to spend part of the sweet month of May in the Isle of Wight, at Osborne.[2] This was a most happy time for me, for you all know how I love Osborne. After many a stormy day, and nights that were all too short for us, we arrived at Osborne quite worn out. Oh! how delicious I found the pure air there, how beautifully the nightingales sang to me, how pleasant was the peace of my lonely room in the tower (others, of course, complained that the weather

---

1 The chronic problem of overcrowding in the churchyards of London was improved when joint-stock companies began to establish suburban cemeteries, the first being Kensal Green in 1832. Brompton Cemetery was consecrated in 1840, and bought from the West of London and Westminster Cemetery Company by the General Board of Health in 1852.

2 The Queen was at Osborne from 10 to 26 May 1856; her birthday visit.

was too inclement, raw and unpleasant, and that it would have been more sensible to remain in London). *'Les goûts sont differents'* – and in any case, you only want to know how I got on. I took to going down to the sea to take the air. Sometimes it was very stormy, but that was good, and after a few days I felt revived, like a half-dead plant. The three weeks passed like three days, I worked hard at my drawing, which I had scarcely been able to do at all in London, and I sewed and patched too, prosaically enough, for my own domestic concerns were beginning to need a little attention. My official duties here, in comparison with London, were mere child's play, for there was no house party and no one in the house. For once we lived an idyllic life.

Only too soon the lovely days were over. I had a cheerful prospect before me, the welcome visit of Captain Schuberg and his wife, who were coming soon. Our work resumed its breakneck pace, *comme à l'ordinaire*, but in a few days there was to be the great firework display to celebrate peace, in the three biggest parks of London – Hyde Park, Green Park, Primrose Hill – that is, there are other bigger ones, but the position of these three is such that one can see something of them from almost anywhere. As the Queen's Palace is situated so that from the roof and from certain windows one could see all three firework displays, you can well imagine that we had the best places without the slightest difficulty. It began at half past nine and lasted until eleven o'clock. Signals were given with cannons, so that all three began simultaneously. It was magnificent: one gazed and gazed and was enthralled. A barrage of rockets and a rain of fire, bigger than anything one could have imagined, filled the sky.[1] The general opinion of the experts, however, was that it lasted far too long and that the experiments were repeated too often to create the right effect. That is no doubt very true, and it quite sums up the English character. They want to have everything in quantity; everything has to cost a great deal of money and therefore last a long time, so that it is worth the expense. They also make their plays long enough to kill you, whereas half or two-thirds of the length would leave a much deeper impression. But I did not find it too long; I did not give much thought to the larger or smaller effects of the whole display, but

[1] For the Queen's own account of the evening *see* Appendix.

simply gazed at the rain of fire for just as long as it lasted, and when instead of half a dozen blue rockets, a few dozen rushed up into the sky in succession, I enjoyed the latter spectacle as much as I had the former.

At this time our Regent[1] had already arrived, and it was of course always a pleasure for me to see him, which I frequently did, from quite close by, in the corridors. I curtsyed to him on various occasions (extremely gracefully and respectfully), which was always acknowledged with a charming kind smile and a majestic nod of the head.

A few days later we went to Windsor for four days for the Ascot Races, horse races. I had never been to the races before. A broad, long track is kept clear, thickly hemmed in on either side with people, carriages and huts. There are some large, very high wooden buildings in which one can buy seats on stands and at windows; then there are special places which the owners of equipages rent, and camp there in their own carriages for the day. The Queen has one of these buildings or stands, in the best place. It is very big and high; on the lower floor are dining-rooms, for one stays there the whole day; on the second floor is the Royal Family, and on the third the Queen's invited guests, of whom there are a great number, and behind them, the upper servants of the Household, again according to rank. All the rooms are open, only covered from above. Only one of us two could go, and Sophie had already seen it many times, so it fell to me. I went with Mary and two of the Queen's pages, driving through the beautiful Park.[2] It was a wonderful drive, between tall, magnificent trees in their richest foliage; I had never been in Windsor in summer before, and the beauty of the Park at this season overwhelmed me.

When we arrived we went to our seats, and I amused myself looking around, for there was an immense crowd; expectation was in the air, for the Queen had not yet arrived and she and her suite always drive slowly down the course in great state, before the races begin. Already from far off one saw the carriages approaching; as they came

1 Friedrich I, 1826–1907. Was Regent of Baden from 1852 to 1856 because of the incurable illness of his brother, Ludwig II. He arrived in England 28 May 1856 and stayed with the Queen before making a tour of the country, leaving on 20 June. It was his sister Alexandrine (who married Duke Ernest II of Coburg) with whom Queen Victoria corresponded about Frieda.
2 Windsor Great Park

closer there was a great waving of handkerchiefs and shouting hurrah.[1] The Schubergs had arrived in London before this, and they had told me that they were coming to Windsor for the races. Herr Meyer's carriage – they were with him – was to be stationed somewhere near us; but although I could see over the crowd it was impossible to recognise a single soul in the crush of carriages and people. Then suddenly a man whom I knew appeared at our stand, and told me that Herr Meyer had sent him to bring me to them during the first interval, for they were nearby. My heart thumped with excitement; just then the trumpet sounded, and about eight horses flew past with jockeys in bright jackets; I tried my best to follow their progress, and in a short time they were back again at breakneck speed, while the crowd roared its applause. Not, of course, quite all together, for the first horse was home and the people who knew its owner took the liveliest interest. It did not make such a striking impression on me as I had expected; I felt sorry for the poor harassed animals. I could see that the fame of English racing is due mainly to the crowds that go to it and the festive atmosphere, for the races themselves are not a particularly memorable spectacle, and only give pleasure to those who are besotted about horses, of whom there are certainly many in England. Nothing gives me less pleasure than the way these poor animals are galloped; people say of course that it gives pleasure and satisfaction to the horses, but I really cannot believe that.

And so now I came down from my stand, and was soon in the carriage with the Meyers and the Schubergs. I was overjoyed, and we watched the races together and had a very merry and enjoyable time. The weather was unfavourable, windy and wet at times, but in spite of that everything went well and cheerfully. After a time I returned to the stand; but I was so happy and delighted to have seen our dear friends that I cannot begin to describe my feelings to you. Soon afterwards we drove back through the magnificent Park to the Castle.

After two busy days we were back in London, where we had to make preparations for a two-day visit to the Camp at Aldershot.[2]

---

[1] The Queen's Journal for the day, 12 June 1856, reads 'At 12, we started for the races . . . Fortunately it did not begin to rain till after we reached Ascot. There was an immense gathering of people and the races were a pretty sight. We saw all, but 2 and came home at ½ p. 6.'

[2] It was quite a new idea in England, actively encouraged by Prince Albert, that the army

Whenever I could snatch an hour or so in the evening, although it was impossible until about nine o'clock, I hurried over to the Meyers, where I found the Schubergs, and was always warmly welcomed.

Aldershot is a huge camp on a heath, where Caesar too once pitched a camp when he came to England. The land is somewhat rolling, and the Queen's Pavilion stands on a height, so that one has a splendid view over the camp. The journey is not long, about two hours by train, then half an hour by carriage, which is an extremely amusing drive.[1] One rides in burning sunlight, shrouded in clouds of dust, in an open carriage over the heath; but the air is good and pure and the sight of the various clubhouses for the royal officers [*sic*], the little shops and inns which stand a short way off, is so intriguing that one gladly puts up with the dust, which after all can be brushed off. Here and there stand groups of soldiers, small carts or workmen's tools. From far off one hears the call of a trumpet or the rumble of a drum; the scene is so new to me and so picturesque that I can hardly put it into words. You must have tried to imagine what Wallenstein's[2] camp looked like: that is the only thing with which I can compare it. But with this difference: instead of the rough, unrestrained spirit which dominated there, here there is a stillness and order that is very much part of the English character.

The Queen's Pavilion is only one storey high, but it is quite charming. The walls and ceilings are draped in tent fashion. The chair covers and curtains are of red and white striped canvas; the legs of the tables and chairs are crossed like camp chairs, and made of white wood. The whole house is built in a style which harmonises with its surroundings, in the way that I have praised before here.

should have a training camp. After a successful experiment at Chobham, Aldershot was acquired in 1854. A wooden building, the site and design chosen by the Prince, was put up there for the Queen. She first stayed in 'our charming Hut, or Pavilion',* on 18 April 1856, commenting in her Journal, 'found it so nice, simple, fresh, and clean. Felt quite delighted at the whole scene, and novelty of the place.' After riding out to watch the manoeuvres the next day, she wrote, 'I had never been so completely *in* anything of this kind before, – surrounded by troops, and I thought it *so* exciting.'

[1] When everyone left Buckingham Palace for Aldershot on 7 July, the luggage left the Palace for Nine Elms Station first, in a van, followed ten minutes later by the 'dressers etc.' in an omnibus and half an hour later by the Queen's cortège. At Farnborough, Frieda would have climbed into the 'fly and pair' provided for the dressers. On the return journey the next day, among the carriages which met the special train at Nine Elms was a carriage and pair for the dressers.*

[2] *See* p. 108.

In the afternoon there was a review of 10,000 men; there is a German Legion[1] there too; the army was drawn up on the nearby heights before the Queen rode out. We watched from the windows, not far off, as the columns marched up and down the hills; it was a wonderful sight. Their weapons glinted in the sunshine; one could not distinguish the different units. Then all at once the familiar strains of the march from the *Freischütz*[2] fell on my ears, and I knew that it was the Germans. It was wonderfully moving; and I must say that I feel sorry for my compatriots, for I cannot believe that it is desirable to be in the service of a foreign country. Later we also drove over to see the Review, but it was so dusty and the heat of the sun was so oppressive that we did not especially enjoy it. But at least we had been there. It reminded me very much of Mr Pickwick's love of reviews.[3]

In the evening, after the Queen's dinner, the Germans (for the Legion has a choral society) were to sing to the Queen[4] on the terrace in front of the windows. I hurried as much as I could to finish my

1 Late in 1854 the government decided to supplement British Forces in the Crimea. The deeply unpopular Foreign Troops Enlistment Bill was passed on 23 December. German (some from the United States of America), Swiss and Italian troops were raised during 1855, commanded by British as well as foreign officers. The German Legion was based at Shorncliffe, in Kent. Queen Victoria inspected over 2000 German troops there, on 9 August 1855, and in December Prince Albert presented colours to the German Legion, the First Regiment of which having already arrived in the Crimea in October. On 16 June 1856 the Germans were newly returned to England when the Queen recorded in her Journal having seen 'the whole of the German Legion, from Shorncliffe, including two fine regiments of cavalry, one Regiment of Swiss, and two batteries of Artillery ... the South Camp was swarming with Germans, whose particular "tenue", cut of features, colouring and light hair, could not be mistaken for a moment. The Germans had only *just* arrived and their horses were all without covering ... The Germans, in spite of their recent arrival, looked uncommonly well and so did the Swiss. The German Jägers, are really very fine, but I cannot admire the German way of marching, which is so stiff; ours I thought contrasted so favourably with them, the marching being so far more natural. The German Cavalry also looked well, – fine and soldierlike looking men. A short impromptu Fieldday now took place, which was excessively pretty to watch, the Germans, for the first time acting together with our men, but they have their own German words of command.'

After the war the disbanded Swiss and Italian units returned home. A contingent of the Germans, still under British Arms, were sent out as a peace-keeping force to Cape Colony as there was tribal unrest in the Cape.

2 (the Freeshooter); Weber's opera based on the tale of the legendary marksman who makes a compact with the Devil, from whom he obtains seven bullets, six of which will always hit their mark; the seventh will hit as the Devil directs. First produced Berlin 1821.

3 *See* Charles Dickens, *The Posthumous Papers of the Pickwick Club* (Oxford, 1979), ch. IV 'A Field Day and Bivouac'.

4 Frieda's account of Aldershot appears to be conflating several visits. There is no mention of this recital in the Queen's Journal for the visit two days after Ascot, 16 June, but on 7 July the Queen records in her Journal that 'some of the German legion sang'. *See also* note 1, page 164.

duties, chose the nearest unoccupied window, and was at my post at ten o'clock, just as the thirty singers marched up. I had not heard a German choir since the St Cecilia Society, and now this, in a foreign country! It was a beautiful evening – the most wonderful moonlight, mild air, and a scene of quiet repose as far as the eye could see. Then all at once they began to sing – just imagine, dear friends – the lovely song I know so well, '*Wer hat dich, du schöner Wald* etc. etc.[1] It sent a cold shiver through me, and I could not help crying. 'A little song from those better days brings back our old happiness.' They sang a few more soldiers' songs and battle songs which I did not know. Although their voices had a rough tone on the whole, they sang very well, and the leader of the choir, a tenor, had a very fine voice and sang the solo in the Waldeslied, 'Farewell, farewell', with much feeling – one sensed that he too had experienced what it means to say farewell to something dear. The Queen enjoyed it very much and sent a message to the singers to tell them so. Our dear Germans are always the same true, warm-hearted people, wherever they are. Although they are in foreign military service they still have a choral society! 'Where there is singing, there you may safely live; evil men have no songs.'

The next afternoon we were to drive over the whole camp to see everything properly. There are no tents, which of course would not do for constant occupation by the troops, but small wooden huts, painted black, each one holding twelve men. The identical size, shape and spacing of the huts give the whole camp an ordered military look. It is like a little town laid out in broad streets. As I was quite sure I would not be needed for two hours in the morning, since the royal party was going out for a long excursion, I went for a walk through the camp, or rather through part of it, for it is very large. I enjoyed this very much; we – Herr Löhlein accompanied me, for it looks too emancipated for my taste for a young lady to walk alone around an army camp – we climbed a small hill on which stands the church, and from which one looks down onto a charming little street. I sat down in a sentry box out of the sun and the dust and made a quick sketch, which although it came out well gives no idea of the charm of the

[1] By Joseph Eichendorff (1788–1857), romantic poet whose joy in nature and religious faith produced poetry which lent itself to song and was often set to music.

scene, for its greatest attraction lies in the grouping of the figures which enliven the view. I saw this at once, but I still deceived myself greatly, for I thought that the place was pretty even without the people. You all know the stunted figures I draw, and my animals with their legs too long or too short! Having already had so little success in copying pictures of living creatures, how much less well could I draw them from Nature? I longed so much to be able to draw figures, for wherever one looked there was a little genre painting to be made. Some were sitting at ease drinking beer in front of the tents; others were cleaning their guns; others were leading horses past, etc. But all this was very quiet, almost silent; whether this was merely the result of the strong discipline, or whether it was wholly or partly because of the English character, I do not know. I am only sure of one thing, which is that the genre scenes one might observe in a French camp would never be so quiet, I mean without the sound of singing, whistling or laughter. The zouaves who formed the guard of honour outside the Palais de St Cloud did not look half as serious as the English in their camp. In the afternoon we drove through the whole camp, and one could not but be amazed at the size, order and cleanliness of everything. We went inside some of the houses and kitchens, and talked to our German countrymen, who were mostly Prussians. I asked if there were any men from Baden there, but I was told that there were only one or two, and these we could not find. To see the sun going down over Aldershot, over the camp, is a sight that has a peculiar charm which I cannot describe to you. Schiller's words in *Die Räuber*, 'Thus dies a hero, worthy of veneration' etc. are especially appropriate.[1] (I thought of Aunt Babette,[2] who once used this passage to describe a sunset in the Castle garden. Oh! if she had only seen the sun go down here! and truly over heroes, for a battalion of infantry which had just returned from the Crimea was marching over the nearest hill back into the camp!)

In the evening from eight to ten o'clock the military band always played beneath the windows, often pieces from operas I knew. This

1 This speech, in which the setting sun is likened to a dying hero, and the speaker remembers his own boyhood wish for such a death, comes in Act III, scene ii of Schiller's tragedy of brotherly betrayal, which was first published 1781 and had been performed at the Hoftheater in Karlsruhe in 1851 and 1852.

2 *See* p.38, note 7.

was always a pleasure for me. There have already been five of these visits to the camp, always for one or two days; I went three times, Sophie twice, for one of us always stays behind.[1] It is one of our most exhausting visits; but I shall say no more! on principle; and it is too dull anyway for such dear spoilt ears as yours, around which the air of home always wafts like a gentle murmur.

In the very midst of an exceedingly busy week of the London Season I was able to snatch a few free hours one day to drive to the Crystal Palace with Herr Rath, the secretary of the young Prince of Prussia,[2] a friend of mine (a grey-haired gentleman with a wife and children). He had never been there and had been waiting for a day when I could go with him. That was a lovely day, and all the more so because it had been so difficult to arrange. I still laugh when I think of how I spent half a day working out how to organise everything as profitably as possible so as to get away in good time. Sophie's cleverness was also a great help. We were to leave at half past ten, and did not have to be back until half past six. I dressed myself up quite carefully, reflecting that no gentleman is so old or so sober that he does not prefer, when he walks out with a lady, that she should look at least a little elegant. I tell you this for the edification of my young friends; one does not learn such things at home, where one lives among friends who know and value our personality more than anything else, and where one does not go out with any gentlemen except brothers, uncles, or at the most cousins. What would people say there, dear God! 'Who's that? Just take a look, Frieda, Amelie, Aurelie etc. etc., with a gentleman!' At least there are no busybodies in big cities, surely one comfort among so many hardships. So take note of that: if you ever go anywhere with any gentleman, old or

1 The Queen's fifth overnight stay at Aldershot was on 30 July 1856. As always, the Queen crammed a great deal into her day. What she wore depended on the weather, but when possible, she would review her troops on horseback, wearing the famous red tunic. The *Morning Post* of 17 July, commenting that she looked remarkably well, reported that 'Her Majesty wore a bonnet of blue and white, trimmed with flowers of geranium colour; a blue visite, and a barege dress of blue and white.' There would be a large dinner in the evening, to which officers would be invited, everyone in evening dress. On 6 November, however, 'We dined . . . in high dresses' and went immediately after dinner to a theatrical performance in one of the huts. This was the year Queen Victoria made the most use of the Pavilion, although until the death of Prince Albert in 1861 she would come regularly three or four times a year.

2 Prince Frederick William of Prussia (1833–88), afterwards German Emperor, who had become engaged to the Princess Royal at Balmoral the previous September.

young, high or low, dress yourselves up a little – it is always wise. I
put on a lilac and white striped silk dress with volants, a green cloak
trimmed with black velvet, and a white hat, yellow gloves and a blue
parasol, and thought myself quite elegant; oh blissful innocence, oh
rapturous self-confidence, how comical you are! To go to the Crystal
Palace dressed in one's best, is exactly the same as when one goes to
the Museum at Karlsruhe in a freshly washed wool dress: one is the
only person who imagines herself as well dressed as the other ladies –
the ladies of rank, I mean, for that is how I wished to look.

We had an open carriage and the drive was very pleasant. The
country is charming and the air in Sydenham is fresh and good. It was
a very fine day, and we reached our destination in an hour. So I went
into this giant temple of the arts for the second time, and this time, in
place of the indescribable astonishment I felt last time, I was filled
with a deep, silent reverence for what I was about to see, knowing
what it would be like. Even if the impression was no longer as
powerful for me, being no longer so new and strange, it is always a
stirring sight. I looked again with renewed and redoubled enjoyment
at everything which had pleased me so well before; I discovered so
much that was new to me, and many things that I had seen in an
incomplete state were now finished. The glorious Alhambra is now
quite complete – and oh, it is enchanting; one small room, only dimly
lit through coloured glass windows, with wonderful mosaics, is
utterly delightful. It was a chamber for resting after meals. One must
indeed have been able to have a siesta full of sweet dreams there, after
a pleasant meal with close friends!

I cannot tell you all the alterations that have been made since last
year; I will mention only the two most important ones. Two
magnificent monuments standing on either side of the central dome:
one was erected after the peace with Russia, the other in honour of
the fallen heroes of the battle of Inkerman.[1] The first, of enormous
size, so that from ground level one can see it properly only from a
considerable distance, represents a female figure, England, with the
palm of peace in her right hand. The figure is of white marble and
stands on a gigantic pedestal, which is also decorated with countless

---

1 Fought on 5 November 1854, in which the Allies repulsed the Russian attack; known as the
soldiers' battle.

figures symbolising appropriate subjects. It is enormous, so much so that the main impression, for me, was only one of amazement, while the admirable details merely distracted me from appreciating the whole. I think it is something which one needs to look at often in order to be able to judge it. The other monument, however, the one to the heroes of Inkerman, I shall never forget. It is of the same colossal size, simple in form, of white marble, with angels at the four corners. These angels must be four to six times human size, but of such simple beauty and repose that they could move one to tears. Their heads are bowed between their long wings, which reach down to their feet; their arms hang wearily downwards, and in their right hands they hold laurel branches, lowered to the ground. Never have I seen such deep and solemn feeling, combined with a divine repose of expression, as in these angels. This monument expresses the most blessed peace after an honourable battle. It is all as simple as one can possibly imagine; the four angels are exactly alike, a symmetry which gives it such devout grandeur. Schreiber once said in his lectures that a symmetrical arrangement in a landscape or genre painting is often stiff, but that in a work of art that has a religious significance or is otherwise intended to make a solemn impression on the mind of the onlooker, it is only with the most perfect symmetry that the most sublime effect can be attained; and this is tangible proof of the truth of his assertion.

This time we looked more closely at the industrial objects, because they interested my companion very much. Machines of the most wonderful kind fill the entire space of the Crystal Palace basement; all are working, and whoever understands such things can see much there; I too saw much, but I can tell you nothing of it; it is too confusing for me. The magnificent park around the Palace has made considerable progress, and the much talked-about fountains,[1] which foreigners have claimed are much bigger than those at Versailles, now play every afternoon from four until five. We planned our tour and our luncheon in such a way that we were ready to go out at four o'clock. From the terrace one looks out over six large pools and one much bigger one. All at once, from countless spouts both large and

[1] The Queen was present for the official inauguration of the fountains on 18 June 1856.

small, the water leaps high up towards the sky. The sun shone down on the scene, colouring the water with rainbow hues, so that one often had the impression of watching Bengali lights in the air. The fountains are indeed wonderful, and perhaps even more impressive than those of Versailles; but I found the latter incomparably more beautiful. It is a completely different style, in the same way as the most perfect modern works of art never can rival the most perfect old masters. Although the former can more easily bewitch the eye with richness of colour and charm of manner, yet the simple grace of the latter is preferable on closer examination. In Sydenham the great fountains are ringed with a multitude of small, very fine water-jets made in such a way that when in play they create a web of translucent beads, so tiny and so numerous that instead of streams of water, millions of droplets fly up into the air. It is like a joyful dance of the elements: when the sun shines one has the impression of drops of water and sparks of fire dancing a giddy reel together. In Versailles, on the other hand, charming nymphs, roguish goblins, mischievous cupids, sea-monsters or wild bears spew out the powerful streams of water or pour it over themselves. There, the whole mighty flood of water rushes out in a single stream, with great force and a roaring noise. The joyous liveliness of the play of the water is given a deeper meaning by the art of the sculptor. I shall always prefer Versailles for that reason, fine and admirable though the fountains at Sydenham may be; and they will be even more so, for scarcely half of it is finished yet. If one did not know that 'Englishmen never begin anything until they have considered what advantage they can draw from it', one could justifiably doubt whether this *huge* expense will ever prove worthwhile. There is still so much work and enlargement going on that the mere costs of maintaining such a building and such grounds must be quite unimaginable. It is being built by selling shares. I must admit that I would not have the courage to buy such shares. My brain cannot take in anything on such a scale.

Satisfied with all we had seen and absorbed with talking about it all, we drove home, both of us particularly aware of the good the fresh air was doing us, for we had lately been shut up in Buckingham Palace for most of the time, and had had little chance of enjoying fresh air.

I also went to a few exhibitions of water-colours in London, where one can indeed see some extremely fine works of art. An important part of the pleasures of my 'Season' consisted as well in the letters I received from home. Whenever one arrived in the morning, I would read it in any corner I could hide in at the time, then put it in my pocket and think about it, and look forward to the evening when I could go to my room, sit down in a large armchair and read it again in peace and at my leisure. On Sunday mornings, when I was not on duty, I went down the Strand to Savoy Street, which was almost an hour's walk, to the German Church,[1] where I heard some very good sermons. When I was on duty, I used this time for writing, or sometimes also for drawing. I painted the view from my window, consisting of the coal-black walls with the main gate of the huge Palace courtyard. Soon the bustle in the Palace was redoubled, as everyone began to prepare for the great departure for our summer visit to Osborne. In our department too there was much hard work. Nevertheless we still devised ways of slipping out for a brief hour from time to time. These were often delightful moments, unhoped-for rewards. I went back to my favourite spot in St James's Park again, and once I went to Regent Street to do some shopping; I also slipped away occasionally to spend a little time in the evening with my friends the Meyers, and drove out with them once again. These moments were little grains of gold that we fished from the sea.

One fine morning[2] we found ourselves sitting in the train, and soon we were sailing over the sea in bright weather, towards the beautiful island, which smiled at us beneath an all-too-sunny sky, for it was oppressively hot here. The first days passed in sorting and tidying; but when the Prussian Royal visitors[3] left after a short time (they had come over with us for eight days), a sense of peace and stillness descended which was like sweet balm to my spirit after all the noise. I made my dear little room as cosy as possible, and I now spend many a peaceful, solitary hour there – for here I have every other day almost entirely to myself. I began to go out for energetic walks, which

[1] German Lutheran Church in the precincts of the Savoy Chapel, (where there were several foreign congregations), built by Sir William Chambers 1766–7, and almost overwhelmed by the approaches to Waterloo Bridge built in 1817. The church was removed about 1876 to make way for a new approach to the Victoria Embankment.*

[2] The Queen went to Osborne 18 July 1856.

[3] William, Prince of Prussia and his wife, the Princess Royal's prospective parents-in-law.

are always so beneficial to my health. I was also diligent with my drawing. All my own little concerns, which had been so neglected, were attended to. Often, oh! so often, I thought of you, my dear, beloved friends – oh! here more than in any other place. I long for home and for you. Here I can think more of myself; here I find rest, but also longing. I often walk quite alone along the sea-shore for an hour or two – oh! if only one of you could be with me! I send you a million greetings over the sea; and were it not for Nature, my eternally faithful Friend who binds me to my home, there are times when I should be very unhappy here. But I am not. I am always cheerful and contented, and sometimes I even enjoy myself very much. One of my pleasures while I am here I have not yet told you about. I have started a museum for myself, and I often go out to look for 'curiosities'. I already have a considerable collection of shells and pebbles, some of which I have found, and others which I have been given. Among other things I have a piece of glass which was excavated at Pompeii. Sometimes I go out on the sea in a little boat, when the weather is calm, by myself – that is, with a sailor to row me. (The Museum, or Natural History Collection, does not travel with me, but stays always at Osborne.)

The Season is behind me; time rolls by so very fast; we are already making preparations to travel to the Scottish Highlands. Wouldn't you like to experience a London Season too some day? I am sure you would gladly do so, and I am confident every one of you would have the courage to brave it once, even if it meant working hard; once is bearable, for a strong soul who does not allow himself to be weighed down by the fog.

Now let me just tell you briefly of a lovely expedition I made on the island, that is, to the well-known sea-bathing resort of Ventnor.[1] We set off in the morning, and had a delightful drive through rolling country, until all of a sudden we turned a small corner and beheld the sea, stretching out before us in all its breadth and glory. If you take a

---

1 A 'handsome modern town and rapidly improving seabathing place . . . Ventnor is now in high repute both as a fashionable summer watering place and as as winter residence for invalids . . . it is considered one of the most favourable places in England for consumptive patients, as it has less rain and damp than other places.'*

map of England and look for the Isle of Wight, Osborne lies on the coast opposite Portsmouth; Ventnor, on the other hand, is quite on the opposite side, looking out towards the endless open sea. You will be able to get a general idea of the difference in scale. The coast at Ventnor is steep and rocky, and between the cliffs and high up on top of them a little town is built, all with flat roofs, quite in the Southern style. The air there is very soft and mild, and one feels as if transported into the South. The sea-shore is delightfully attractive, not a tree, not a blade of grass, not a flower, only small pebbles of the same sort as those from Blackgang which I sent you, but bigger, which cover the endless stretch of beach at ebbtide, glittering and (I only wish I could see Georg burrowing in the sand on such a beach!) sparkling in the sunshine like treasures in a fairy-tale; and then the tall steep cliffs and the glorious sea with its foaming waves. The sea here is very rough even in the clearest weather. Unfortunately our time was too short to linger for long on this enchanting sea-shore; our drive home took two hours. I picked up many pebbles, and I mean to send you some of them some time. If only you could look just once at this little town – oh! a single glance would be enough to make an everlasting impression! Unfortunately this lovely spot is a place of much sadness, for it is said of it that people go there to die. The air is so mild, even in the middle of winter, that there could be no better place for people with chest diseases. So only too often people are sent there who have already been given up for lost, and who can thus only go on living there for a few weeks or months. If – as also often happens – the invalids go there in good time, however, it is said that many benefit from staying there. There are always many visitors there as well who go simply for pleasure or to take sea-baths, but only from September onwards, because it is apparently too hot there in summer for healthy people. We thought the sun was trying to thrust a dagger through us for the few hours that we spent there. We drove most of the way home along the sea, which was an unforgettably lovely drive; never, never can I say enough of the enchantment and power of the sea with its ceaseless waves. Many beautiful stones are found here, which are used for brooches and all kinds of things. To burrow about on the shore and dig out the treasures of the sea-goddess is a beguiling pastime for mind and fantasy, in which one could indulge all day long in perfect silence. Adieu!

Letter 11

SCOTLAND

1856

Once more the Court was on the move. Among the dressers, it was Frieda's turn to leave Osborne first, with the heavy luggage. The Queen came on to Buckingham Palace later in the day. The next morning, 28 August 1856, at the Great Northern Railway Station, King's Cross, one observer noted that only a few moments sufficed to transfer what he coyly called 'the travelling appendages'* into the train. Everything would have been ready for the train to pull out as soon as the Queen arrived with her escort of Light Cavalry. If Frieda realised that the author of Uncle Tom's Cabin, Harriet Beecher Stowe, was waiting to meet the Queen on the platform (carpeted for Her Majesty with crimson cloth) she makes no mention of it.

The train consisted of the royal saloon carriage, a saloon for the princesses, a saloon for Prince Alfred; two family carriages, one for the ladies and one for the gentlemen of the suite; three first-class carriages for servants, pages, attendants and the directors of the railway company; two carriage trucks; two break vans, and an engine bearing the royal insignia, specially used on the Great Northern for the conveyance of the court, decorated with flowers and a couple of banners. The royal saloon was 'copiously supplied' with maps and charts of the line of the railway, and copies of the daily newspapers. The 399-mile rail journey to Edinburgh took the royal train via Huntingdon (where a loyal address was handed in through the window to Her Majesty), Grantham, Doncaster and York, where the royal party lunched at the station. The North Eastern Railway took the train from York to Berwick, and the North British Railway from Berwick to Edinburgh.*

*I*t was a cloudy day, with quite a strong wind blowing, when we left Osborne, on 27 August 1856 at six o'clock in the morning. I was to go ahead, accompanied only by Mary, Mr Cart and a manservant. We had the steamer all to ourselves, and so we chose the best places. When the boat began to pitch I was very nervous, but it soon became quite calm, and we sailed away quietly and safely, in a pleasant, refreshing morning breeze. It was very still; there was scarcely a ship and nothing else to be seen. That strange grey veil which often covers the landscape in the morning when there is no sun had spread itself over the sea, and gave the waves a curious, sombre look which contrasted strangely with their lively motion. But how dead and monotonous this description seems, my friends: you have never seen the beguiling dance of the waves over the sea, and cannot picture it to yourselves.

We arrived in Southampton an hour before the train left, and made use of this time to go for a walk along the shore. The sea-shore at Southampton is not particularly beautiful, there is so much shipbuilding and all kinds of business being carried on. It looked very dirty and untidy, even more so because it was eight o'clock, and too early for work to have started. I walked, as I always love to do, down by the sea as close to the water as possible, and amused myself watching the waves. The sky cleared, and I saw the sun's cheerful morning greeting to the sea before I had to leave.

We travelled to London on the train without any adventures or noteworthy happenings, and when we arrived, there was plenty to do in preparation for the next stage of our journey next morning at eight o'clock. I said goodbye to my last and only friend and companion on my way to Scotland; Sophie was leaving for Germany[1] the following day. Now for the first time I was quite alone in the great wide world; not a single close friend was near me any more. This is such an overwhelmingly painful feeling that the very severity of one's loss itself gives one the strength to bear it. I saw her leave with unbearable yearning, and gave her countless messages for all of you; my whole inner life went with her. I had leisure to reflect on this, for the train travelled on without stopping for a moment until two o'clock, when

[1] Sophie was not, as Frieda's agonies suggest, leaving for ever.

we got out for a meal (although in the carriage on the way we ate all kinds of things).

Our journey continued until seven o'clock in the evening. At several stations which we passed there were bands playing, and at all there were crowds of people, relative to the size of each place. This amuses me each time I see it: the endless curious, enthusiastic faces, the shouts of 'Hurrah!' and the waving of handkerchiefs.

Arriving in Edinburgh, we drove at once to the dark old Palace of Holyrood.[1] It was still broad daylight, and so here too we had the opportunity of admiring the inquisitive faces of the population, who seemed to have turned out to a man. We were favoured with a few deep curtsies from old ladies, because there was a royal coat-of-arms on our carriage, and we received these attentions with a gracious acknowledgement. The younger generation is less respectful, and they stared at our carriage and at us quite openly, and showed no sign of wanting to greet us. I do not know whether I should consider our generation too wise and sophisticated to salute an inanimate object like a carriage; or should I simply say that manners have become more relaxed. I am too prejudiced in this respect, so you must decide, as I enjoyed these curtsies so much that I should gladly have been curtsied to by everyone. We laughed so heartily about it at Holyrood, and I imitated these obeisances when we were in the Queen's ante-room, which made the old lady who lives at Holyrood as a kind of housekeeper and who is so overcome with awe when the Queen comes that she can only stammer instead of speaking, quite beside herself at the sight of us performing such antics. But by dint of a few civilities, which in her eyes were an immense honour, coming from me, the Queen's dresser, I was soon able to win her over so completely that I never had to fear that the good old lady would think me lacking in respect towards her earthly gods.

The few permanent inhabitants of Holyrood, that is to say the people of greater or lesser importance needed to look after it, have something curious and old-fashioned about them that gives one the impression that they are as old as these strange old walls they live in. No doubt these peculiar surroundings exercise a peculiar magic on

---

[1] *See* p. 137.

the people who inhabit them. They seem to me to be the type of whom Gotthelf[1] says, 'They are like cats, they are more attached to the place than to the inhabitants'.

The evening was taken up with duties, and a hearty supper: travelling gives one a good appetite, and since I began to eat well on journeys I find I can bear them much better. I arranged as much as I could for the following day, the whole of which we were to spend in Edinburgh, in order to be able to save time during the day and to go out. The next morning we were greeted by a clear sky and bright sunshine: it was the sunniest day we had had for a long time. The Queen was kind enough to remember at once that I had not yet seen Edinburgh, and she allowed me to go out in the morning and in the afternoon for as long as she herself was out, and to see as much as possible.[2]

The morning I spent in a lovely drive along the foot of a hill, where one has the most perfect views over the beautiful old city. What shall I tell you about Edinburgh? Edinburgh is lovelier and more striking than any place I have ever seen. Without being as grand as London or as elegant and gay as Paris, Edinburgh is far superior to both. Scotland has something so simple and magnificent in its natural beauties that it cannot be compared with anywhere else. Edinburgh has a glorious position: on one side wild rocky mountains, on the other the sea, and in the distance, picturesque hills and charming valleys. All this one sees almost in one glance, and in the midst of it lies the city, built on hills, so that each part of it affords a separate and delightful picture. The old and new towns are joined by an enormous bridge[3] which soars high above the roofs of the low-lying quarters. For the city is built chiefly on two hills, apart from a few other, smaller hills, so that this bridge makes communication between the two main parts of the city much easier, as one does not have to go down and then climb up again. I only wish, my dear friends, that I could grant you a single look at this wonderful city. In the last two

1 Jeremias Gotthelf was the pseudonym of Albert Bitzius (1797–1854), a Swiss pastor and author, noted chiefly for his moralising novels illustrating the home life of the Bernese peasantry.
2 The Queen drove round the city in the morning 'Great crowds out, – all, very friendly and very noisy'. At 4 p.m. she went on 'a long and very pretty' expedition to the ruins of Craigmillar Castle.*
3 North Bridge; founded 1763, widened 1876, demolished and replaced 1896–7.

years I have seen countless beautiful things, and although everything interests me deeply, even the smallest things, and I have certainly not lost my sense of delight at a tiny flower or a clear brook, nevertheless the stupefaction that seizes one at the first sight of something magnificent gradually lessens, that I can feel. One can admire, one can be delighted, enthusiastic, or profoundly moved; but to be transfixed with amazement is no longer in one's power; it seems no longer possible to have that involuntary reaction at the sight of something astonishing. But Edinburgh made me speechless with delight. We drove through part of the city, and on the way back stopped to take a closer look at Sir Walter Scott's Monument.[1] It stands in a large open square with gardens all around. It is a splendid, very beautiful memorial, immensely tall, like a kind of shrine, with Sir Walter Scott seated in the centre, a book on his knees and a pen in his hand, his head bent, with an expression of profound calm and gentle gravity. The whole monument is very skilfully and artistically modelled, with arabesques and figures representing characters in his works. But Sir Walter Scott needs no stone monument in order to live on in our memory: his characters come to life for anyone who has travelled in Scotland. I declare freely and openly to all whom I have often heard describing his novels as tedious and rambling, that they have failed to understand and absorb the profound truth, the pure, natural poetry of his language. He who can write in such a way that his whole story comes to life as soon as one breathes the air in which it was written, is indeed great, immortal! I respect my dear mother much more for having always admired Sir Walter Scott so much, since I have been in Scotland, and I only wish that she could once see Edinburgh, with its dread dungeon,[2] as her just reward!

Before dinner I snatched a few more moments to make a little sketch of the old Chapel in Holyrood, at which Mary Stuart was married to Darnley.[3] This gave me much pleasure, although it was

[1] In Princes Street Gardens, in the form of an elaborate Gothic steeple, all pinnacles and crockets. Designed by George Kemp in 1840 and completed 1846.
[2] Frieda uses a somewhat literary turn of phrase in German, '*Edinburg mit seinem festen Kerker*'. She may have in mind the Heart of Midlothian, the name given to the city's old jail or tolbooth in which Scott set the opening of his novel *The Heart of Midlothian*.
[3] Her second husband, on 29 July 1565.

but a brief and fleeting moment, and I hope I shall be able to show it to all of you soon.

After dinner, to my great joy, I saw Frau Hähnisch for a few moments: she lives in Edinburgh. We spoke at length about Karlsruhe and its inhabitants. There we sat, the two of us, in the heart of glorious Edinburgh, in the lovely old Royal Palace, and praised above all else our cosy old town with its parallel streets and its *very interesting* buildings, such as the Mint, the church etc. etc. (the contents of the former are, no doubt, unsurpassable). In the afternoon we drove first to a churchyard, quite far away, to visit the grave of my unfortunate predecessor, Fräulein Bonanomi. It was a lovely drive; the churchyard is in a beautiful spot, and her grave was marked with a simple, pleasing tombstone, and flowers.[1] I drew it for Sophie. She has found a peaceful resting-place, so far from her homeland. Next morning, as we left the palace in the grey light of early dawn, I could not help thinking constantly of her. It must have been on just such a morning, exactly two years ago, that she was left behind, poor creature, all alone and ill. The band was playing a melancholy Scottish folk-song, 'Annie Laurie', and the notes of this song were the last echoes she heard of the presence of the Queen and her suite. The next evening she was dead.

But now we wanted first to see the famous old Castle[2] that stands on a height, and yet in the middle of the city. The view from up there is wonderful and full of contrasts. The Castle itself is built on an enormous and massive scale. All the historical memories connected with it were explained to us in great detail, but I cannot repeat them here, and they would sound dead to you, in any case. But I shall always remember it with the liveliest wish to see it again. Afterwards we went for one more drive from one end of the city to the other, which we enjoyed immensely, for the entire populace was in the streets, dressed in their best, and on the lookout everywhere, as if they would never tire of staring, lest they miss the long-awaited moment when the Queen passed by. The Queen had not been in Edinburgh

[1] In the grandest and most expensive avenue in the relatively new Rosebank Cemetery, opened 1846. The headstone, of polished granite surmounted with a draped funereal urn, reads: 'Sacred to the memory of Miss Ida Bonanomi, the faithful and highly esteemed dresser of Queen Victoria, who departed this life Octr 15th 1854, in the 37th year of her age. Beloved and respected by all who knew her. This stone had been placed by Queen Victoria as a mark of her regard.'
[2] Edinburgh Castle.

for several years, except to spend the night, and so everyone was delighted and curious to see her. The streets were decorated, and Herr Hähnisch told me he had never before seen the city so cheerful and lively. We looked around in all directions, and were ourselves stared at by the idle young men in the streets, and gazed at from the windows lined with faces, which sometimes turned to watch us until something more interesting came along. We had given orders to be driven very slowly (of course we had an open carriage) so that we could see everything. The beautiful city, and the amusing scenes which often met our eyes, put me into such a happy mood that I could not restrain myself from making various comments which made us all burst out laughing so much that we could hardly preserve the decent composure required when one is out in the streets; but soon we had to tear ourselves away from this merry scene, for it was time to return, which we did without delay. There was plenty of work to do until late at night, in order to be ready for the journey next morning.

The court travelled on to Balmoral by the alternative route to that which Frieda and the Messenger had used the previous year. From the private station of St Margaret's, the Edinburgh and Glasgow Company took the royal train to Stirling, where the engines were changed for those of the Scottish Central. The Queen went via Perth to Aberdeen, where she passed onto the Deeside Railway as far as Banchory. The entire rail journey from London was 576 miles, and she had been the responsibility of six railway companies in turn along the way.

The carriages ordered to be ready at Banchory station at 2.40 p.m. on 30 August consisted of five travelling landaus and fours; a charabanc and pair; a small fourgon and pair for loose luggage. Four horses were also required for the dressers' coach; four horses for the Queen's fourgon, or luggage van; and a pair of horses for Prince Albert's fourgon.* The dressers' coach, fourgons, and three vans had, as last year, been sent to Aberdeen by steamer.*

Eighteen fifty-six was a disastrously wet year and today was no exception; the Queen noted in her Journal for 30 August that they had had to close the carriages. She went on, 'Got to Balmoral at 7. The Tower is now finished, as well as all the offices and the poor old house has disappeared. The whole has a *very fine effect. No-one but ourselves to dinner . . . our house is really lovely and the rooms so very pretty.' She rather enjoyed the business of arrival: 'all was bustle and unpacking, the good Highlanders carrying about the things',* and later recalled fondly how 'The first morning after our arrival we generally had to unpack'.* Frieda did not experience a similar enthusiasm.*

———

I had very little time to sleep that night: long before daybreak I had to be ready again; then came another train journey, from eight o'clock until four, with a mere twenty minutes' stop for dinner; and from four until seven we travelled by carriage through the mountains. Unfortunately it rained so hard during the last part of the day that one could not enjoy the landscape at all. When at last we arrived I was dead tired; but we could not think of resting for one moment. To arrive like that at a house where one's only welcome is from endless boxes with still more endless contents to unpack, is dreadful beyond description. I cannot tell you how glad I was when I could at last close my tired eyes, late that night. After a few days I had put everything in order, and the glorious Scottish air and the delightful view of the lovely mountains had strengthened me wonderfully; my fatigue had vanished and given way to a cheerful contentment at being in the mountains.

Now I began to go for walks in the hills in my free hours, with great energy and enjoyment. I made all kinds of sketches, which were always improved by the thought that I would be able to show them to you some day.

My first drive was to the Garrawalt Falls, the great waterfall of which I told you last year. I was entranced by it again, and I made use of a quarter of an hour's free time to draw a sketch of the upper part of it, which will give you some idea of it (some day). Unfortunately, however, we could not simply stop anywhere we pleased, because as always our every minute was numbered. Another time we drove to the Pass by Ballater, the cliff road which I also visited last year. If that first surprise of novelty is somewhat reduced, when one visits a place of natural beauty for the second time, another, almost more delightful feeling takes its place, as if one were greeting a dear acquaintance, for when a magnificent natural scene makes a deep impression on us, a longing to see it again remains with us, even when we are far away, and the fulfilment of this longing brings great happiness. I also sketched the Pass this time. I have become extraordinarily bold in this way: the conviction that I shall never have another chance has given me the strength and courage to think ten minutes long enough to capture at least something, and I hope it will make it easier for you to imagine. The dear, pretty little town of Ballater looked so quiet and peaceful in the lovely valley; the sun sank slowly in a magnificent glow behind the mountains, and peace descended on the landscape and filled my heart.

On the way home we sang together: a Frenchman, an Englishman, a Belgian woman and I. Such glorious harmony – at one moment it was '*les beaux yeux bleus de ma belle Jeannette*', the next 'My heart is in the Highlands', or '*Von meinen Bergen muss ich scheiden*', which rang out the clearest. Thus we arrived back at the Castle just in time to resume our duties again as quick as lightning.

Another interesting expedition was to Braemar Castle,[1] where a popular festival, the 'Gathering', was being held – a relic of those old rallies of the Scots in their mountains of which Sir Walter Scott and others tell. Braemar Castle is very ancient, and was famous and important at the time of the Scottish Rebellions; a battle was fought very near it, and it is said that various Scottish noblemen lie buried here, having fallen in the battle. The site of the Castle is very attractive and open. The Castle itself is ancient and therefore interesting: you shall see a faithful sketch of that too, in my book. A broad, open area in front of the Castle was set aside for the usual games and dancing, and on a small bank there were seats for the Queen and her suite, for she attends the festival every year.[2] The other spectators, whether on

[1] Strategically placed at the centre of communications in the area, the Castle was built by the Earl of Mar in 1628 and burnt out during the Rebellion of 1689. In 1715 the Earl of Mar raised the Jacobite standard in Braemar village. Defeat came swiftly. The second Jacobite attempt having been quashed in 1745, the government took Braemar Castle on a ninety-nine- year lease in 1748, the ruinous Castle was restored for occupation, and became a military garrison until 1797.

[2] The first Highland Games at Braemar were traditionally supposed to have been held by Malcolm Canmore in the eleventh century. At the time Frieda was watching, they were organised by the Braemar Highland Society, a benevolent society, but were subject to local disputes. The Queen wrote of that afternoon, 'After an early luncheon, we drove over to Braemar for the gathering which was not full, the Duffs not bringing over their men!'*

foot or in carriages, took up their allotted places. We remained sitting in our carriage and had a comfortable view over everything. The different clans, dressed in their own plaids, were grouped picturesquely together and danced and performed figures, a kind of gymnastic exercise which was accompanied by the loud shrilling of the bagpipes. The traditional costumes and characteristic arrangement of the whole spectacle made a most striking and attractive impression. It was a fascinating experience for me to watch this festival; but one could not quite banish the feeling that it was only a shadow of what it must once have been. Even if the destructive and yet creative spirit of the age cannot penetrate so rapidly and devastatingly into the mountains of Scotland, and the people can therefore preserve their nationality and individuality better than many others, the spirit of the age still filters slowly and steadily through and succeeds little by little in destroying the old ways. Even if vast stretches of the Highlands are almost impenetrable, innumerable roads have nevertheless been built, allowing strangers, and with them strangers' ways, to enter. The people begin to recognise their own great poverty and deprivation, and nearly all the younger people leave the mountains in order to earn themselves more than their mountains can yield, for the Scots are in general extremely intelligent and acquisitive.

One of the most important landowners in the area, on whose land Braemar Castle is situated and who has the keys of the Castle, although it belongs to the nation,[1] had prepared a great feast in the Castle. Within its great, rough-hewn walls, where before there had been barracks, he had had fir branches hung on the walls, and on one floor he held a banquet for himself and his company of ladies and gentlemen, while on another floor a second was given for the Highlanders. A servant of the house came to invite us in, to see the inside, and we went over the whole Castle. It looks remarkably old and austere inside, and there are only blocks of wood to sit on. We were obliged to take 'a drop of whisky' and eat Highland bread; the kitchen, which is underground, is so dreadful that the poor cooks seemed to me much to be pitied. An enormous fire burns in the

[1] It seems Frieda's information was a little out of date; by 1856 the castle had passed out of government hands, and belonged to the Laird of Invercauld.

middle, and around it hang huge joints of meat. All the smoke and fumes, which are no doubt expected to go out through a small slit window, instead remain inside, so that through the dense cloud of smoke only the naked flames can be seen leaping in the fireplace, with an occasional glimpse of a figure at work in the midst of the smoke. Of course only a meal of a very simple kind can be prepared there.

We could not remain for more than a very short time, for we had not been able to leave Balmoral until after the Queen, and had to be back before her. She left Braemar after the games were over and when the feast began. The celebrations are said to have continued until five o'clock in the morning: the people amused themselves the whole night through with eating, drinking and dancing. At ten o'clock the host's party withdrew to his residence nearby, and left the joys of food and drink to the Highlanders, who without doubt made the best of them.

Another time I visited a charmingly situated Scottish farm, first to enjoy the view, and then to acquaint myself a little better with the character of the local inhabitants. I was given a most hospitable welcome, and was shown over the whole establishment, a very orderly farm and farm-house. As I later discovered, these were very rich farmers I was visiting. The kitchen was especially simple and typical, and so I made a sketch of the fireplace as a souvenir. On leaving, I had to drink more 'Visky', with the whole family drinking out of the same glass. The next day my good opinion of the natives was somewhat reduced, however, as was my great satisfaction with my visit: I told my English companions at table about my visit, and did not omit to give due credit to the great hospitality of the Scots towards a complete stranger, for the English generally dislike the Scots. But instead of the effect my tale was intended to have, I was myself laughed at for my trustful nature; for the farmer, they told me, was an old fox who supplied butter and flour for the Royal Household, and often came to Balmoral. He knows all the Queen's people very well, and so never fails to pay them every attention. Although I could not deny that there must be some truth in this, I tried to point out other examples of occasions when we had been out driving, and had stopped to water the horses at small inns, where the people had always invited us in to try their whisky etc. But I was told that the Queen's horses and carriages were known far and wide, and that I would only truly be able to praise the hospitality of the Scots, and their good nature, if I travelled one day alone, and on my own account. No doubt that will never happen; but all the same I shall not stop thinking well of the Scots, and however much I find to praise in the English, I shall never admire their characteristic dislike of hearing others praised.

We went on a few pretty little drives to the little old town of Castleton, or to Abergeldie,[1] the Duchess of Kent's residence, or to Birkhall[2] and other small places. These drives were always in the afternoon when we had an hour or two free. We would always choose a place from which we could get back in time without exhausting our trusty steed too much. The wonderful, healthy air, the delightful light, the lovely views over and into the mountains, these were the greatest attractions of these little drives. Sometimes we were caught in quite a downpour; but we defied the rain, safely wrapped up in our plaids and waterproofs. Once we even had an adventure that could very easily have cost us our lives. The horse shied, and in doing so kicked over the traces, which got under its hooves, and this frightened and enraged the poor creature so, that it reared and struggled violently, breaking its reins and traces into pieces. Our coachman – who was nothing of the kind, but only an amateur, Monsieur Nestor,[3] *le coiffeur de Sa Majesté*, an experienced and *extremely* careful but not particularly *cuirassé* cavalier – was able to jump down in good time and hold the horse; but it had become so wild that he could not hold it for more than a few moments, which he at once realised, and told us to jump down as quickly as we could, which we three, Mary, Lydia[4] and I, did at once, quite nimbly and quickly and with good cheer, for we were not afraid, not realising what great danger we were in. The carriage was but an inch away

1 Neighbouring castle on the Dee leased by the Queen.

2 Property bought for the Prince of Wales in 1848, and rented out until his majority. One of the guests staying there in 1856 was Florence Nightingale.

3 Jean Nestor Tirard, hairdresser to Her Majesty since 1846, when he had taken over from his father-in-law, Monsieur Isidore Marchand. He also worked for the Queen's mother, the Duchess of Kent, and as the Queen's daughters grew up he did their hair also, so his salary was increased to £400 p.a. He retired from regular service in 1867, and died in 1888.

4 Lydia Greatorex, wardrobe maid since at least 1849. She left the Queen's employ in June 1857.*

from a rocky precipice. Mary and I unfastened the traces on either side, while Monsieur Nestor held the horse. It was so terrified that it was trembling all over. By walking it slowly and calmly up and down he succeeded in pacifying it; but there lay our beloved dog-cart, shattered. A little way off was a house, so Mary and Lydia hurried there to get help, that is to say, to try to get some ropes; Nestor and I stayed with the horse and dog-cart. The two girls set off cheerfully across country, but found themselves wading ankle-deep through a marsh, and became quite drenched. Meanwhile I tried with great expertise and prudence to gather together the pieces of reins and traces. It was then that I became aware for the first time of the deathly pale face of our cavalier, and asked him very anxiously whether he had been hurt. He could hardly speak, and said, 'Thank God, no', and thank God we were not hurt either; but his anxiety for us, as he knew what danger we were in, had thrown him into a cold fever. Later, on the many occasions when the incident was discussed and laughed over, he gave us a glowing testimonial for our excellent, brave and competent behaviour. He said that if any of us had begun caterwauling, as is so typical of the weaker sex, he would have given us all up for lost; he did not think he would have been able to do anything else, for '*Bon Dieu!*' he exclaimed, '*retourner à Balmoral sans une, deux ou vous toutes les trois, c'était impossible pour moi: je suis heureux que vous êtes si courageuses, Mesdames, mais j'ai appris que la responsabilité d'avoir la charge de trois dames et d'un cheval est trop pour un seul homme; pour le futur je ne prendrai que deux de vous et un autre monsieur, pour mon assistance, au cas d'un accident, mais je ne crois pas pour cette fois-ci qu'un Monsieur aurait été plus utile que vous.*' But now came the greatest embarrassment: in the house Mary and Lydia found no one but a poor, miserable, dirty, deaf old man, to whom they could hardly make clear what they wanted, and they realised in any case that he could not be of much help. An old iron chain was all they could find when they searched the hut. This they took without further ado, and gave the old man some money, whereupon he followed them willingly. Monsieur Nestor now investigated the damage, and the old man and I together held the horse, which meanwhile had become quite quiet. He was a little afraid, and so was I: he wanted to leave me holding the horse alone, and said, 'I am not at all accustomed to do such a thing.' 'Nor am I', was my reply, spoken with the deepest conviction. But needs must, and so we held on, while Mary laughed at us from a safe distance, and called us grooms of Her Majesty's horses. The whole scene made a very funny sight; for strangely enough all three of us (but not Monsieur Nestor) treated it all as an amusing adventure. Luckily – as otherwise I do not know how our adventure would have ended, for Monsieur Nestor knows very well how to tie a garland of flowers, but managing chains and reins was too much for his delicate hands – luckily, as I said, two strong men, workmen from Balmoral, came along the road towards us. One took charge of the horse, the other of the carriage, with such strength and skill that with the aid of a few ropes which they had with them, in a very short time they assured us the carriage could safely be used. But the horse was so absurdly frightened, for such a great big animal, that it refused to be harnessed again. Our two bold cavaliers knew how to manage that, and now the question was, would we dare get into the carriage again? Lydia said firmly, 'I shall certainly never get in'; Mary was doubtful, and I looked at the time and reached the conclusion that on foot – it was about an hour's walk from Balmoral – we could not get back in time. And in any case there was practically no firm ground to walk on; it was wet and muddy. As the men thought it quite safe and were willing to lead the horse for a while, I decided to get into the carriage; the two others then followed suit after all, and so we arrived home quite safe and sound and in good heart. Had not my handkerchief, which was holding together a broken rein with a large white knob on the horse's back, aroused the suspicion of the groom who took hold of the horse on our arrival, no one would have noticed from our demeanour that we had been in danger of our lives. Of course the incident was much talked and laughed over after that. At first, of course, everyone was simply relieved that it had turned out so well. The Queen was of the same opinion as Monsieur Nestor; she forbade us to go out in the dog-cart without two gentlemen. But later, when the shock was over, the Dog-Cart Accident became a constant source of laughter and teasing at table, and as Monsieur Nestor always took such a delight in teasing others, he was now mercilessly teased himself. We ladies, however, always took his part, and called him our cavalier. As a result he was always called 'the

Ladies' Man', and at every opportunity people said 'What clever coachmen Frenchmen are'. They said he had been too afraid to drive home alone, and so he had forced us to get into the carriage again after the accident, which we, however, completely disproved, as soon as the dog-cart was repaired, by refusing all other coachmen and insisting that henceforth we would only drive with Monsieur Nestor.

These were my most memorable experiences at Balmoral this year, enriched with moments of greater or lesser delight, such as the view from a window in the evening by clear moonlight, or half-an-hour's stroll by the river in the morning etc. etc. Duties I had in plenty too, and in the evening, when I was tired, I was sometimes overwhelmed by a feeling of sadness at the thought of having lost, in Sophie, the last kindred spirit anywhere near. But the feeling passed quickly; and if it persisted, I turned to my well-tried remedies, and they worked at once. Often in the evenings I derived much pleasure from reading the poems which Byron wrote in memory of Scotland and of his youth, which he spent not far from Balmoral.[1] He sings the praises of the highest mountain in the region, the sight of which has often delighted and enthralled me, so beautifully that I learned the poem by heart, and have copied it out for that purpose. I enclose it with this, as belonging to this account, and my friends who know English can enjoy reading it and tell the others what it says. When Lochnagar is before one's eyes, when one wanders in the dark valley at its foot, every line of this fine poem speaks vividly to one's heart; and more than once on my solitary walks I have cried out with the deepest conviction, 'England! Thy beauties are tame and domestic etc'.

I also read, while I was in Scotland, *The Lamplighter*,[2] a simple tale

---

[1] George Gordon, Lord Byron (1788–1824) was sent, as he put it, into the Highlands about Invercauld and Braemar in 1795–6, to recuperate after scarlet fever. He always entertained romantic dreams of his Scottish childhood and in 1806 recollected his Highland sojourn in 'Lachin Y Gair', which Frieda quotes, in which he celebrates the mountain:

> England! Thy beauties are tame and domestic,
> To one who has roved on the mountains afar;
> Oh! for the crags that are wild and majestic,
> The steep, frowning glories of dark Loch na Garr

[2] A book of this title, by Miss Maria Susanna Cummins, was first published in England in 1854, and went into many editions. A tale of rags to riches through virtue. The lamplighter, Trueman Flint, rescues little Gerty from the horrors of orphaned life and she ultimately, with many moral signposts along the way, achieves happiness and wealth – finds her long-lost father and marries her childhood sweetheart.

with many shortcomings and absurdities, but with an appealing sincerity of feeling, a profound moral, and many very charming descriptions of characters, so that it kept me quite absorbed for a considerable time, and I have become the richer by a quantity of good intentions since reading it. But what are intentions? How few we fulfil! I should like to advise you all to read this book, for I am certain that in spite of our many differences of character and attitude, we enjoy such harmony of spirit that a book which absorbed, moved and amused me could not displease you.

I have just realised that I have forgotten to mention one of my loveliest and most important expeditions, to the 'Linn of the Dee'. This is the source of the River Dee, many miles away from Balmoral. We left the house at two o'clock, and did not return until seven o'clock in the evening, and we had to go in a carriage with two horses, for our dog-cart was too light for such a long expedition. The road is difficult and we had to change horses twice. As most of our other expeditions had been away to the right of the Dee, I knew only a small part of this side, and was quite enchanted with the beauty of the river banks. Our drive followed the river the whole way. High rocky cliffs, stretches of beautiful pine and fir woods with small cottages or farms here or there, were all that there was to see, but together they formed a most delightfully composed, varied picture, and one could not imagine anything prettier. The highest mountain peaks were covered with snow, and above them the sky was clear and glowing. The river became broader and calmer at first, but then ever narrower and rushing with ever greater force. The nearer we came to our goal, the prettier and more charming the landscape became. It was plain that we were approaching some habitation, and soon a pretty little house came into view, close to the river, and just then a very beautiful, lively looking young lady with a cheerful friendly expression passed us, driving her own carriage. It was Lady Agnes Duff, a close relation of Miss Mary Duff, Byron's first love: when he was still a boy and lived in these mountains, Mary Duff, a grown girl, older than he, was his frequent companion in his many wanderings, and a few lovely poems from that time are addressed to her, as is the beautiful 'Well! Thou art happy', which was written after he saw her again later in Edinburgh, when she was married.[1] The Duff family owns much land on the Dee, and its source is also on their property. We left our carriage near the farmhouse, and had to walk through a small coppice which was quite dark; only a loud roaring betrayed the proximity of our goal. Suddenly we emerged from the trees and were confronted by an enormous cliff, from the middle of which the water cascaded in a snow-white foaming stream, forming a broad waterfall. A bridge crosses above it, which gives the scene an even more picturesque air, and we gazed in delight at the scale and strength of Nature here. I also made a sketch which I am very pleased with. It is very wet and damp everywhere – the spray flies out so far that one is quite drenched. The rocks are completely smooth, like ice, from the action of the water; and I again gave my philistine companions something of a fright by taking a delight in running about on them. But I am not frivolous, I assure you, and I am no mountain goat. We could not stay long; we had a light meal in the open air – it was very cold, and so we drank whisky. On the way home yet another pleasure was in store for us, a surprise prepared for us by our companions. We were told to get out of the carriage, which was kept waiting, and after a short, pretty walk we came to the Falls of Corriemulzie, which are truly magical. The earth there is so damp and rich and the vegetation is so luxuriant, that everything is veiled in green, with ivy, ferns and climbing plants. The water falls from a very great height, pouring down not out of the rock, but apparently from a tangle of foliage, like pearls and dust. This waterfall is the prettiest and most romantic I have ever seen. I also saw the Falls of the Muick, another time; these are quite different again from all the others, enormously wide and interrupted by boulders, while below on the river-bed there is such a bubbling and splashing of water that one feels lured, enticed to plunge into its depths, where joy and happiness seem to reside. Water, whether it is the sea or a river, always conceals a mysterious magic in its depths, and I confess that if

[1] It is hardly surprising that Frieda has confused several of the Marys in the young life of the legendary lover. 'When I roved a young Highlander' is probably the only poem of several to 'Mary' which clearly refers to Mary Duff. She and Byron, distant cousins, were both eight when they met briefly in Aberdeen and he fell in love with her. He was devastated when, at sixteen, he was told of her marriage, but shortly fell hopelessly in love with the eighteen-year-old Mary Chaworth. She too married, and 'Well! Thou art happy', was written on seeing her for the first time since her marriage.

there is anything in fairy-tales which I can believe in, it is the nymphs and their palaces of crystal under the water.

On October 15th we left, in the morning. The first day as far as Edinburgh, the second to Windsor, the same way as we had come.[1] The journey was very tiring. I read the whole day in the carriage, each day a volume of *The Counts of Harten*. This held my interest completely; it was raining, and there was little that was new to look at outside. In Windsor I found Sophie: the endless boxes were unpacked with much gossip and many tales of Karlsruhe, and in the evening hours there were questions to be asked and answers to be given until late at night. My experiences in Scotland were intertwined with news of you, my dear friends! Oh, may our lives, near or far, remain closely linked for many years to come! Adieu!

---

[1] Two very long days: the Queen left Balmoral at 8.30 a.m., arriving at Edinburgh at 6.30. She left Edinburgh the following morning at 7.30 a.m., arriving at Windsor at 7.45 p.m.* Arrangements on the royal train were comparable to those on the outward journey.

Letter 12

SCOTLAND

1857

A year has passed; once again it is autumn and time for Balmoral. In the meantime, on 14 April 1857, the Queen was safely delivered of her ninth child, Princess Beatrice, while preparations were in hand for the wedding of the Princess Royal. In June the thorny question of her husband's rank was finally settled as the Queen created him Prince Consort. Hideous reports of the Mutiny began to come in from India. The most important event in Frieda's life, however, was that she had been back to Karlsruhe. There is no evidence as to how long she was away, but if she was allowed as long as Sophie had had the year before (from 29 August to a date shortly before the Queen's return to Windsor on 16 October) then we could assume that Frieda too had been away for the best part of six weeks, and had left England about 18 July, when the Queen went to Osborne.

> *The life of yesterday returns today*
> *And Phantasy alone is ever young.[1]*

So I have been back to Scotland too!
I had only arrived in the Isle of Wight, at Osborne, from Germany three days earlier, when we left the island, on a very hot, beautiful morning.[2] The sea was so clear, the sky so blue, and the landscape so bright and peaceful. This was the first quiet moment, since my return, when I could really think back over my most recent activities, and I sat on the deck, as quiet and motionless as the sea

---

[1] Frieda's epigraph is taken from Schiller's poem on a subject very much after her own heart, 'To my Friends'.
[2] 27 August 1857.

beneath me, and thought of you. After an hour we landed in Portsmouth, where a Scottish regiment (Highlanders) was drawn up. They were to sail for India in a few days, although they had not long returned from the Crimea, where they had suffered considerable losses. They paraded before the Queen – they were all fresh, strong young men – God knows how many of them will be sacrificed in this terrible conflict,[1] or have perhaps already fallen victim to the effects of the climate. It takes almost four months for them to reach the place they are posted to, so they will only be approaching it now.[2] I have rarely been as strangely and sadly moved by anything as I have been by the sight of regiments parading for the last time before their Queen as they leave for the battlefield. I saw all the regiments which went to the Crimea. Oh! but I saw the remainder return too, and what a contrast! If death on the battlefield were not in itself something great and honourable, the sight of an army departing would be heart-rending indeed; but the thought of a hero's death at least adds something uplifting and softening to the pain. Here again I saw how rarely one's youthful impressions fade (as if my present impressions were those of old age!): the description in Rellstab's *1812*[3] of the soldiers marching out of Warsaw imprinted itself so strongly on my memory years ago that I could not help being constantly reminded of it at the departure of the soldiers, however different that departure was from those I saw!

Two hours later we arrived in London by train, and were back in gloomy Buckingham Palace. We stopped there only for a brief night's rest, and then it was on to Edinburgh the next day.[4] There is no question that travelling by railway can hold no charms for someone who has rattled all the way from Cologne[5] to London only a few days

---

[1] The Indian Mutiny.

[2] This remark indicates that Frieda is writing in December.

[3] Ludwig Rellstab (1799–1860), artillery officer turned author and journalist. His historical novel, *1812*, published in 1834, was his most successful work.

[4] The Court Circular assured its readership that all the 'usual regulations' for the royal train had been adopted. The line and stations were kept clear half an hour before the train was due, and all traffic stopped until the royal engine and the pilot engine following had passed. The train was accompanied by its own fitters, lampmen and greasers, and had a telegraph officer on board. At the stations where it was timed to stop, the public were kept within barriers on the down platform, so as to prevent their crowding upon the royal carriages, while those who were admitted to the up side were confined to the platform and not allowed upon the line.*

[5] Presumably Frieda had come down the Rhine by steamer from Karlsruhe.

before; and so I remained in a state where my body simply endured the journey while my mind was lost in thought, until Edinburgh, whose ancient streets received us in the twilight and brought us to Holyrood, that ever solemn, forbidding Palace.

Here too the night's rest was all too short, alas, and before eight o'clock the busy wheels of the railway carriage had set us in motion again. We were to take a different route from the usual one this time, for the last part of our journey; that is to say, we were to cross the mountains the same way that I had gone two years earlier with the Courier, partly by night and partly by the light of dawn, when I travelled up alone after the others.[1] I do not know whether you still remember that story; at any rate I was very happy to travel through this magnificent region again by day.

It was a hot, wonderful day, and everything glowed in the bright daylight. The mountains, otherwise bare, were covered with beautiful heather at the height of its flowering. Again we travelled on for mile after mile, from posthouse to posthouse, without meeting a single living soul. But this time our travelling party, consisting of nine carriages a charabanc and a few fourgons, brought life enough with it, except that it often happened that one was alone for a time and lost sight of the others. But that was nothing like the solitude of last time.[2]

When we reached the Devil's Elbow we got out of our carriages again and climbed this steep mountain on foot. That was a sight! The sun was just going down, and sank with such magnificence, such calm and majesty, between the mighty mountains which threw deep, dark shadows into the abyss on either side, while their summits glowed the fieriest red. Oh! If you could only draw a single breath of that fresh mountain air! Although it was hot, there was a freshness, indeed one would say a chill in the air if it were not a contradiction, which gave

[1] Recounted in Letter 8.

[2] They left Holyrood at 9.30 and arrived at Blairgowrie at 12.30, where three landaus and fours and a sociable and pair were ordered to be waiting for Her Majesty, Royal Family and suite; besides a charabanc and pair 'for pages etc.', a new four-wheel dog-cart and horse, a no. 5 van and pair for loose luggage, and four horses for the dressers' coach.* 'Very hot sun,' wrote the Queen in her Journal, 'but fresh air, and the country quite beautiful. The road very tedious.' With fresh horses required at each stage, the combined resources of three postmasters were necessary to convey the Queen over the mountains. Messrs Mclaren and Moon's horses took the cortège from Blairgowrie to Percy to the Spittal of Glenshee, which the Queen reached by three o'clock, and there stopped for lunch. Mr Grant's horses took them to Braemar and Mr George Clarke's from Braemar to Balmoral.*

one new life, rather in the way that a glass of champagne fresh from the ice is at once fiery and cooling. There is nothing more appropriate to compare it to. My vital forces were at their lowest ebb physically, and only the powerful effect of Nature could arouse me and banish my desire to lie down and fall asleep for ever. No one can imagine the effect which travelling for days by train has on one; I felt as if my limbs had been broken on the wheel, and on top of that I felt sick and dizzy from riding in a carriage immediately afterwards. Not an enviable state to be in! One consolation was left to me: we were going farther and farther away from all railways, which were the bane of my life at that time, and the thought of the impossibility of hearing a steam whistle for the next six weeks was delightful to me.

We reached Balmoral at half past eight;[1] it was a Saturday evening. After the usual exhausting uproar of unpacking we went to bed, and the next morning I awoke as from a dream, for I had the beautiful mountains before my eyes again. After two days, when everything was quite in order, a new stillness seemed to come into my life, and I had time to take in the realisation that I had indeed seen my dear home again, and everything I love, ah yes! everything I live for, and had enjoyed a blissfully happy time, except that I had also known that I should have to leave it all again for a long time, without knowing when I would come back.

As the weather was extremely favourable, we went on many expeditions, and I went back to all the places I wrote to you about before. But if last year I saw and admired the various waterfalls in the rain and in storms, so that they were at their most wild and swollen, this year their waters were lower, but gilded with bright shafts of sunlight, so that it is difficult to say which is preferable.

I saw the charming little town of Ballater at sunset, and oh! how beautiful, how magical it looked – it was wonderful! I visited the lovely dark lake, Loch Muick, twice this year, but I never had time to reach the far shore to see my dear little girl. I hear she is quite well, however, and has a little brother now. I also spent a night with the Queen in the little house called Altnaguithasaich;[2] it was so cold

1 Much later than the Queen, who had arrived at seven.*
2 17 September 1857. The little shiel or mountain hut, which had been enlarged in 1849, had 'a charming little dining room, sitting room, bed-room and dressing-room, all *en-suite*' for Queen and Prince, with a room for the Lady in Waiting and a room for the dresser. There were huts behind for the kitchen and staff.* All through the 1850s, with the exception of 1855 and 1858, the Queen and Prince spent a night or two here every time they came to Balmoral.

there, and there was such a wind in the valley, you cannot imagine what it was like. My duties did not allow me to go far from the house that time; but I explored the immediate surroundings thoroughly: it is a mixture of wilderness and civilisation. A small garden has been made in the middle of an area of dark pines and rocks, with lovely flowers blooming in it. The little plants smiled sweetly at me; but it seemed strange and odd to see roses blooming amongst pines and heather. The rose, the symbol of love, penetrates even into the most isolated regions, as does its lovely meaning, delighting those who see them – few though they be – with its scent and wounding them with its thorns.

It is well worth spending a night in the mountains, for the utter silence, the black darkness, with from time to time the rustling of the tops of the pine trees and the muffled bleating and roaring of the red deer is curious and pleasing, provided of course that one has a roof over one's own head! I went out in a little boat on the lake, which looked black like a magic looking-glass, and Sir Walter Scott's beautiful poem 'The Lady of the Lake'[1] seemed to come to life before my mind's eye.

My chief expedition, and almost the only completely new one, was to Lochnagar,[2] the place I had longed to go to every time I was in Scotland. I left Balmoral at eleven o'clock in the morning, alone except for a servant and a Highlander to act as a guide. This time there was no one from the house who came with me, as on other expeditions, for most of them had already been up there, and were not anxious to face the ardours of the climb a second time, while others lacked the courage to face it at all. I was very happy to go up, and with a good escort too, for the servant who went with me was one who had already been up many times with the Queen and knew the way thoroughly, as did my guide. We were all three on *horseback*. I was wearing thick woollen clothes, a quilted jacket (made from my old coat from home), a round brown straw hat against rain and sun, and my raincoat was strapped to my horse with Wilhelm Gastel's useful strap, for the sky was clear and the sun was shining. My guide had a thick plaid for me on his horse and the servant had a little basket

1 *See* p. 135.
2 3789 feet (1155 metres).

of provisions, and held my horse on a long rein, in case it decided to bolt with its experienced rider, for it is impossible to catch up with these creatures: as soon as one begins to chase another, it gallops all the faster. My noble Rosinante was, however, a gentle creature, and had no such evil intentions: she ambled along quite happily between my guides where the path was wide, and behind them on the narrow mountain paths. The first half-hour I kept my eyes on my horse's ears all the time, and watched the movements of its head, which seemed to me to threaten my downfall. But soon I found this as monotonous as it was useless, and I began to look around me, and enjoy the delightful scenery, the cool air and the pleasant ride. We rode for most of the time at a walking pace, on a narrow path which climbed all the time, and we could see our destination in front of us, sometimes in clear sunshine, sometimes wreathed in clouds. So it continued for about two and a half hours, a most cheerful and satisfying ride, until all at once the narrow path came to an end, and we had to ride over rough ground. We had to pick our way between stones two to three feet high, and I thought I would not be able to stay in the saddle, although the Scotsman had dismounted and given his horse to the servant to lead, while he led mine. Sometimes I thought my backbone would snap, I was jolted so much on my pony. I wanted to get off, and thought I would find it easier to walk, but my guide advised me against this as it would have taken too long; with one step my pony could get over a stone which I would have had to struggle to climb over. We continued thus for a brief hour, and then dismounted as we could not take the horses any further. A Highlander was waiting for us there; he had been sent in advance and stayed with the horses. We armed ourselves with the sticks he had ready for us, and continued our journey on foot. It was very steep: the guide went ahead and sought out the best places, then I followed, and the servant walked behind me. It began to get cold, and I tied a scarf over my round hat to hold it together. But in spite of the cold air one got as hot from climbing as in high summer. After half an hour we arrived at the lake, which lies almost at the summit of this great mountain, broad, deep and black between rocky cliffs which surpass all human imagination. The sight of this lake, so high up, is overwhelming, and it was as if I now grasped for the first time what rock is, what a wilderness is. The depth of it is precipitous and terrifying, the water black; no man has ever dared so much as to dip his hand into it, it is enclosed with such horrifyingly steep cliffs. The sun was no longer shining now, and it was dark, which gave the sight before us an even more uncanny air. We were not so very far from our goal now, and we pressed bravely on, although not without some effort. A rock only big enough for four people to stand on is the highest point, and when we were still a few steps away from it my guide poured some whisky into a little cup, for we were so overheated that we could not stand still in the strong cold wind without warming ourselves from within. He let me go ahead so that I should be the first to climb up, and as soon as I had set my foot on the top he handed me the cup, which I put to my lips with the words 'God save Queen Victoria'. The two others had also climbed up, and raised a cheer to the Queen.

The view that met my eyes there was *wonderful! magical, indescribable*. The sun emerged from the clouds and gave me – if only for a few minutes – a vision which I shall never forget. Then all at once everything was blotted out by a cloud, and there I stood on this towering mountain, enveloped in a damp grey mass in which I could not make out a single object, not even five paces away. My guide had spread out my plaid on the sheltered side. I wrapped myself up in my raincoat and lay down on the plaid, quite exhausted, but utterly delighted and satisfied. I kept hoping that the sun would break triumphantly through the clouds again, but in vain. My companions went to a nearby spring to fetch water, and so for about a quarter of an hour I was left alone, far away from the world, lying in a cloud on a mountain-top. They soon came back with some water; it was about three in the afternoon, and we now consumed with hearty appetites a meal of chicken, bread and wine. My guide, a true Scot, praised my stamina in walking, and said that there might well be many fine ladies in Britain who could ride better than I, but none could surpass me on foot, and he asked me whether all German ladies are as good at walking. He himself was not at all tired, in fact, and would on no account sit down, however often I invited him to do so; this is how respectful these people are, and how strong. The manservant did not sit down either. Both had often walked the whole way up before. I asked the Scotsman to sing me a national song, knowing that he was a good singer, and he willingly did so, in a very original way. Then I drank the health of my dear mother, and we all three drank a toast to 'absent friends'. We stayed up there for half an hour, and then we had to leave. There was no hope of having a second look at the view; it was getting darker and darker around us and we climbed down very cautiously. The lake and everything had disappeared, and we could not even risk going back towards that side, for the danger of falling down the precipice was too great, and it taught me how dangerous it is to travel in such regions without absolutely trustworthy guides. After a while it grew lighter, and we heard whistling, which was to guide us to the spot where our horses were waiting behind a rock to protect them from the wind. It is a strange feeling to go out walking in the clouds like that; I wish you could try it some time. We mounted our steeds and rode cheerfully on; but riding downhill is much more tiring, and the wily creatures knew that they were on their way home, and constantly tried to break into a trot, which my back could never have endured. The lovely view which had delighted me on the way up was enveloped in a grey gloom, and a fine drizzle was falling, which then grew heavier and heavier so that we found ourselves riding for about an hour and a half in pouring rain. But you must not think that that was a misfortune! oh no, it is nothing at all. My clothes kept me perfectly dry, and it did not in the least matter that my face was quite wet.

At half past seven in the evening we reached home safely; I was well satisfied with my day, and although I was tired, I was not as tired as I had expected. The next day, however, I felt so utterly exhausted that I should gladly have sat down in any chair to sleep. After a second night's rest I was quite recovered, and I am ready to ride up there again another year. It would have been an everlasting pity to have been at Balmoral without going up Lochnagar.

I made a few other less dramatic excursions on horseback with Sophie and Mary, which gave rise to much laughter and many an amusing comment, for it is too comic what a figure we three novices cut on our ponies. I made a few little sketches, and went for many a lovely walk by myself, while many charming drives and various visits to the cabins of the natives in the neighbourhood gave me much pleasure.

But all this passed, and the moment of our departure approached. We were to travel via Aberdeen this time, a route which was quite new to me. Our first day's journey took us to Haddo,[1] the country seat of Lord Aberdeen, fifty English miles away from Balmoral. We travelled by carriage. The weather was fine and the country we passed through most beautiful, in quite a different style from the region we had seen on our way to Balmoral. This region is flatter and more populated, less wild but extremely pretty.[2] The Queen had never been to this part before, which was why the people flocked towards the road from far and wide and stood on either side. There were welcoming ceremonies prepared for the Queen everywhere. Although I have often seen these, and far more brilliant ones, this was something new again, and characteristic of country people, and it gave me particular pleasure. Every little cabin along the way was decked out with as many flowers as possible, as were their inhabitants, of whom each and every one, down to the babes in arms, were standing at their front doors and curtsying and bowing again and again to each carriage that rolled by. We responded with great good cheer to every honour accorded to our carriage. The throngs of people of every sort who were at the posthouses were indescribable. In the villages and little towns through which we passed the people lined the roads with staves in their hands and ribbons on their hats. When we reached Lord Aberdeen's land four hundred farmers came to meet us on horseback. From Balmoral to Haddo we passed through eleven triumphal arches in all, of which some were really beautiful. Sophie, Mary and I were together in the carriage, which with four horses and two postilions in front and two men-servants behind, in spite of its weight, rolled along amazingly fast. It was such a pleasant, cheerful journey, and to my great good fortune I felt better than I had ever felt, and the driving did not upset me at all this time.[3]

[1] 14 October 1857. The Earl of Aberdeen had been Prime Minister from December 1852 to February 1855.

[2] The Queen's opinion of the country was equally decided; from Inverary 'the country became frightful, the hills totally disappearing – dreadfully flat, and nothing but stone walls . . . the air very different from the dear Highlands and one sadly missed the mountains.'*

[3] Frieda was travelling ahead of the Queen. At Inverary the carriages with royal attendants were reported to have passed through three-quarters of an hour before the Queen. The excitement of the day was captured by the *Banffshire Journal* on 20 October 1857: 'all were on tiptoe of expectation for the Sovereign. Suddenly there was a movement seen among the crowd on the hill . . . those on higher parts . . . got up a cheer . . . the carriage, drawn by four

After arriving at Haddo[1] we saw to our duties, had an excellent supper, and went to bed, to continue our journey next morning at eleven by carriage, travelling about ten more miles to Aberdeen. The country here is very well cultivated, and handsome farms of a size one rarely finds in other districts are to be seen on all sides. Here too we passed under many triumphal arches and were welcomed in the same way everywhere. In Aberdeen, however, a new and truly magnificent spectacle awaited us. Aberdeen is a large, rich town in Scotland in a beautiful setting and with very loyal people. Already a good way out of the town the road was lined with citizens, and the streets in the town were so richly decorated that we were quite amazed! One immensely long street was lined on both sides with platforms, which were adorned with crowds of charming and elegantly dressed ladies. The houses were lavishly bedecked with tartans, plaids etc. and flowers, and there were crowds of cheerful people everywhere. It looked quite lovely! Manchester[2] was miserable in comparison; the whole impression was more nearly to be compared with Paris. At the station there was a band and soldiers to receive us. There luncheon awaited us, after which we departed by train, leaving behind all these charming and cheerful scenes, and arriving feeling tired at Holyrood in the evening, only to continue our journey by train next day, from morning till night, reaching Windsor at about eight o'clock. But by the time you receive this letter we shall have set off again.

The Arrow and the Song[3]

I shot an arrow into the air,
It fell to earth; I knew not where
For so swiftly it flew, the sight
Could not follow it in its flight.

horses, dashed up, and was seen to contain nobody! It was the royal luggage van! About this time, a lady and gentleman, mere passing travellers, drove through in a gig, and the crowd most wickedly cheered them the whole way, persisting in affecting to believe they were of royal blood. Next came two or three more carriages, evidently a portion of the royal cortège, some containing servants, and others only luggage.'

1 which the Queen summarised as 'plain, about 100 years old, with 2 flights of steps leading up to it . . . Our rooms are small but comfortable, consisting of a sitting and dressing room for us each, and a bedroom. Ours and the children's rooms open into a lobby.'*

2 The Queen had visited the Art Treasures Exhibition in June 1857. She stayed at Worsley Hall and Frieda had time to sketch the view from one of the windows.

3 Frieda is quoting Henry Wadsworth Longfellow (1807–82).

I breathed a song into the air,
It fell to earth, I know not where;
For who has sight so keen and strong,
That it can follow the flight of song?

Long, long afterward, in an oak
I found the arrow still unbroke;
And the song, from beginning to end
I found again in the heart of a friend.

Postscript

After 1857, Frieda wrote no more of her letters or 'tales', as she once called them. None of the letters she undoubtedly continued to write to individual family members survives, and her subsequent career can only be pieced together from fragments and snippets.

In January 1858 the Princess Royal married Prince Frederick William of Prussia. Among Frieda's carefully preserved little paintings is one of a brooch in the form of three rings, the central ring set with six bluish stones, possibly crystals; the back of the painting is inscribed 'From Princess Royal as a remembrance of the days at her happy home give[n] before she left Windsor'. A second little painting depicts a gold brooch in the form of a ribbon decorated with a key pattern, a present from Prince Frederick William. The Princess Royal probably gave presents to many of the servants before she left home for good, but Frieda and the other dressers would undoubtedly have been very much involved in the preparations for the trousseau which she took to Berlin; 'I hear from all sides', wrote the Queen to her fledgling daughter, 'how much your dresses and toilettes are admired, so I take a good deal to myself as I took such great pains with your dresses.'*

The drawings in Frieda's sketchbooks provide further clues to the rest of her period of service with Queen Victoria. Two drawings of White Lodge Richmond Park are dated 16 May 1858, when the Queen spent the night there; Frieda was with the Queen at Osborne in May, and at Aldershot on 5 and 6 July. In August the Queen went to Berlin to see her daughter's new home for herself. The royal yacht left from Gravesend. Frieda drew the scene from on board; but alas for Frieda, she never improved as a sailor; the waters of the harbour are represented with an oily calm, but underneath is written, 'poor Miss Arnold! Sick to a degree, oh!!' The Queen stayed at Schloss Babelsberg in Potsdam; Frieda sat out in the park there and drew the topmost tower and the Havel in the background. She started a water-colour of the Schloss Berlin and also drew the Pfaueninsel, or Peacock Island, at Potsdam. The drawing is dated 18 August, which the Queen spent at Babelsberg, without making any long expedition during which Frieda could have escaped. In the evening the Queen took a boat to the island and with a large gathering of royalty took tea in the Palm House and sat in the balmy air enjoying the band playing. Either Frieda had the day off, or, more likely she was there with the Queen, invisible but to hand with her sketchbook, filling in the time until she was needed. Frieda accompanied the Queen to Balmoral in the autumn, commemorated by a single drawing 'New Bridge at Balmoral from Haran's farm 1 of Oktober 1858'.

In July 1859 came the parting of the ways. On the 11th the Queen travelled from Aldershot to Osborne; Frieda went in the opposite direction to London,* and on to Karlsruhe. She was receiving medical treatment there, for an unspecified condition, from 20 July to October; the bill, presented by Dr Adolph Polz, was paid by the Queen.* These weeks in Karlsruhe are a corresponding period of time to Sophie's home leave in 1856 and Frieda's own in 1857, but Frieda's term of service ended on 30 September 1859, the last date on which her name appears in the accounts of the Department of the Mistress of the Robes.* Her health may have been a reason for Frieda's departure, but it is more likely to have been that she had accepted a proposal of marriage from Ernst Wilhelm Müller, a publisher in Karlsruhe.

Frieda was in Karlsruhe on 7 October, when the Princess Royal saw her and her replacement, Emilie Dittweiler, and told the Queen 'I was very glad to see them',* but at the end of October Frieda went back to England, it seems to collect her belongings. The question of her return to Germany with her not inconsiderable luggage appears to have been the occasion of a brisk passage of arms between Frieda and the redoubtable Marianne Skerrett, who wrote that Miss Arnold 'still continues insistent for someone going with her and will not consent to her things being sent for her. She has got 4 or 5 great boxes or cases and I do not suppose she could look after these things herself but if she would [allow] them to be sent . . . she could then very well go alone. She is in a great hurry to go as it appears in Germany they cannot be married in advent, I do not know why and then she would have to wait till Christmas.'*

Frieda, never one to give in lightly, won her point. The Queen's courier, Joseph Julius Kanné, arranged Frieda's passport and visa, a cab to Waterloo Station, and no less than three cabs to go to London Bridge with her luggage. He paid her fare from London to Cologne (£3 9s. 6d.) and for the luggage to go from London to Cologne (£7 17s. 6d.).* It is not clear why only to Cologne and not all the way to Karlsruhe, perhaps because that was as far as the railways could take her (*see also* Letter 12, p. 191). Kanné accompanied her, as she had wished, as far as Calais.

On 28 November 1859 Frieda married Ernst Müller. He was fifteen years older than her, and had already buried two wives, the first, Wilhelmina Fecht, in 1852, and the second, Wilhelmina's sister Henriette, in 1856. He had two sons, Max, born in 1849, and Albert, born in 1854. Frieda's first daughter Victoria Alberta Müller was born in 1863. The Queen was godmother to the child. A second daughter, Bertha, was born in 1866, and died of diphtheria in 1875. The royal grapevine kept Her Majesty in touch with the family: the Queen's half-sister wrote to her in 1866, 'I was to tell you, from the Grand Duchess [now Louise, daughter of King William I of Prussia], that the operation performed on the eyes of Müller, the husband of your former dresser Arnold, had succeeded quite well at Heidelberg. I daresay you know it already.'* Sophie Weiss stayed on with the Queen until 1864. The Princess Royal wrote from Karlsruhe in 1872 to say that she had seen 'your' Sophie Weiss and Frida [*sic*] Arnold 'both looking very well'.*

When the Queen went to Baden Baden to see her sister in 1872, after luncheon one day she saw 'Frida [*sic*] Arnold, my former maid, and Sophie Weiss, who had also been with me'.* Again, when the Queen was in Baden Baden in 1876, she mentioned having seen '2 old former maids of mine, who live at Karlsruhe'.* Frieda's daughter was also there, and all her long life remembered being summoned for an audience. Queen Victoria 'had a lively conversation with the ladies' and then gave her god-daughter a set of jewellery, ear-rings and pins in the form of beetles; of violet-blue 'Scottish stones', the legs and heads of gold. She remembered being received several times at Baden, and the Queen giving 'Mama' engravings and photographs.*

When Ernst Müller died in June 1890 the Queen wrote, in German, from Balmoral:

My dear Frieda,

These lines accompany an enamelled photograph of your dear husband which I have made for you. Please accept also the expression of my deep sympathy on the irreplaceable loss which you have suffered.

May God console and protect you!

> *Your*
> *affectionate*
> *VRI*

17 October 1890

Frieda herself died on 28 September 1901.

Appendix

The Queen was watching too, and described the evening in her Journal for 29 May 1856: 'Dinner over, we went upstairs to Albert's rooms, which overlook the Park. It was one dense mass of people, so closely packed, that a pin could not have been dropped . . . At ½ p. 9 punctually the fireworks began and all excepting Mama, Leopold, and a few others, went out on the terrace or balcony where a tent had been erected, covering only a small part. With cloaks and wraps (for it was very cold) we sat out there till ½ p. 11. It was dry and a favourable night for the fireworks, which were magnificent, particularly the aerial ones, which were finer than I had ever seen. We could see those in Hyde Park, quite distinctly, also those on Primrose Hill, and faintly, those in Victoria Park. George [Duke of Cambridge] and [Prince] Edward [of Saxe-Weimar] said the noise reminded them of the shells and of the firing of musketry, at Sevastopol. The finale, was an indescribably splendid bouquet of endless rockets and streamers, which quite filled the sky. Frequently the light was brilliant enough to light up the countless thousands assembled. Our roof was occupied by our servants and there were seats also below, and tickets given to many in the outer courtyard. When all was over, we . . . went downstairs where refreshments were served, and where we were quite glad to have something warm to drink. At 12 we all separated, pleased with this very successful and fine sight and were quite surprised to see that the people had already all dispersed.' If Frieda was among the servants on 'our roof', she had the better viewpoint.

Reference Notes

Note on Abbreviations

ILN   Illustrated London News
PRO   Public Record Office
RA   Royal Archives
RC   Royal Collection
RL   Royal Library

Notes to Introduction

PAGE

1 **begun her duties** RA QVJ, 20 December 1854
1 **the Crimea** Queen Victoria to King Leopold, 13 October 1854 Christopher Hibbert (ed.), *Queen Victoria in her Letters and Journals* (London, 1984), p.125
1 **on 15 October, died** Staatsarchiv Coburg LAA 8647 Nr. 567, Queen Victoria to the Duchess of Coburg, 16 October 1854
2 **quite overset me** RA Y 99/37, Queen Victoria to King Leopold, 18 October 1854
2 **never be replaced** RA Z 480/132, Duchess of Gloucester to Queen Victoria, 19 October 1854
2 **lay her mistress out for burial** RA QVJ, 30 April 1857
2 **known to Queen Victoria** RA Y 99/29, Queen Victoria to King Leopold, 1 August 1854
2 **the King's recommendation** RA Add C 4/231, Marianne Skerrett to Charles Andrews, 25 April 1854
4 **duties which are my lot** Letter from Sophie Arnold to Mathilde Arnold, 1845
6 **three months' trial** Staatsarchiv Coburg LAA 8647 Nr. 573, Queen Victoria to the Duchess of Coburg, 18 November 1854
6 **new dresser from abroad** RA PP Ledger January 1853–December 1860, p.147 and Journal, July 1853–June 1856 p.259

207

PAGE

6 **service with the Queen began** PRO LC 13/3, p.32

6 **enormously tall** Staatsarchiv Coburg LAA 8647 Nr. 577, Queen Victoria to the Duchess of Coburg, 18 December 1854

6 **a cultured girl Frieda was** Staatsarchiv Coburg LAA 8647 Nr. 578, Queen Victoria to the Duchess of Coburg, 23 December 1854

7 **attendence on the sovereign** RA Z 202/168–9, 2 March 1868

7 **letters to tradespeople** C. Grey, *The Early Years of the Prince Consort; compiled under the direction of HM The Queen* (London, 1868) p. 348

7 **23 October 1857** RA Z 276, p. 20

7 **going to town and back** Ibid., p.36

8 **Her Majesty's wardrobe** PRO LC 13/3

8 **satisfaction in her service** RA Add C 4/244, Marianne Skerrett to Charles Andrews, 20 November 1854

8 **discretion and straightforwardness** C. Grey, *The Early Years of the Prince Consort* (London, 1868) p.348

8 **very plain spoken** RA Add C 24/17, 18 December 1861, Lord Torrington to Delane

8 **likings and dislikings** RA Add Q 1/17, 16 September 1859, Sir Charles Phipps to Queen Victoria

8 **second dresser** RA Add C 4/248, James J. Kinloch to Marianne Skerrett, 9 December 1854

8 **paid quarterly** PRO LC13/3, p.44

9 **favourite horses** RL Catalogue of the Paintings, Sculpture, and other Works of Art at Osborne (London, 1876)

9 **boot cupboard** RC Inventory of Furniture at Osborne up to 1900, p. 56

9 **ironing trestles** RC Inventory of Works of Art and Furniture at Osborne, 1904

11 **style of countenance requires** Mrs Isabella Beeton, *The Book of Household Management*, new edition (London, 1869), pp.1018–25

11 **properly attended to** RA Z 202/62 Memorandum, undated, bound between letters dated 1866

11 **must obey them** RA Z 202/55 Memorandum, March 1866

11 **the dress in particular** RA Add C 4/231, Marianne Skerrett to Charles Andrews, 25 April 1854

12 **last thing at night** RA Add J/1591

12 **one who was at dinner** RA Z 202/55 Memorandum, March 1866

12 **go out at other times** RA Add C 4/231, Marianne Skerrett to Charles Andrews, 25 April 1854

12 **eau-de-Cologne** RA Add J/1592

12 **the Queen's lamp** RA Add J/1593

13 **20 m to 12** RA Z 491, Queen Victoria's Reminiscences 1840–1861, p.19

13 **even if Papa is with me** Queen Victoria to Princess Frederick

PAGE

William of Prussia, 11 June 1858, Roger Fulford (ed.), *Dearest Child; Letters between Queen Victoria and the Princess Royal, 1858–61*, (London, 1957), p.112

13 **peculiar duties** RA Y 99/29, Queen Victoria to King Leopold, 1 August 1854

13 **books and drawings** RA Add C 4/231

13 **were not put in** RA Z 491, pp.21–21a

14 **concert takes place** Frieda Arnold, *Letter 10*, p. 147

14 **opals and diamonds** *The Times*, 13 March 1856

14 **was much admired,** *Illustrated London News*, 19 April 1856, p.403

14 **diamond circlet** *The Times*, 16 April 1856

14 **two months later** Ibid, 26 June 1856

15 **correspond to the train** Ibid., 30 May 1856

15 **and silver ribband** Ibid., 21 June 1856

15 **green leaves and diamonds** Ibid., 18 June 1856

15 **jewels of the crown** *Morning Post*, 6 June 1856

15 **diamond ornaments** Ibid, 7 July 1856

16 **green silk parasol** *Morning Chronicle*, 24 April 1854

16 **hunting Stewart tartan** *Banffshire Journal*, 20 October 1857

16 **and white bonnet** *Illustrated London News*, 31 May 1856

16 **according to a watercolour** RL 20234

16 **a white bonnet** *Illustrated London News*, 7 June 1856, p.264

16 **dress of blue and white** *Morning Post*, 17 July 1856

16 **at the levee** Roger Fulford (ed.), *Dearest Child; Letters between Queen Victoria and the Princess Royal, 1858–61*, (London, 1957) p.83

17 **improves her excessively** Eleanor Stanley, *Twenty Years at Court*, (London 1916), p.309

17 **the expanding circumference** RA Add U 32, p.178 Queen Victoria to Princess Frederick William of Prussia, 21 July 1858

17 **will be necessary** Ibid.

17 **questions of toilettes** RA QVJ, 11 August 1855

17 **I am glad to hear** RA QVJ, 1 September 1855

17 **a poodle in gold** E. Saunders, *A Distant Summer*, (London, 1947) p.93

18 **over-ornament in dress** *Illustrated London News*, 1 September 1855, p.258

18 **smart new gown** RA Z 491, p.26a

18 **Christmas morning also** Ibid., p.32

18 **admire my new dress** Ibid., p.31

18 **lace veil, as a shawl** RA QVJ, 10 February 1858

18 **smart morning dresses** RA QVJ, 20 March 1856

18 **mousseline de soie** RA QVJ, 26 August 1856

18 **the crown diamonds** Ibid, 25 January 1858

18 **white feathers on my hat** Ibid., 18 April 1856

19 **wearing a scarlet tunic** Ibid., 16 June 1856

PAGE

19 **striking and beautiful** *Illustrated London News*, vol. 28, 26 July 1856, p. 80

19 **not a little proud** RA QVJ, 17 July 1856

19 **detailing was superb** Two versions of the tunic are preserved in the Museum of London: A19072 and D328

19 **crimson bullion tassels** *Illustrated London News*, vol. 29, 16 August 1856, p. 169

19 **graceful costume** *The Times*, 30 July 1856

19 **very minute proportions** *Morning Post*, 8 November 1856

20 **of great use – hereafter** RA Add U 32, Queen Victoria to Princess Frederick William of Prussia, 7 September 1858

20 **bear this in mind** Ibid., 9 June 1858

20 **later in the day** Queen Victoria to Princess Frederick William of Prussia, 11 June 1858, Roger Fulford (ed.), *Dearest Child; Letters between Queen Victoria and the Princess Royal 1858–61* (London, 1957) p.112

20 **same night shift** Roger Fulford (ed.), *Dearest Mama; Letters between Queen Victoria and the Crown Princess of Prussia, 1861–4* (London, 1968), p.192

20 **with guipure lace** RA QVJ, 29 April 1857

20 **the Empress's dressing gown** Queen Victoria to Princess Frederick William, 1 April 1858, Roger Fulford (ed.), *Dearest Child; Letters between Queen Victoria and the Princess Royal, 1858–61* (London, 1957), p.83

20 **on 30 April** RA QVJ, 30 April 1857

20 **as long as we like** RA Add U 32, p. 97, Queen Victoria to Princess Frederick William of Prussia, 17 March 1858

21 **England was at war** Vera Watson, *A Queen at Home: An Intimate Account of the Social and Domestic Life of Queen Victoria's Court*, (London 1852) p.124

21 **Duke of Genoa** RA Annual Report of the Proceedings in the Lord Chamberlain's Department, 1855

21 **six months mourning** Eleanor Stanley, *Twenty Years at Court* (London, 1916) p.320

21 **over her shoulders** Ibid., p.323

21 **and green leaves** *The Times*, 10 July 1857

21 **band of black crape** Ibid., 27 June 1857

21 **refurbish it for the season** RA Y 42/35 Princess of Hohenlohe-Langenburg to Queen Victoria, 4 March 1860

21 **my toilettes succeeded** RA Add U 32, Queen Victoria to Princess Frederick William of Prussia, 7 February 1858

22 **with silver blonde** *The Times*, 8 May 1856

23 **left royal service** RA PP 2/36/10420, and *see also* p.202

23 **quick and active** RA Y 99/29, Queen Victoria to King Leopold, 1 August 1854

23 **good temper** RA Add C 4/231, Marianne Skerrett to Charles Andrews, 25 April 1854

PAGE

23 **was living before** Queen Victoria to Princess Frederick William of Prussia, 21 October 1858, Roger Fulford (ed.), *Dearest Child; Letters between Queen Victoria and the Princess Royal, 1858–61* (London, 1957) p.141

23 **every day into my room** Ibid., 29 November 1858, p.147

23 **breaking in his new valet** Ibid., 4 December 1858, p.149

23 **this hurry scurry** Ibid, 6 February 1858, p.33

23 **belonging to her family** RA HH 1/75, November–December 1869

23 **treating them kindly** RA Add A 3/101, 22 November 1867

24 **very particular about** RA C 64/77, August 1874

24 **will not tolerate it** RA Add A 25/388, 22 November 1873

24 **with perfect civility** RA Z 202/54, 27 February 1866

24 **attendance on Herself** RA Z 202/55, Duties of Her Majesty's Wardrobe Maids, March 1866

24 **going into dinner** RA Z 491, p.16

24 **a 'block book'** RA Add O68/65

25 **and small pearls** RA Add O68/78

25 **etui for needlework** RA Add O68/87

25 **of gold hairpins** RA Add O68/99

25 **return to Osborne** RA Z 279, Copy of the Journal of Queen Victoria's visit to Germany, p.3

25 **leave for Woolwich** RA QVJ, 9 August 1845

25 **retain it. It is quite lovely** *Leaves from a Journal; being a record of the Visit of the Emperor and Empress of the French to the Queen and of the Queen to the Emperor of the French, 1855* (Private printing, c. 1881) 26 August 1855

25 **accepting it. It is quite lovely** RA QVJ, 26 August 1855

Notes to Letter 1:

28 **Princess Helena** RA PP Minute Book 1, p.206

32 **instalments of £500** Oliver Millar, *The Victorian Pictures in the Collection of Her Majesty the Queen*, (Cambridge, 1992) p.321

32 **Karlsruhe in 1852** *Verzeichnisses der Kunstgegenstande in der Grossherzoglichen Kunsthalle zu Carlsruhe*, 2nd edition, (Karlsruhe 1852)

34 **at 1/2 p.5** RA QVJ, 9 January 1855

35 **at Spithead** RA Court Circular, 5 January 1855

41 **reckoned at 640lb** RA LS Statement of Expenses in the Department of the Lord Steward , 1851, p.35

42 **visitors to Her Majesty** William Strange, *Sketches of Her Majesty's Household* (London, 1848), p.87

Notes to Letter 2:

43 **government hunting errand** RA QVJ 5 February 1855

PAGE
43 **the box lobby** RA PP Household 229
43 **at Windsor since 1848** RA Z 171/37
51 **comfort to us** Theodore Martin, *The Life of the Prince Consort*, vol. iv
     (London, 1879) p.281

Notes to Letter 3:

56 **on white silk** RA Queen Victoria's Playbills, *Harlequin Bluebeard*, 16
     February 1855
57 **wedding breakfast also** Ibid.
57 **previous June (see Letter 4)** Ibid.
64 **every sort and kind** *Leaves from a Journal; being a record of the visit of the
     Emperor and Empress of the French to the Queen and of the Queen to the
     Emperor of the French, 1855* (Private printing, c. 1881), 16 April

Notes to Letter 4:

70 **transport of troops** *The Palace and Park: General Guide Book* (London,
     1854), p.142
70 **May it be prosperous** Owen Jones and Joseph Bonomi, *Description of the
     Egyptian Court* (London, 1854), pp.14–15

Notes to Letter 5:

78 **as a father** RA QVJ, 23 July 1855
79 **fashionable bathing place** William White, *History, Gazetter, and
     Directory of Hampshire and the Isle of Wight* (Sheffield, 1859) p.145
81 **in Karlsruhe in 1852** Eugen Kilian (ed.), *Beitrage zur Geschichte des
     Karlsruhe Hoftheaters unter Eduard Devrient* (Karlsruhe, 1893)
83 **and autographs** Charles Knight (ed.), *London* (London, 1842), vol. ii,
     p.243

Notes to Letter 6:

88 **faster than anything else** RA Add A 29/19
88 **anything else we have** RA Add A 29/11
89 **by sea to Boulogne** RA MOH AR 1/94
89 **on the Queen did not** RA Add A 29/24
90 **and 5 footmen** RA HH 1/19 List of staff accompanying H.M. and
     arrangements for their transport
94 **at le Vesinet** Blanchard Jerrold, *The Life of Napoleon III* (London, 1874),
     vol. ii, p.88

PAGE

96 **bewildered but enchanted** *Leaves from a Journal; being a record of the visit of the Emperor and Empress of the French to the Queen and of the Queen to the Emperor of the French, 1855* (Private printing, c. 1881), 18 August 1855

97 **walk so lightly** Ibid., 19 August 1855

98 **and is small** Ibid., 20 August 1855

98 **as could be wished** Dean of Windsor & Hector Bolitho (eds) *Letters of Augusta Stanley* (London, 1927) p.69

99 **instructive, and melancholy** *Leaves*, 21 August 1855

100 **diamonds and blue flowers** Ibid. 22 August 1855

101 **are, quite safe** Ibid., 23 August 1855

102 **in Paris** Ibid.

102 **half past twelve** Ibid.

103 **was loudly cheered** Ibid., 24 August 1855

104 **and the** *Gendarmerie* Ibid., 27 August 1855

109 **shawls and bonnets** Ibid.

Notes to Letter 7:

111 **packing for Scotland** RA QVJ, 30 August 1855

111 **gone to Scotland** RA Add C 4/213, 5 August 1852, Marianne Skerrett to Sir Edwin Landseer

113 **retired in 1856** RA PP Osb 704

117 **required in 1855** Figures supplied by R. D. Ridding

Notes to Letter 8:

119 **everything perfection** Queen Victoria, *Leaves from the Journal of our Life in the Highlands, from 1848 to 1861*, (London, 1868) p.149

120 **fetched by post horses** RA Y 125/41, Queen Victoria to Augusta Princess of Prussia, 30 August 1855

120 **£4 19s 9d** RA PP 2/13/5834

124 **post boys and expenses** RA MOH 7/436, David Robertson to Mr Moon, 22 August 1855

129 **Balmoral in 1851** Delia Millar, *Queen Victoria's Life in the Scottish Highlands depicted by her watercolour artists*, (London, 1985) p.59

132 **came to 5937** RA LS Statement of Expenses in the Department of the Lord Steward 1851, p.36

136 **horses can be got** RA MOH 7/437, James Ross to J. R. Groves, 24 August 1855

138 **and ill-fated rival** Thomas Carlyle, *Life of Schiller*, 2nd edition (London, 1845), p.134

138 **two carriage trucks** RA Court Circular, Monday, 15 October 1855

PAGE

Notes to Letter 10:

149 **expunged from the text** Charles Kean, *Shakespeare's Play of the Winter's Tale, Arranged for Representation at the Princess's Theatre, with Explanatory Notes, as first performed on Monday 28 April, 1856,* (London, 1856) p.6

149 **impressed and enchanted** RA QVJ, 28 April 1856

153 **their dreamy life there** William Howitt, *The Rural and Domestic Life of Germany* (London, 1842) p.247

153 **parts of London** Peter Cunningham, *Handbook of London Past and Present* (London, 1850)

154 **and Afghanistan** George Eyre-Todd (ed.) *The Autobiography of William Simpson* (London 1903)

160 **Hut, or Pavilion** RA QVJ, 16 June 1856

160 **for the dressers** RA MOH Carriage Orders and Memoranda, 7 and 8 July 1856

168 **the Victoria Embankment** W. J. Loftie, *Memorials of the Savoy: The Palace, the Hospital, the Chapel* (London 1878) p.184

169 **and damp than other places** William White, *History, Gazetteer, and Directory of Hampshire and the Isle of Wight* (Sheffield, 1859) p.147

Notes to Letter 11:

172 **travelling appendages** And details of the royal train and route from the *Morning Post*, 29 August 1856.

262 **Berwick to Edinburgh** RA Court Circular, 29 August 1856

175 **Craigmillar Castle** RA QVJ, 29 August 1856

178 **Prince Albert's fourgon** RA MOH Carriage Orders and Memoranda, 30 August 1856

178 **Aberdeen by steamer** RA MOH AR1/143

179 **carrying about the things** RA Z 491, p.52

179 **had to unpack** Ibid., p.53

180 **bringing over their men!** RA QVJ, 10 September 1856

183 **in June 1857** PRO LC 13/3, p.73

187 **Windsor at 7.45 p.m.** RA QVJ 15, 16 October 1856

Notes to Letter 12:

191 **upon the line** RA Court Circular, 26 August 1857

192 **the dressers' coach** RA MOH Carriage Orders and Memoranda, 29 August 1857

192 **from Braemar to Balmoral** Ibid.

193 **who had arrived at seven** RA QVJ, 29 August 1857

193 **the kitchen and staff** Delia Miller, *Queen Victoria's Life in the Scottish*

PAGE

Highlands, (London 1985) p.130

198 **missed the mountains** RA QVJ, 14 October 1857

199 **open into a lobby** Ibid.

Notes to Postscript:

201 **with your dresses** QV to Princess Frederick William of Prussia, 18 February 1858, *Dearest Child*, (London 1957) p.49

202 **opposite direction to London** RA PP 2/36/10420

202 **paid by the Queen** RA PP 2/39/10723, Marianne Skerrett to Sir Charles Phipps, 30 October 1859

202 **Mistress of the Robes** PRO LC 13/3, p.93

202 **glad to see them** RA Z 8/57, Princess Frederick William of Prussia to Queen Victoria, 7 October 1859

203 **wait till Christmas** RA PP 2/39/10723, Marianne Skerrett to Sir Charles Phipps, 30 October 1859

203 **to Cologne (£7 17s. 6d.)** RA PP 2/38/10697

203 **know it already** RA Y 44/42, Feodore, Princess of Hohenlohe-Langenburg to Queen Victoria, 18 May 1886

203 **looking very well** RA Z 27/21, German Crown Princess to Queen Victoria, 5 December 1872

203 **also been with me** RA QVJ, 30 March 1872

203 **live at Karlsruhe** RA QVJ, 6 April 1876

204 **engravings and photographs** Personal note by Victoria Weltzien, written in 1945

Index

216